WHY ENVIRONMENT

This book is for those who are not just interested in the ways humans have harmfully altered their environment, but instead wish to learn why the many governmental policies in place to curb such behavior have been unsuccessful. Since humans began to exploit natural resources for their own economic ends, we have ignored a central principle: nature and humans are not separate, but are a unified, interconnected system in which neither is superior to the other. Policy must reflect this reality. We failed to follow this principle in exploiting natural capital without expecting to pay any price, and in hurriedly adopting environmental laws and policies that reflected how we wanted nature to work instead of how it does work. This study relies on more accurate models for how nature works and humans behave. These models suggest that environmental laws should be consistent with the laws of nature.

JAN LAITOS holds the John A. Carver, Jr. Chair in Environmental and Natural Resources Law at the University of Denver Sturm College of Law. He has previously published natural resources and environmental law books and treatises with all the major law publishers in the United States as well as several in Europe. He has taught and lectured throughout America as well as in Spain, Hungary, Argentina, Ireland, Turkey, and Scotland. He is a graduate of Yale College and the University of Colorado Law School. He has a Doctorate in American Legal History from the University of Wisconsin Law School.

WHY ENVIRONMENTAL POLICIES FAIL

JAN LAITOS

University of Denver Sturm College of Law

WITH JULIANA OKULSKI

CAMBRIDGE
UNIVERSITY PRESS

University Printing House, Cambridge CB2 8BS, United Kingdom

One Liberty Plaza, 20th Floor, New York, NY 10006, USA

477 Williamstown Road, Port Melbourne, VIC 3207, Australia

4843/24, 2nd Floor, Ansari Road, Daryaganj, Delhi – 110002, India

79 Anson Road, #06-04/06, Singapore 079906

Cambridge University Press is part of the University of Cambridge.

It furthers the University's mission by disseminating knowledge in the pursuit of education, learning, and research at the highest international levels of excellence.

www.cambridge.org
Information on this title: www.cambridge.org/9781107546745
DOI: 10.1017/9781316343326

© Jan Laitos 2017

First published 2017

Printed in the United States of America by Sheridan Books, Inc.

A catalogue record for this publication is available from the British Library.

Library of Congress Cataloging-in-Publication Data
Names: Laitos, Jan, author.
Title: Why environmental policies fail / Jan Laitos.
Description: Cambridge, United Kingdom, New York, NY: Cambridge University Press, 2017. |
Includes bibliographical references and index.
Identifiers: LCCN 2017000354 | ISBN 9781107121010 (hardback) |
ISBN 9781107546745 (paperback)
Subjects: LCSH: Environmental law. | Environmental policy. | Nature –
Effect of human beings on. | Human behavior. | Human ecology. |
BISAC: LAW / Environmental.
Classification: LCC K3585.L345 2017 | DDC 333.7–dc23
LC record available at https://lccn.loc.gov/2017000354

ISBN 978-1-107-12101-0 Hardback
ISBN 978-1-107-54674-5 Paperback

To
Erik Jan Peter Laitos

May you live in a world where you and your
environment are in harmony

CONTENTS

ACKNOWLEDGMENTS

A book of this scope is due to the insight, inspiration, support, and encouragement of many people. I would like here to acknowledge some of those who helped contribute to the ideas and arguments set forth in many of the chapters. Certain people directly educated me in matters about which I had a thin background. Either directly or metaphorically, they sat me down and "taught" me the science behind our natural environment. Or they wrote about environmental law and policy, and about how policy has too often fallen short, or how it has been endlessly tinkered with in attempts to make it more effective. Some of these sources have written about concepts, usually grounded in science, that I have relied on to make proposals about how better to shape workable environmental policy. Some have written groundbreaking studies about humans and their environmental surroundings, pointing out how law and policy have often conspired to facilitate anthropomorphic alteration of Nature, natural resources, and natural systems. Others have simply directly encouraged me, or have made it possible for me to acquire the best thinking out there on this important topic, and to analyze just why some of our best ideas about affecting our natural world have not been able to slow the pace of environmental damage. To each of them, listed here, and cited elsewhere in the book, I am grateful. Although I am solely responsible for the contents of this book, and although there is only one "author," that author is indebted to a number of scholars, thinkers, scientists, and truly creative individuals who helped educate and inspire in countless ways.

First and foremost, I must acknowledge and express my gratitude to Juliana Okulski. In many ways, this book is as much her idea, her product, as it is mine. She was the one who first introduced me to the importance of science – particularly biology and the workings of Earth's natural systems – as an important element in environmental policy that too often has been underplayed by policymakers. She also introduced me to how modern ecologists perceive Nature, and humans' effect on Nature, and how Nature operates. She also alerted me to the role humans play in affecting the interconnected human-Nature unit, termed a Social Ecological System. She was the first one who urged me to explore the underlying explanations for policy ineffectiveness, instead of simply focusing on the effects of policy disappointments and then proposing some grandiose solution. She helped me understand how policy models, when flawed, cause policy failures, and how many of the models that we have been using are flawed because they are too often not based on good science. This book is a testament to all of her hard work, and infinite patience in me. She has been, in effect, my copilot on this journey.

Several people set in motion events that permitted me to think through, organize, propose, and write this book. I must acknowledge the support and confidence in me by John Berger, Senior Editor at Cambridge University Press. John too has been patient with me, and had confidence in the idea of a book that dealt with the "why" question of environmental policy failures. I am grateful that he waited for me to hatch the concept, and stood by me when I first raised with him the central idea behind the book. Dean Marty Katz of the University of Denver Sturm College of Law was also supportive. He granted me a timely research leave in order to allow me the time to actually sit down and write the book. Micah Desaire, part of the support staff at my law school, labored through draft after draft of the book, mastering without complaint topics far from traditional legal scholarship, such as complex adaptive systems management, behavioral economics, the science of symmetry, and Einstein's "unification" principle, extending even to the underlying unity of humans and Nature originally espoused by Taoism.

Several prominent American law professors have been either influential in guiding my thinking while I worked through the book's many chapters or directly supportive of me when I was initially proposing the book to Cambridge University Press. Professor J. B. Ruhl of the Vanderbilt Law School is someone who did both. He is one of the giants in the world of environmental law trying to figure out how laws can be made more suitable to addressing environmental and natural resource issues. His numerous articles on environmental policy have been seminal to a generation of academics and policymakers (and me). J. B. also helped me focus my topic and my approach to my topic, as well as to realize the daunting task ahead for me. I thank him for his insight and backing. Other law professors have also considered some of the same issues that are contained in the book's chapters, and I have read, pondered, and been influenced by their thinking (although they were not in direct contact with me). Professor Robin Kundis Craig of the Utah Law School and Professor

Eric Biber of the University of California Law School at Berkeley have engaged in scholarship that I found incredibly useful – indirectly helping me in their various articles to test my ideas against their well-thought-through arguments about environmental policy. Professor Dan Tarlock from IIT Chicago Kent College of Law was and is a scholar who long ago saw that environmental policies were too eager to return the planet to some kind of ideal natural "baseline" that in fact never existed. I have been influenced by his thinking. Professor Mary Christina Wood from the University of Oregon Law School and Professor Michael Blumm from the Lewis and Clark Law School are two nationally leading advocates of the public trust doctrine as potential paradigm-shifting environmental policy, and I have cited and referred to their influential thinking. Professor Shi-Ling Hsu has also been influential with respect to his important scholarship in the field of resource economics.

The writings, scholarship, and findings of other ecological scientists and Earth system academics have been useful to me throughout the writing of the book. A number of ecologists, environmentalists, and resource academics have changed the way we perceive Nature and Earth systems, as well as the impact humans are having on natural goods and capital, ecosystem services, and planetary boundaries that permit humans as a species to survive. Rather than list all of these researchers and commentators, I offer here the names of the leading authors of the works via which they, along with a long list of other authors, have advanced the groundbreaking ideas essential to the arguments in this book. The names of these leading authors of the key articles on scientific environmental realism, which have changed the thinking of so many policymakers, scientists, academics, and researchers, are Carl Folke, Simon Levin, Johan Rockstrom, and Will Steffen. They appear most frequently at the forefront of the lists of numerous contributors who are beginning to alter how we perceive the world around us and our place in that world. Behavioral economics has also helped transform how we, and how policymakers, understand how humans respond to environmental policy. I have been greatly influenced by the significant scholarship advanced by Professors Cass Sunstein and Richard Thaler, who have caused us to rethink how laws can best reach the roots of humans' behavioral dynamics.

Other researchers have written on disparate topics that were instrumental in some of the conclusions and proposals offered in the book. Mario Livio and Frank Wilczek have written extensively and eloquently on the Law of Symmetry. Their scholarship and explanations of the ubiquitousness of symmetry in Nature helped persuade me that symmetry needs to underscore any environmental policy designed to address Nature. Mario Livio's important book – The Equation That Couldn't Be Solved (2005) – was a catalyst for much of my thinking laid out in Chapter 9 of this book. Similarly, the earlier writings of the late Willard Hurst, one of America's most outstanding legal historians, helped me, and many others, see how laws themselves could contribute to and even encourage the eradication of natural goods and ecosystem services. I have tried to acknowledge the influence Hurst has had on my thinking, particularly in Chapter 2.

Finally, I wish to acknowledge that much of what appears in the first two chapters first appeared in articles I have had published elsewhere. These are the *Environmental Law Reporter*, Volume 45, No. 5 (May 2015) (coauthored with Juliana Okulski) (Chapter 1), and the *William and Mary Environmental Law and Policy Review*, Volume 39, Issue 1 (Fall 2014) (coauthored with Lauren J. Wolongevicz) (Chapter 2).

~

Prologue

This is a book about environmental policy, and how this policy, in its many forms, has largely failed to prevent a human-caused deterioration of the Earth's natural systems. There are three storylines. First, there is an economic system, embraced by most societies on this planet, that rewards and encourages anthropogenic growth and development. Second, there are the Earth's natural systems, ranging from stock resources like soil and minerals, to renewable resources like water and fisheries and trees, to environmental sinks like the atmosphere and the oceans, to ecosystems. These have been the preconditions to capitalist production. These natural systems have either been "fuels" used and exploited by humans to achieve economic growth, or a seemingly limitless dumping ground for our wastes and by-products of resource development. Third, when human societies began to realize that economic growth had overused or destroyed natural resources, and failed to internalize the environmental social costs of pollution and waste disposal, they turned to legal-governmental institutions. These institutions were tasked with devising environmental policy in order to address the disturbing consequences of our unchecked reliance on earth systems and natural resources for economic success.

The focus of this book is this third storyline – the saga of various proposed and tried environmental policies and their disappointing or failed record. The book reviews the history of these policies and critiques their outcome. It then attempts to explain *why* these good-faith attempts at environmental policy have all failed to do what they were intended to do – mitigate anthropogenic changes to natural systems and restore environmental conditions on this planet to the point where humans can continue to survive and even thrive. The book then proposes a new policy paradigm that might bring about a happy ending to this third storyline. This proposed policy will hopefully have a better chance of success than past and present policies because it seeks to conform to a universal truth that is consistently followed by Nature on Earth, as well as the larger forces of the Universe.

But before we consider the failed policies, we should have as our starting points the first and second storylines, because they caused the initial
need for environmental policy. It was an anthropocentric choice to create
societies that coveted a particular kind of growth, economic growth, that
in turn put growing pressures on the natural world. There have historically
been close links between social economic systems and the natural world.
However, human activities based on economic drivers have so expanded
recently that the planet's natural environment is for the first time being
altered not by natural forces, such as glacial epochs or asteroids or volcanoes, but by purely anthropogenic actions.

A. The Economic System

The chief "driver" behind these human activities affecting our environmental surroundings has been a generally shared belief among organized societies and nation-states about the benefits of economic development and
capitalistic production and material accumulation of goods and wealth.
This resource *use* is elevated over collective stewardship and conservation
of natural resources and environmental goods and systems. Faith in economic growth has meant that the natural world around humans – trees,
minerals, land, water, air – has been seen as a means of achieving human-
centric ends such as population growth and urbanization, higher gross
domestic product, increasing personal wealth, more carbon-based energy
use, and competitive market advantage.[1] As a result, this natural world has
been overused, degraded, polluted, poisoned, and sometimes destroyed,
because prior to the advent of environmental policy, Nature had no voice
and no legal protection. It was just there to be taken, or to be used as an
endless waste dump, usually free of charge.[2] The dominant worldview that
emerged from Judeo-Christian and Greek thought characterized Nature
as nothing other than an array of seemingly limitless raw commodities,
to be exploited, used, and changed to benefit people. Nature became com-
modified; land and natural resources belonged to humans.

This emphasis on economic, material prosperity, fueled by resource
use, overuse, and abuse, has been grounded in several near-irrebutable

[1] Gar Alperovitz, America Beyond Capitalism: Reclaiming Our Wealth, Our Liberty, and Our
Democracy (2d ed. 2011); Cormac Cullinan, Wild Law: A Manifesto for Earth Justice (2d ed.
2011); Charles Derber, Greed to Green: Solving Climate Change and Remaking the Economy
(2010); William Greider, The Soul of Capitalism: Opening Paths to a Moral Economy (2003).
[2] Elizabeth Kolbert, Field Notes From a Catastrophe: Man, Nature, and Climate Change
(2006); David Korten, The Great Turning From Empire to Earth Community (2006).

presumptions. One has been the presumption that the present is more valuable than the future. We can phrase this principle using a scientific example. If we can benefit today by cheaply or freely emitting greenhouse gases that will adversely affect global temperatures fifty years from now, we should not sacrifice now, by reducing reliance on cheap carbon-based fuels, to gain benefits or to avoid costs fifty years from now. Or to put the presumption even more succinctly, we prefer instant, real-time present gratification, even if by doing so we are sacrificing the benefits that could be experienced by others in the (not so) distant future.

Most legal policies, even environmental policies, are skewed toward the present while marginalizing the future. For example, it is quite difficult for anti-pollution rules to reflect in present emission control rules the damage that continual emissions will cause later. It is difficult because policymakers have a hard time determining how much future pollution mitigation is worth to us today.[3] And policymakers have an even more difficult political task in convincing constituents that a (relatively) distant future in which there is less pollution should be preferred over present needs that are satisfied by polluting enterprises.[4] This reality has led environmental policy, affected by economic growth pressures, to discount the value of future benefits while encouraging choices that yield present benefits.

Another presumption justifying a close connection between economic systems and the natural world has been the Myth of Inexhaustible and Unpollutable Resources. For centuries, humans believed that the Earth's natural bounty was so large and plentiful as to be, in effect, infinite. No matter how many trees were cut down, or fish caught, or oil pumped out of the earth, or water diverted, the assumption was that there would always be more of the needed resource available for both present and future use. A parallel belief arose about the three great environmental "sinks" that humans used as waste receptacles: the planet's atmosphere, the world's water sources, particularly the oceans, and the soils and dirt under the earth's surface. Each was so vast that none could ever be permanently impaired by pollution.

A textbook example of the Myth of Inexhaustible Resources is the case of Easter Island. The Easter Island "natives" first arrived on an island that

[3] See, e.g., Laurie T. Johnson & Chris Hope, The Social Cost of Carbon in U.S. Regulatory Impact Analyses: An Introduction and Critique, 2 Journal of Environmental Studies and Sciences 205 (Sept. 2012).
[4] Jacob Hacker and Paul Pierson, American Amnesia (2016); Daniel A. Farber & Paul A. Hemmersbaugh, The Shadow of the Future: Discount Rates, Later Generations, and the Environment, 46 Vanderbilt L. Rev. 267 (1993).

supported a healthy, subtropical forest whose trees were suitable for building homes and seaworthy canoes so that the island inhabitants could live
off a steady diet of ocean porpoise. The trees could also be used to make
rope latticing so that the great stone Easter Island statues could be moved
from the rock quarries to their positions overlooking the ocean. Because
of the Myth of Inexhaustible Resources and the revealed time preference
where the present benefits of tree harvesting outweighed future benefits of
forest conservation, the island's forests were eventually decimated and the
last tree was finally cut down. Deforestation caused the quality of life for
the Easter Islanders to plummet, and the society there collapsed.[5] The key
natural resource on Easter Island was not inexhaustible, and when it was
gone, it would never return there. The notion that there was always one
more tree to cut down turned out to be a myth.[6]

The parallel Myth of Unpollutable Resources was based on the sheer
size and power of the Earth's atmosphere, oceans, waterways, and land.
There was just so much there on this planet that it seemed inconceivable
that puny humans could ever have much of an effect on them, or their
functioning, no matter how many gigatons of waste we put in them. And
not only were these sinks unimaginably large; there was "bad science"
that for years held that they could not be polluted. For example, it took a
long time to refute the hoary canard that "running water purifies itself to
drinking water quality" within a stated distance.[7] Indeed, throughout the
nineteenth century, air pollution was not feared, but considered a sign of
economic progress; smokestacks belching black smoke were sought after
for their symbolic value connoting a vibrant, thriving community.[8]

Another presumption was that the Earth's natural resources were
there for a reason, which was for humans to exploit, develop, and use
them. Moreover, much of American legal activity during the eighteenth
and nineteenth centuries sought to further this larger purpose by devising ways to transfer natural resources – agricultural land, water, timber,
mineral deposits, and energy resources – from public, state ownership to
private control. That transfer was necessary so that these resources could
be extracted and used, through an economic system based on private

[5] See Jared Diamond, Collapse: How Societies Choose to Fail or Succeed (2005).
[6] The same Myth of Inexhaustible Resources drove the deforestation of the vast virgin forests of Wisconsin throughout the nineteenth century. J. Willard Hurst, Law and Economic
Growth: The Legal History of the Lumber Industry in Wisconsin, 1836–1915 (1964).
[7] U.S. Food and Drug Administration, PMO 2007: Appendix D-Standards for Water Sources
at 10 ("the old saying ... is false").
[8] Jan Laitos, Legal Institutions and Pollution: Some Intersections Between Law and History,
15 Natural Resources Journal 423 (1975).

incentives and market transactions. In other words, legal policy assisted in creating the close link between the private economic system and the natural world.[9]

B. The Earth System

When the humans on this planet pursue economic growth requiring natural resource use and development, there will be effects on the Earth's natural systems.[10] There will be, and there has been, intensified use of Earth's resources, higher levels of pollution, loss of ecosystems, natural capital, and biodiversity, and changes to the world's oceans. There has been an anthropogenic alteration of the planet's biosphere, that thin layer on this Earth occupied by living organisms on the surface, atmosphere, and hydrosphere. Our use of natural resources has grown so dramatically that we are endangering the key environmental systems that we rely on. The Earth possesses the only known biosphere in the universe, and its stability and suitability for human life is now threatened.[11]

The most notorious and well publicized of these changes to the Earth system involves the phenomenal amount of atmospheric emissions of greenhouse gases, such as carbon dioxide, methane, and nitrous oxide, which have caused climate change and global warming. The United Nations Intergovernmental Panel on Climate Change (IPCC) predicts that without significant mitigation of greenhouse gas emissions, the world will face a mean surface air temperature increase of $3\,°C$ in less than two decades.[12] Worse, these predicted temperature increases could be irreversible.[13] Already these changes in the concentrations of greenhouse gas have caused unprecedented record heat; loss of forests, freshwater systems,

---

[9] Paul W. Gates, History of Public Land Law Development (1968); J. Willard Hurst, Law and Conditions of Freedom in the Nineteenth Century United States (1956); Harry N. Scheiber, Ohio Canal Era: A Case Study of Government and the Economy, 1820–1861 (1969); Gary Lidecap, Economic Variables and the Development of the Law: The Case of Western Mineral Rights, 38 J. of Economic History 338 (Jun. 1978).

[10] Peter Victor, Questioning Economic Growth, 468 Nature 370 (Nov. 2010).

[11] World Wildlife Fund for Nature, Living Planet Report 2016; Bill McKibben, Earth: Making a Life on a Tough New Planet (2010).

[12] Intergovernmental Panel on Climate Change, www.ipcc.ch; Robin Kundis Craig & Stephen R. Miller, Contemporary Issues in Climate Change Law and Policy: Essays Inspired by the IPCC (2016).

[13] Patrick J. Egan & Megan Mullin, Recent Improvement and Projected Worsening of Weather in the United States, 532 Nature 357 (Apr. 2016); Kirstin Dow & Thomas A. Downing, The Atlas of Climate Change: Mapping the World's Greatest Challenge 40 (3d ed. 2011).

land, and biodiversity; melting glaciers and ice sheets; and significant sea
level rises.[14]

Another Earth system affected by humans is ecosystem services. Such
services encompass benefits people obtain, at no cost, from functioning
ecosystems. Ecosystem services provide food, fresh water, fuel, and fiber;
they regulate climate and water-cycles and they support soil formation
and nutrient cycling. Land-based ecosystem services have been compromised because of ecosystem loss, caused by climate change, pollution,
resource overexploitation, and land-use changes resulting in loss of open
space.[15] Ocean ecosystem services have also been impacted by accelerating
loss of marine populations and species, caused by human overfishing and
pollution.[16]

Human economic activities have disrupted the Earth's natural nitrogen
and phosphorous cycles. Anthropogenic emissions of reactive nitrogen
to the atmosphere and water bodies damage human health and ecosystems. For both developing countries and wealthy established countries,
the global nitrogen footprint has grown.[17] Similarly, the quantity of phos-
phates flowing into the oceans and rivers from crop fertilizer runoffs has
increased exponentially in the last 100 years. This alteration of the natural
phosphorous cycle causes algae blooms and an oxygen deficit for marine
life.[18]

The purely anthropocentric need for cropland and grazing areas, in
order to feed the growing world population, has put enormous pressure
on existing forests. Yet, forested ecosystems store more carbon than any
other land cover type per unit area. They host a considerable percentage of
global biodiversity and provide ecosystem services essential for humans.
They also play a key role in the global climate system. Despite being an
important constituent in the Earth system, humans have so deforested the

[14] Fifth Assessment Report of the United Nations Intergovernmental Panel on Climate
Change (2014); John Metcalfe, The U.S. Hits Never-Before-Seen Milestone for Warmth,
CityLab (April 13, 2016).

[15] United States Dept. of Agriculture, Forest Service, More About Ecosystem Services, www
.fs.fed.us/ecosystemservices.

[16] Boris Worm, et al., Impacts of Biodiversity Loss on Ocean Ecosystem Services 314 Science
787 (Nov. 2006).

[17] The nitrogen footprint is the sum of emissions of ammonia, nitrogen oxide, and nitrous
oxide to the atmosphere, and of nitrogen exportable to water bodies. Azusa Oita, et al.,
Substantial Nitrogen Pollution Embedded in International Trade, 9 Nature Geoscience 111
(2016).

[18] Eric Roy, et al., The Phosphorus Cost of Agricultural Intensification in the Tropics, Nature
Plants #16043 (2016).

planet that now three-quarters of the Earth's terrestrial, ice-free surface is tree-free, and appropriated for human use.[19]

Human economic activities have brought about species extinctions and loss of biodiversity. High rates of extinctions have been due to habitat loss, overharvesting, and pollution, all caused by humans seeking to economically develop land and resources. Loss of biodiversity is not simply a problem because humans may not be able to see charismatic animals like polar bears or wolves except in a zoo; it is an Earth system problem, because biodiversity effects reduce plant production and damage entire ecosystems. In fact, it appears that loss of biodiversity affects ecosystems as much as do climate change, pollution, and other human-caused environmental stressors.[20]

Despite their impressive size, the Earth's oceans have not been able to escape the effects of anthropogenic actions. Rising dissolution of human-generated carbon dioxide in seawater causes ocean acidification and desalination. This ongoing, and excessive, carbon dioxide–driven acidification/desalination has disastrous effects on the ocean's phytoplankton.[21] But humans do more than just dump greenhouse gases into the Earth's oceans. We also dump plastic, mountains of it, into the oceans. It has been estimated that the quantity of plastic that ends up in the ocean is equal to five plastic grocery bags per every foot of coastline around the globe.[22]

Three powerful conceptual frameworks have been proposed to capture the sheer scale of the human influence on Earth systems. One is the suggestion, now largely accepted, that we have entered a new post-Holocene geologic epoch, called the "Anthropocene."[23] This new era marks the time when purely human activity expanded to the point that anthropogenic choices made a global imprint in the geologic record. All of the aforementioned changes in Earth systems, from climate change to ocean acidification, are due to anthropogenic actions. Nature and Earth systems, for the very first time in the Earth's 4.5 billion-year history, are responding to the decisions of one species – humans. These actions have been driven by economic influences. Although there is no consensus on when the

[19] Karl-Heinz Erb, et al., Exploring the Biophysical Option Space for Feeding the World Without Deforestation, 7 Nature Communications #11382 (Apr. 19, 2016).
[20] National Science Foundation, Ecosystem Effects of Biodiversity Loss Rival Climate Change and Pollution, www.nsf.gov/news (May 2, 2012).
[21] Feng-Jiao Liv, et al., Effect of Excessive CO_2 on Physiological Functions in Coastal Diatom, 6 Scientific Reports #21694 (Feb. 15, 2016).
[22] Laura Parker, Eight Million Tons of Plastic Dumped in Ocean Every Year, National Geographic (Feb. 13, 2015).
[23] P. Crutzen, Geology of Mankind, 415 Nature 23 (2002).

Anthropocene began, it appears to have its genesis in the industrial revolution of the nineteenth century, when carbon-based energy fuels began to be burned and initiate the steady growth of greenhouse gas pollution of the Earth's atmosphere.[24]

Another marker demonstrating the extent to which the forces of economic growth have affected the natural world is the concept of "Planetary Boundaries."[25] The idea behind planetary boundaries is that there is a "safe operating space for humanity" to exist on this planet, but if anthropogenic actions push certain critical Earth systems outside of this safe place, then human life is no longer sustainable.[26] Evidence suggests that some of these boundaries have already been exceeded, and others are heading toward dangerous levels.[27] Scientists are warning that we may be "at a planetary tipping point ... incompatible with the planet on which civilization developed ... and to which life is adapted."[28] More ominously, some commentators have correctly pointed out that there is a distinction between boundaries we can breach and fixed limits that we cannot, because once fixed limits are crossed, humanity can never repair the damage and restore the boundary. We may be precariously close to breaching some of the latter, fixed-limit boundaries.[29]

A third realization about the scale of human influence on Earth systems is the idea of a "Great Acceleration." In updating an earlier 2004 analysis of twenty-four indicators of global change in the natural world,[30] researchers saw a steepening of trends since about 1950 toward intensified use of Earth's natural resources, higher levels of pollution, and more anthropogenic alteration of Earth systems. They termed this speeding up of anthropomorphic environmental change "The Great Acceleration."[31] The

---

[24] Damian Carrington, The Anthropocene Epoch: Scientists Declare Dawn of Human-Influenced Age, The Guardian (Aug. 31, 2016); F. A. Jonsson, The Industrial Revolution in the Anthropocene, 84 The Journal of Modern History 679 (2012).

[25] J. Rockstrom, et al., A Safe Operating Place for Humanity, 461 Nature 472 (2009).

[26] Alastair Brown, Planetary Boundaries, 5 Nature Climate Change 19 (2015).

[27] Jonathan Foley, Boundaries for a Healthy Planet, 302 Scientific American 54 (2010).

[28] James Hansen, et al., Target Atmospheric CO_2: Where Should Humanity Aim?, www.columbia.edu.

[29] For example, fertilizer is often produced from rock phosphate, and phosphorous, an ingredient in fertilizer, is a key plant nutrient. If we use up all of the earth's supply of rock phosphate in fertilizer, it is then gone and there is no more. A boundary with fixed limits will have been breached. Simon L. Lewis, We Must Set Planetary Boundaries Wisely, 485 Nature 417 (May 2012).

[30] W. Steffen, et al., Global Change and the Earth System: A Planet Under Pressure (2004).

[31] W. Steffen, W. Broadgate, L. Deutsch, O. Gaffney, & C. Ludwig, The Trajectory of the Anthropocene: The Great Acceleration, 2 Anthrop. Rev. 1 (2015).

notion of a Great Acceleration indicates that from the starting point of the Anthropocene Epoch,[32] the current trajectory is rapidly moving toward a breaching of Planetary Boundaries, not in the distant future, but in the near term.[33] In short, the close links between the world's economic system and the natural world lead to only one conclusion: human activity affecting the natural world, and Earth systems, is not sustainable for continued human life on this planet.

C.   The Policy System

There is a growing agreement among academics and commentators that the United States, along with all other policy-driven countries, can no longer adopt a "business-as-usual" approach to these anthropogenic changes to the Earth system. There is near-universal adoption of the view that "[w]orking only within the [existing] system will, in the end, not succeed."[34] If there is "inertia" in environmental policy, then humans are heading to an inevitable rendezvous with global environmental disaster.[35] Even when there is a worldwide agreement, such as the 2015 Paris "Agreement" on Climate Change,[36] acknowledging the need to rein in certain human activities that are altering basic Earth systems, there is skepticism that the policy will actually yield results that will slow the Great Acceleration.[37]

Apart from a shared reluctance to use traditional environmental policy tools to address Earth system changes, there has been a collective embrace of the need for a "transformative change in the system itself."[38] As one leading book on ecological survival puts it, "[I]t is impossible to think that

[32] See *Jonsson, supra* note 24.
[33] Editorial, Our Planet and Us, 8 Nature Geoscience 81 (2015).
[34] James Gustave Speth, The Bridge at the End of the World: Capitalism, the Environment, and Crossing from Crisis to Sustainability 86, 225 (2008).
[35] William D. Nordhaus, Managing the Global Commons: The Economics of Climate Change (1994).
[36] Doyle Rice, 175 Nations Sign Historic Paris Climate Deal on Earth Day, USA Today (Apr. 22, 2016).
[37] Indeed, even ardent supporters of the Paris Treaty acknowledge that it will do little to actually slow global warming. The United Nations estimates that if every country were to make every single promised carbon cut between 2016 and 2030, carbon dioxide emissions would still only be cut by one-hundreth of what is needed to keep temperature rises below 2°C. Bjorn Lomborg, Trump's Climate Change Plan Might Not Be So Bad After All, The Washington Post (Nov. 27, 2016); Karl Ritter, Huge Cuts Are Needed to Meet Emissions Goals: Even Paris Agreement Targets Not Enough to Avoid Dangerous Temperature Change, Associated Press (Nov. 4. 2016); Eli Kintisch, After Paris: The Rocky Road Ahead, 250 Science 1018 (Nov. 2015).
[38] *Speth, supra* note 34.

policy responses to our 'planetary emergency' can be successful without innovative transformative action."[39] This call to arms for "transformative" and "innovative" environmental policy has not gone unheeded. Creative, imaginative, exciting new approaches to environmental policy have been powerfully and effectively advanced by authors suggesting, for example: (1) a reconceptualization of the human "right" to a clean and healthy environment and the modern rediscovery of the "commons"[40]; (2) that instead of viewing economic growth as the cause of an ecological crisis we view targeted environmental economic investments as the solution to the crisis[41]; (3) the need to rely on economic optimization and economic modeling[42]; (4) integration of truly science-based environmental policy with the behavioral drivers behind human choices[43]; (5) another look at non-regulatory "collective" action[44]; (6) resurrection and expansion of the "public trust" doctrine[45]; and (7) an acknowledgment and legitimatization of "nature's rights."[46]

These and other "innovative" environmental policies certainly fill in the third storyline of how societies, and governments, might address the near-catastrophic consequences of economic systems that plunder and contaminate the natural world. But what is needed, before one turns to new policy, is an understanding of *why* old policy or existing policy has failed. This book seeks to supply that understanding, that explanation for the question: Why do environmental policies fail?

Without considering the reasons for the failure, policymakers (and commentators) are simply leaping from failed policies to suggestions

---

[39] Burns W. Weston & David Bollier, Green Governance: Ecological Survival, Human Rights, and the Law of the Commons xxiii (Cambridge 2013).

[40] *Id.* at xix–xx.

[41] Ted Nordhaus & Michael Shellenberger, Break Through: Why We Can't Leave Saving the Planet to Environmentalists (2009).

[42] William D. Nordhaus & Joseph Boyer, Economic Models of Global Warming (2000); Daniel Fiorino, Making Environmental Policy (1995).

[43] Oswald Schmitz, The New Ecology: Rethinking a Science for the Anthropocene (2016); Michael Marchetti and Peter Moyle, Protecting Life on Earth: An Introduction to the Science of Conservation (2010); Cass R. Sunstein, Why Nudge? (2014); Alessandro Tavoni & Simon Levin, Managing the Climate Commons at the Nexus of Ecology, Behavior, and Economics, 4 Nature Climate Change 1057 (2014).

[44] Elinor Ostrom, Governing the Commons: The Evolution of Institutions for Collective Action (1990).

[45] Mary Christina Wood, Nature's Trust: Environmental Law for a New Ecological Age (Cambridge 2013).

[46] Jan G. Laitos, The Right of Nonuse (Oxford 2012); Susan Emmengger & Axel Tschentscher, Taking Nature's Rights Seriously: The Long Way to Biocentrism in Environmental Law, 6 Geo. Int'l Envtl. L. Rev. 545 (1994).

of alternative policies that hopefully will slow the Great Acceleration and thereby provide humanity with a "safe operating space." But there is another step that needs to be analyzed, before offering grandiose proposals for alternative environmental policy, and that step is the topic of this book – the one that answers why past and current environmental policy has failed. Once we have an idea why present (or even proposed) policies have failed, we can construct a policy that is more likely to succeed, because it avoids some of the underlying causes for other policy failures.

In Part I, we begin with a summary of the two central themes featured in the book: why environmental policies have failed, and what a proposed policy would have to do to succeed (Chapter 1). Part II is both a history and an assessment of traditional environmental policies. The history of environmental policies in the United States reveals how laws first encouraged natural resources use and exploitation, and then, for purely anthropocentric purposes, sought to preserve natural spaces and clean up polluted environmental sinks (Chapter 2). The upshot of this legal legacy has been a natural world anthropologically altered by climate change, global warming, ecosystem and biodiversity loss, pollution, and ocean acidification and contamination (Chapter 3).

Part III discusses the first category of reasons for the failed policies recounted in Chapter 3. Part III argues that these failures were due in part to several recurring faulty assumptions that traditionally have grounded environmental rules. Among these have been a false worldview of humans' relationship to nature, premised on the twin beliefs that we are both separate from and superior to our environmental surroundings (Chapter 4), an incorrect model of how Nature works (Chapter 5), an equally incorrect model of how we should perceive and value Earth systems (Chapter 6), and an unrealistic model of how humans behave (Chapter 7). Part IV then takes up the second category of reasons for failed policies: internal limits and weaknesses embedded in virtually all tried and proposed environmental policies. Chapter 8 considers each type of policy that has been suggested as a solution to global environmental changes, and points out how each contains flaws that interfere with its effectiveness.

Part V seeks to offer a policy that might avoid failure because it (1) hopes to avoid the false models and flawed assumptions outlined in Parts III and IV, and (2) tries to conform to certain universal truths that are followed by Nature and Earth systems. Chapter 9 advances the proposition that environmental policies need to reflect, and be consistent with, the universal "laws" and "truths" that guide how Nature works. The most central of these truths is the all-encompassing principle of symmetry. Notions of symmetry, along with derivative concepts of equivalence, unification, and conservation, seem to guide, if not control, much of what is in the natural universe. Policy that wishes to have an impact on the natural world needs to obey these same rules that are followed by Nature and environmental systems.

Part V then offers an environmental policy that both rejects the flawed assumptions and models that have been the basis for much past and present policy and embraces the universal requirements of symmetry that seem to influence many natural processes. In Chapter 10, it is suggested that for symmetry to be satisfied, the policy must do more than just create a legally enforceable *right* to a natural world conducive to human survival. The policy must also impose a correlative *duty* to make conditions compatible with planetary boundaries providing humans with a "safe operating space." The right is held by humans and their ecological surroundings, not just by humans. The duty is imposed only on humans. And unlike most negative duties embedded in current policy, which tell humans what *not to do*, the duty suggested here is a positive one, urging humans *to do* certain acts that ameliorate the effects of Anthropocene alterations on Earth systems. Such an affirmative obligation is more consistent with how humans naturally wish to behave.

I

Nature: Humans and Their Environmental Surroundings

Before one can examine the question of why environmental policies fail, it might be useful first to establish the meaning of the phrase "environmental policies." An environmental policy is governmental philosophy that guides decisions, often implemented as a rule or law, that address environmental issues. A policy can originate with an executive decision, such as by the President of the United States, and then become a positive law or rule, as a result of legislative action followed by administrative rulemaking. Policy is the philosophy triggering the eventual laws that impact human behavior regarding the natural environment.

The word "environmental" is usually ambiguously defined, and subject to many definitions and meanings. It is therefore important to articulate up front how the noun "environment" and the adjective "environmental" are used in the pages that follow. The "environment" is the sum of all of Nature and the natural world which surrounds humans and their activities. "Environmental" describes something which is a component of Nature and this natural world. "Environmental" surroundings consist of Nature, Natural Resources, Environmental Goods, Natural Capital, and Earth Systems (or Earth-based systems, or planetary systems). Each of these words is defined below in this introduction to Part I. Humans now affect all parts of Nature and the natural world surrounding humans, which means that Nature in a pre-human context no longer exists on this planet.

Some of the words used to describe "environment" and "environmental" are "terms of art" and have generally accepted, precise meanings. Some of these words are used in a particular way, unique to this book, in order to make a very particular point.

One of the central points in the book, and one of the answers to the question of why environmental policies fail, is that humans traditionally, and wrongly, have assumed that they are somehow separate from their environmental surroundings. In truth, of course, humans are not *apart from* their environmental surroundings; humans are just *a part of* those surroundings. If policies presume a separation between humans and their natural environment, then these policies will tend to fail, because humans are in fact integrated within and connected to their natural environment. Human actions affect their environmental surroundings, and our environmental surroundings in turn affect us. An entire academic discipline – Earth Jurisprudence – has arisen, based on the essential unification of humans and their natural environment.[1] The underlying philosophy of Earth Jurisprudence is that the Earth itself is an entire "earth community," where humans are only one part of the community, and not necessarily the dominant part.[2]

To reflect the absence of separation between humans and their environmental surroundings, this book uses the encompassing and inclusive terms "Earth" and "Nature" to describe a space on this planet consisting of (1) humans and (2) all the other nonhuman members of the Earth community. These coupled human-natural systems are sometimes called social ecological systems (SES). The nonhuman members of the SES and the space they occupy on the planet will be termed the "Earth's environment" or human "environmental surroundings." The Earth's *environment*, or human environmental surroundings, in turn consist of "natural resources," "environmental goods," "natural capital," and "earth systems." This environment is more than the biosphere because it includes both living organisms (e.g., microbes and plants), and nonliving substances that make life possible (e.g., oxygen and water).

Natural resources include land, oceans, waters, hard rock minerals, energy minerals, common variety minerals, soils, sand, timber, rangeland, agricultural goods, and wildlife.[3] Often these resources have enormous economic value when they are used by humans, often as a commodity.[4]

Environmental goods include the air, water, land, and subsurface parts of the Earth, which are essential to the existence of the planet's biosphere – the zone of life on Earth. Humans often use environmental goods as free environmental sinks for our waste, garbage, and pollution. Environmental laws are enacted, and environmental policies are often adopted, to try to curb our relentless desire to exploit these environmental sinks.

---

[1] Peter D. Burden, Earth Jurisprudence: Private Property and the Environment (2015); Cormac Cullinan, Wild Law: A Manifesto for Earth's Justice (2011); Cormac Cullinan, Principals of Earth Jurisprudence, http://therightsofnature.org.

[2] Judith E. Koons, Earth Jurisprudence: The Moral Value of Nature (2008).

[3] Jan Laitos and Sandra Zellmer, Natural Resources Law (2015).

[4] Jan G. Laitos, The Right of Nonuse 24–47 (2012).

Natural capital is the stock of natural ecosystems that yields a flow of valuable ecosystem "goods" and "services."[5] Ecosystem goods would include such items as trees or fish, which in the absence of humans should be sustainable indefinitely. Natural capital ecosystem services would include wetlands that filter wastes or forests that provide erosion control. The collective benefits of ecosystem goods and services, flowing from natural capital, become the basis of all human economic activity.[6]

Earth systems, Earth-based systems, or planetary systems define the biophysical subsystems and processes that permit the biosphere to exist, and that are necessary for the presence of human life. These include photosynthesis, the hydrologic cycle, the overturning and thermohaline circulation in the oceans, the nitrogen and phosphorous cycles, and planetary climate conditions that permitted human beings to evolve during the stable Holocene Era.[7]

Each of these components of the Earth's environment, each of these ingredients of our environmental surroundings, is being changed by human activities. Environmental policies seem to be unable to deter these human actions. Nature will eventually adapt to this anthropogenic change,[8] but humans may not be able to survive in their post-Holocene world.[9]

This new epoch, dubbed the "Anthropocene," began when human activities started to have significant global impact on Earth's ecosystems and conditions necessary for the survival of homo sapiens as a species.[10] Human actions have so altered natural, pre-human processes that there is now real question of whether our species can adapt to an Earth whose atmospheric, hydrologic, and biospheric systems may no longer be conducive to human life.[11] It is important therefore to try to ascertain: Why Have Environmental Policies Failed?

[5] Robert Costanza, Natural Capital, www.eoearth.org/view/7/31/2008; Gretchen C. Daily, Nature's Services (1997).

[6] Robert Costanza et al., The Value of the World's Ecosystem Services and Natural Capital, 387 Nature 253 (May 15, 1997).

[7] See, e.g., Johan Rockstrom et al., A Safe Operating Space for Humanity, 476 Nature 282 (Aug. 2011).

[8] Marissa Fessenden, Here's What our Future World Might Look Like, Smithsonian.com (Sept. 3, 2015); Lizzie Wade, Earth in 16,000 years, The Atlantic (Sept. 7, 2015).

[9] Nadia Drake, Will Humans Survive the Sixth Great Extinction? National Geographic (June 23, 2015).

[10] Andrew Goudie, Anthropocene, Oxford Bibliographies (Sept. 29, 2014); Paul Crutzen, Geology of Mankind, 415 Nature 6867 (2002).

[11] Will Steffen, Paul Crutzen, & John McNeil, The Anthropocene: Are Humans Now Overwhelming the Great Forces of Nature? 36 AMBIO: A Journal of the Human Environment 614 (Dec. 2007).

The Gardener and the Sick Garden*

A. Introduction

When humans first began to notice that the planet's natural resources were not inexhaustible, and then later when they realized that the earth's environment could eventually become poisoned by human-generated waste, they turned to government policies to regulate and impose limits on the human tendency to exploit the planet's natural goods. Virtually all of these institutional responses have presumed that humans were like metaphorical gardeners trying to enjoy a garden. What the gardener realized was that the garden was being both depleted and contaminated by the gardener's bad habits. Humans were exploiting and exhausting the Earth's many natural resources for their own selfish interests. Legal institutions and environmental policies then sought to control the destructive gardener (truly, the *self*-destructive gardener) and to manage the garden.

Since the beginning of the twentieth-century, various rules have been imposed on humans intending to limit their obsession with damaging their garden, which is the planet Earth. During this time, different management techniques have been tried to ensure that the garden could continue to provide the resources and natural systems for humans to survive (see Chapter 2). But despite all these rules, laws, and institutional commands, the garden seems to be getting sicker. Why have these environmental policies not worked? Why have these governmental responses neither deterred the exploitative self-destructive gardener nor helped the garden regenerate?

These important questions can be answered in part by examining the worldview that humans have persistently and continuously adopted when fashioning legal policies intended to improve our relationship with our natural environment. This human worldview has been, and is,

---

* A modified and abbreviated version of this chapter earlier appeared in Laitos and Okulski, The Gardener and the Sick Garden: How Not to Address the Planet's Environmental Issues, 45 Envtl. L. Rev. (Envtl. Law Inst.) 10391 (May 2015). An even more abbreviated version of this chapter was presented as a paper at the AUBEA 2015 Conference in Sydney, Australia (Australasian Universities Building Education Assoc.).

wrong. It has been based not on reality or scientifically proven fact, but on false assumptions and unsubstantiated hope. And because our view of humans in the natural environment is fundamentally incorrect, three central models that historically have served as the foundation for policies that define and direct our actions toward our natural environment are flawed. These models set out (1) how Nature works; (2) how humans assign value to natural resources and environmental goods; and (3) how humans behave. Our environmental policies have failed because the assumptions that underlie each of the three central models are faulty. As a result, humans continue to pollute environmental goods and deplete the planet's resources. The self-destructive gardener has not been successfully regulated, and eventually the garden may not be able to provide for the gardener's needs.

If environmental policies are to succeed, they need to be based on an accurate view of humans' relationship with their natural environment. Policies should be built on three fact-based models that answer these questions: (1) How does Nature really work? (2) What is the proper value that humans should give to natural resources and environmental goods? (3) How do humans behave and make choices? A worldview of our relationship with Nature must not be predicated on wrongheaded beliefs about what we think that relationship *should be*. A model of how Nature works should not be based on how we *want* Nature to work. A model capturing the value of natural resources should not be grounded on how we *want* to use resources in the near term. And a model of how humans behave should not be formulated on how we *assume* humans behave. Instead, these models should reflect accurate, scientific reality.

When reality replaces wishful thinking, several realizations follow. First, since current environmental policies – typically either regulatory mandates or economic market-based instruments – are based on a fundamentally skewed worldview, and are grounded in three flawed models, these policies have little chance of long-term success. Second, an alternative, more workable and effective strategy, would start by relying on a fact-based view of humankind's relationship with Nature. Effective environmental policy would rely on better, more realistic, and empirically accurate models.

To avoid failure, environmental policy would also need to reflect, and obey, a fundamental principle that governs effective laws addressing earth-based systems and human behavior: The Requirements of Symmetry. The laws of "nature" are governed by symmetry, so any environmental policy seeking to succeed must be consistent with three universal requirements of symmetry. These are (1) the *equivalence* principle, (2) the concept of *unification*, and (3) the law of *conservation*.[1]

To be consistent with the equivalence principle, a policy should *not* be based on the traditional premise that humans are superior to, and more worthy than, other components of their natural environment, the biosphere. The gardener is not somehow more exceptional than the garden. To reflect the concept of unification, we should fashion policy that assumes that humans and their natural environment are not separate, but are one holistic reality – Nature. The gardener and the garden are not apart; they are two parts of the same system.

The law of conservation follows from another recognized principle, which holds that when there is symmetry, which there is in Nature, there is a corresponding conservation.[2] One such conservation law is that Nature usually opts for the simplest, most economical solution. This law is sometimes known as Occam's Razor (attributed to the medieval philosopher William of Occam). Occam's Razor admonishes that when choosing from a set of otherwise possible models of a given phenomenon, the simplest one is usually the correct one. The simplest environmental policy (and one that conforms to traditional bilateral symmetry) would embrace two correlative legal norms: (1) we should recognize a "positive" *right*, held by both humans (the gardener) and their natural surroundings (the garden), to environmental conditions that may sustain human survivability[3]; and (2) we would impose an affirmative *duty* on humans to promote and support natural systems.[4] The gardener has a responsibility to the garden that goes beyond the duty not to harm the garden; the gardener has an obligation to regenerate the garden.

---

[1] Mario Livio, The Equation That Couldn't Be Solved: How Mathematical Genius Discovered the Language of Symmetry 209–218 (2005); See also Frank Wilczek, A Beautiful Question: Finding Nature's Deep Design (2015).

[2] This principle is otherwise known as "Noether's Theorem," named after the early twentieth-century mathematical genius Amalie Noether. She showed that to every symmetry recognized by the laws of physics, such as the equivalence principle and the concept of unification, there exists a corresponding conservation law.

[3] As discussed later, "nature" alone does not need to be protected or conferred a special right, because nature, natural systems, and environmental goods will adapt to any and all human-caused exogenous changes to, or alterations of, purely ecocentric, non-anthropomorphic natural conditions. It is not Nature or the environment that needs to be protected; what needs protection are humans.

[4] As explained later, such a duty would not be the correlative of a negative right, i.e., a duty not to intrude on the right, but rather a positive obligation to provide something.

B.   A Realistic Picture of Nature and Humans and Their Natural Environment

Our legal responses to what appear to be "problems," "harms," or "negative changes" to the environment have typically been based on an overall worldview of humans in their natural environment, and on models that traditionally have defined our perceptions of humans and nature. For environmental policies to be effective, they must reflect an understanding of nature and humans grounded in truth and science, which requires that reality moor both the human worldview and the foundational models for legal action.

1.   A Proper Worldview of Humans' Relationship with Their Environmental Surroundings

In 2015, the Australian federal government approved the $1.2 billion Shenhua Watermark coal mine, expected to produce 268 million tons of coal in its 30-year life. The mine's approval was controversial because it would remove more than 35 square kilometers of some of Australia's most productive farmland. It would be expected to "destroy" almost 800 hectares of an endangered ecological community. The coal mine was nonetheless approved because the Australian government imposed on the project "18 of the strictest conditions in Australian history." Moreover, the mine was touted as "making a big economic contribution to the region, including much needed jobs."[5]

The approval of the Shenhua Watermark coal mine reflects a particular worldview of our relationship with our environmental surroundings. First, it seems to be environmental madness for government policy to greenlight an enormous coal mine (whose coal would be shipped primarily to China) at a time when greenhouse gases (from burning coal) seem to be contributing to relentless climate change and global warming.[6] But the approval nevertheless took place because policymakers *hoped* that the "18 of the strictest conditions in Australian history" would somehow lessen the mine's (and the coal's) impact on environmental conditions. Wishful

---

[5] Peter Hannam, Farmers Lament Massive Coal Mine, The Sydney Morning Herald 9 (July 9, 2015).

[6] Global Analysis – June 2015, The National Centers for Environmental Information (NDAA – July 23, 2015) (The combined average temperatures over global land and ocean surfaces for June 2014 was *the highest* for June in the 136-year period."). (Emphasis added.)

thinking about humans' ability to affect their environmental surroundings is often part of the human worldview.

Second, the fact that Australian policymakers imposed 18 "strict" conditions on the mine is consistent with the notion that humans (and particularly human policymakers) have *superior* and *exceptional* skills that permit them to manage and control Earth systems. Those 18 conditions reflect an anthropocentric arrogance about human knowledge of, and power over, the actual workings of our environmental context.

Third, both the mine and the coal emerging from the mine are viewed as being *separate* and *segregated* from human experience. Any harm associated with the mine is seen as being limited to its destructive potential to 35 kilometers of farmland and almost 800 hectares of endangered ecological community. It is as though the farmland and the endangered ecology are distinct and apart from humans, when in fact humans, and the new mine, will both affect the farmland, and be affected by the loss of ecological community. The distinction between "natural" and "anthropogenic" is artificial and not consistent with ecological reality. Ecosystems are influenced by humans, and humans are influenced by ecosystems.[7]

Our overwhelming anthropomorphic ethics have far too long insulated humans from our connections to, and dependence on, nature. Modern lifestyles and technological advances mask many of the usual linkages between humans and their surrounding natural systems, obscuring the normal environmental feedbacks.[8] For example, although resource consumption choices in one part of the world may have dramatic consequences for countries that supply the resources, the consumer usually never knows of these effects, and is oblivious to the real global environmental effects of the consumptive choice.

The reality, of course, is that humans are a part of, and entirely dependent on, the natural systems that surround them. Humans also certainly affect environmental goods and natural systems, contextualizing those human actions. Natural resources, environmental goods, and natural systems are absolutely necessary to support human life. The availability of natural resources, and the continued functioning of ecosystems and Earth-based natural systems, ensures that the biosphere operates to meet

---

[7] J. B Ruhl, The Myth of What is Inevitable Under Ecosystem Management: A Response to Pardy, 21 Pace Envtl. L. Rev. 315, 318–319, 320–322 (2004).

[8] Emilio F. Moran, People and Nature 69 (2006); John Cairns, Jr., Eco-societal Restoration: Re-examining Human Society's Relationship with Natural Systems, ch. 2, in Goals and Conditions for a Sustainable World (ESEP Books 2002).

the specific environmental conditions required for human life.[9] Indeed, human evolution itself – the emergence of *homo erectus* two million years ago – seems linked to, and probably caused by, environmental variability then taking place in East Africa, which affected local ecosystems.[10] All the component parts of the Earth-based community evolved in relation to one another. Humans and the natural environment that humans inhabit are all created by the ongoing relationships between the subjects and systems that make up the planet, its biosphere, and natural resources.[11]

Not only do humans and their natural surroundings exist in a mutualistic, interdependent relationship in which they co-evolve together. Humans and the environment are also not two separate entities, with one "superior" to the other. The gardener is not somehow better, compared to the garden. Our belief in human exceptionalism is misplaced. In fact, humans and their planet are a single system that responds to the continuously changing dynamics of human actions and environmental reactions. Insects, earthworms, bacteria, and photosynthesizing plants play a greater role in planetary systems than do humans.[12] Modern scientists have correctly adopted the term *social-ecological systems* to refer to a holistic planetary reality comprised of coupled human and ecological systems, with no hierarchical divide between them.[13]

2.   Three Models That Should Become the Foundation for Environmental Policies

In order for environmental policy to be effective, it should be built on models of environmental dynamics, policymaking, and human behavior that maximize the likelihood that such policies will in fact guide human

---

[9] Carl Folke, et al., Reconnecting to the Biosphere, 40 Ambio 719 (2011); Mathis Wackernagal & William Rees, Our Ecological Footprint: Reducing Human Impact on Earth 4–5 (1996); P. Wesley Shultz, Inclusion With Nature: The Psychology of Human Nature Relations, in the Psychology of Sustainable Development 61–66 (P. Schmuck et al. eds. 2002)

[10] C. Magill, G. Ashley, & K. Freeman, Ecosystem Variability and Early Human Habitats in Eastern Africa, 110 PNAS 1167–1174 (Jan. 22, 2013).

[11] Cormac Cullinan, Wild Law: A Manifesto for Earth Justice 115 (2002).

[12] Cormac Cullinan, Do Humans Have Standing to Deny Trees Rights? 11 Barry Law Rev. 11, 12, 14 (2008).

[13] Carl Folke, et al., Adaptive Governance of Social-Ecological Systems, 30 Annual Rev. Envtl. Resources 441, 443 (2005); Simon Levin et al., Social-Ecological Systems as Complex Adaptive Systems: Modeling and Policy Implications, 18 Environmental Development Economics 111–132 (Dec. 2012); Stephen Kellert, Birthright: People and Nature in the Modern World (2012).

choice so that the surrounding natural environment can sustain anthropomorphic existence. The policy goal should not be to "protect" the natural environmental so that it is not "harmed" by anthropocentric actions.
The natural environment surrounding humans will eventually adapt to
anthropogenic acts that affect environmental-ecological systems.[14] But
humans may not be able to adapt in time if the Earth's natural systems are
so altered by anthropogenic behaviors that the *homo sapien* species can no
longer survive.[15] Environmental policy needs to be grounded in realistic,
scientifically based models if this policy seeks to modify human behavior
so that our natural environment remains conducive to human life. Such
models, discussed more fully in Chapters 5–7, will ensure that any resulting policy will reflect (1) how Nature really works, (2) how humans should
value their natural environmental surroundings, and (3) how humans in
fact behave and make decisions.

a.   Model #1: How Does Nature Really Work?

In Moffat County, in the northwest corner of Colorado, a majority of the
land is owned by the U.S. federal government. The land is chiefly valuable to Moffat County residents for mining, oil, and gas operations, as
well as sheep grazing and herding. About 60 percent of the county is sage
grouse territory, and federal policymakers are drawing up plans to protect breeding areas and restore sage brush territory for the bird, in order
to keep it off the endangered species list. Protection of the sage grouse
could close federal lands in Moffat County to both grazing and oil and gas
development.[16]

The environmental policy of closing federal lands in Moffat County
to resource development because of a wild bird, the sage grouse, reflects
three assumptions about the workings of Nature: (1) humans are fundamentally apart from environmental goods, like the sage grouse; (2) there
is some "natural baseline" for the environment that policies should restore
or preserve; and (3) Nature is essentially static and, if left alone by humans,
will achieve some state of equilibrium. The reality of how Nature actually
works belies each of these assumptions.

First, although it may appear that the sage grouse of Moffat County is
a component of the natural order that is separate from the miners and

---

[14] S. A. Levin, Ecosystems and the Biosphere as Complex Adaptive Systems, 1 Ecosystems
431–436 (1998).
[15] J. Rockström, J. W. Steffen, K. Noone, et al., A Safe Operating Space for Humanity 461
Nature 472–475 (2009).
[16] Mark Jaffe, The Changing West, The Denver Post 1A (June 28, 2015).

ranchers whose activities seem to threaten the bird, the reality is that there is no separation between these humans and their environmental surroundings, such as the sage grouse. To biologists and ecological scientists, the concept of "Nature" is nothing but a shorthand for (1) the Earth's natural systems (e.g., ecosystems, atmospheric climate, photosynthesis), (2) the living organisms of the biosphere (e.g., grassland, protozoa, and yes, even humans), and its (3) environmental goods (e.g., the air, water, land, and soil). Indeed, as one leading scholar has correctly proclaimed, "naturalness is a human conception."[17]

Second, a policy of protecting a wild bird whose existence may be threatened by anthropogenic change in Moffat County reflects a traditional feature of natural resource and environmental policymaking – a desire to restore or preserve an environmental good that has been affected by humans. Policies commonly first seek to reverse human-caused changes to restore an area or an environmental good, so that it is returned to some more "natural" baseline.[18] Alternatively, environmental policies attempt to preserve ecosystems or natural landscapes or wildlife in a desired, non-anthropogenically altered, more "natural" state.[19] Both the restoration and preservation paradigms presume that there is a normal, or natural non-human-induced state for environmental goods, and that the goal of policy should be to mitigate or minimize human change, so that Nature either returns to or remains in this idealized baseline.[20] However, the reality is that a policy will fail if built on an expectation that ecosystems are stable, or that a particular environmental baseline must be sustained. In truth, an equilibrium model for nature is not scientifically accurate anymore. Environmental policies addressing environmental goods or systems must start with the recognition that change, not stasis, is norm.[21]

Third, environmental policy that seeks to keep natural resources in a particular state of being is a policy that presumes the planet's biophysical

[17] J. B. Ruhl, The Pardy-Ruhl Dialogue on Ecosystem Management, Part IV: Narrowing and Sharpening the Questions, 24 Pace Envtl. L. Rev. 25, 31 (2007).

[18] J. Hobbs & A. Viki Cramer, Restoration Ecology: Interventionist Approaches for Restoring and Maintaining Ecosystem Function in the Face of Rapid Environmental Change, 33 Ann. Rev. Envt'l. Resources 39, 40 (2008).

[19] Ted Nordhaus & Michael Shellengerge, Break Through: From the Death of Environmentalism to the Politics of Possibility 24–26 (2007).

[20] Robin Kurdis Craig, "Stationarity Is Dead" – Long Live Transformation: Five Principles for Climate Change Adaption Law, 34 Harv. Envtl. L. Rev. 10, 31–35 (2010).

[21] Daniel B. Botkin, Discordant Harmonies: A New Ecology for the Twenty-First Century 4 (1990).

subsystems and processes are static. The scientific reality about Nature is that it has no "natural baselines" to restore or preserve. Rather, the ecological reality is one of constant complex change, where natural dynamism is the rule.[22] Humans and their environmental surroundings are best seen as an integrated, holistic *complex adaptive system* (CAS).[23]

A CAS consists of individual agents able to change, learn from experience, evolve over time, and exploit their own agendas. It is a highly dynamic system able to adapt and evolve with a changing environment. There is no separation between Nature and its surrounding environment and critical players (i.e., humans). Nature is closely linked with all other related systems that act on it or affect Nature's evolution. Nature does not just adapt to humans; there is inevitable change by both humans and nature when they interact – there is co-evolution. The central features of CAS are resilience, diversity, redundancy, complexity, connectivity, and nonlinear spatiotemporal interactions. A CAS, like Nature, pushes away from and rejects equilibrium.[24]

While Nature can adapt to human activities, many of the subsystems of Nature turn out to be sensitive when various threshold levels are crossed. For example, when humans disrupt Earth-system processes such as climate, biodiversity, stratospheric ozone levels, global freshwater, atmospheric levels of carbon dioxide and other chemicals, and ocean acidification, there may be unacceptable environmental change – that is to say, unacceptable for human survival. When these thresholds are crossed, the Earth's subsystems may shift into a new state, with potentially disastrous consequences for humans. In short, even though a CAS can "adapt" to human development, when it adapts to the point at which planetary boundaries are exceeded, the resulting environmental change makes the Earth no longer conducive to human survival.[25]

---

[22] Robert L. Glicksman, Ecosystem Resilience to Disruptions Lined to Global Climate Change: An Adaptive Approach to Federal Land Management, 87 Neb. L. Rev. 833, 852–856 (2009).

[23] J. B. Ruhl, Thinking of Environmental Law as a Complex Adaptive System: How to Clean Up the Environment by Making a Mess of Environmental Law, 34 Hous. L. Rev. 933, 940, 968–975 (1997).

[24] Simon Levin, et al., *supra* note 13; R. M. May et al., Complex Systems: Ecology for Bankers, 457 Nature 893 (2008); S. A. Levin, Ecosystems and the Biosphere as Complex Adaptive Systems, 1 Ecosystems 431–436 (1998).

[25] Will Steffen, et al., Planetary Boundaries Guiding Human Development on a Changing Planet, Science (Jan. 15, 2015); John Rockstrom, et al., A Safe Operating Space for Humanity, 461 Nature 472 (Sept. 2009); The Nine Planetary Boundaries, www.stockholmresilience.org/21/research (2014).

b.   Model #2: How Should Humans Value Their Environmental Surroundings?

In 2015, the developer of the Village at Wolf Creek agreed to delay further construction of the residential village while a lawsuit filed by Friends of Wolf Creek and San Luis Valley Ecosystem Council challenged a policy of the U.S. Forest Service permitting a public-private land swap that expanded access for the proposed village. The Forest Service had "given" the private developer 205 acres of federal land connected to his property atop Colorado's Wolf Creek Pass in exchange for 177 acres of wetlands the developer gave the Forest Service. The lawsuit argued that the Forest Service had violated federal environmental law by not adequately considering the impact the land swap would have on "the human environment."[26] This "human environment" included the large village planned for 8,000 people who would live on Wolf Creek Pass as well as the surrounding national forest.[27]

Environmental policy that considers only the impact of human behavior on "humans" and "the human environment" values anthropocentric consequences. Such a human-focused policy asks these questions about proposed action: What impact does that land swap have on the future village and its 8,000 human residents? What impact will 8,000 new humans have on the surrounding trees in the national forest? Will those trees still be available to harvest? But what is missing from this kind of traditional policy valuation is some analysis of the impacts on a variety of natural systems and the humans who depend on them. The combined, integrated combination of human-natural systems is termed a socio-ecological system, or SES.[28] Environmental policies should be concerned with the effects of human actions on SES. These anthropogenic actions operate on complex ecosystems and SES and set in motion feedback loops and

---

[26] The environmental statute at play in this case is the National Environmental Policy Act (NEPA), which requires policymaking agencies such as the Forest Service to take into account the impact of their policies on "the quality of the *human* environment." 42 U.S.C § 4332(2)(c) (emphasis added). The "human environment" is further defined as "includ[ing] the relationship of people with the environment." 40 C.F.R § 1508.14.

[27] Jason Blevins, Lawsuit Puts Hold on Project: The Village at Wolf Creek Will Not Begin Construction Until the Case Is Resolved, The Denver Post 12A (July 16, 2015).

[28] "Socio-ecological systems, social-ecological systems, and coupled human-environmental systems … describe systems of human-environmental interactions." Elinor Ostrom, Marco Janssen, & John Anderies, Going Beyond Panaceas, 104 Proc. Nat'l Acad. Sci. 15, 176 (2007). See also note 13, *supra*.

nonlinear changes that can result in the irreversible crossing of ecosystems thresholds.[29]

To avoid this bleak prospect, environmental policy should take into account, and value, the dynamic complexity of natural systems and the relationships that SES have with such systems. Such policy would begin by first adopting an *ecosystem management* framework in the context of environmental sites and objects undergoing systemic changes.[30] The village of Wolf Creek must be considered in the context of the surrounding ecosystem. Next environmental policy should acknowledge how SES are dependent on *natural capital* and *ecosystem services*.[31] The trees next to the village of Wolf Creek are not just an economic commodity; they are natural capital that provide humans with free ecosystem benefits. Environmental policy should then ensure that environmental and natural resources law increases the capacity of SES to continual transformation – what some scholars term the increase in an SES's *adaptive capacity*.[32] Whatever policy is initially adopted to oversee the Wolf Creek land swap, it must have the capacity to adapt and change in light of new future environmental conditions. And finally, policy should reflect *ecological resilience*, the ability of ecosystems to take on alternative states, when the magnitude of an exogenous disturbance triggers a shift to an alternative regime.[33] Forest Service policy needs to be aware that a new village of 8,000 persons could cause the Wolf Creek ecosystem to manifest ecological resilience by dramatically transforming the nature of the surrounding ecosystems after the completion of the village.

c.   Model #3: How Do Humans Really Behave?

An executive order from President Barack Obama requires that the U.S. Environmental Protection Agency (EPA) analyze the costs and benefits

[29] Intergovernmental Panel on Climate Change 2014: Mitigation of Climate Change 113–114 (2014); U.S. Climate Change Sci. Program, Synthesis & Assessment Product 4.2: Thresholds of Climate Change in Ecosystems viii (2009).

[30] The Laws of Nature: Reflections on the Evolution of Ecosystem Management Law & Policy (K. Robbins ed. 2012); Robert L. Fischman, From Words to Action: The Impact and Equal Status of the 2006 National Wildlife Refuge System Management Policies, 26 Stan. Envt. L.J. 77, 82–84 (2007).

[31] J. B. Ruhl, Steven E. Kraft, et al., The Law and Policy of Ecosystem Services (2007).

[32] *Craig, supra* note 20 at 39.

[33] Michael Ungar, The Social Ecology of Resilience: A Handbook of Theory and Practice (2012); Adapting Institutions: Governance, Complexity, and Social-Ecological Resilience (E. Boyd & C. Folke eds. 2012).

of its regulations. The assumption is that both policymakers and human decision-makers make choices based on a weighing of costs and benefits of alternative courses of action. In order to measure the economic benefits of restrictions on greenhouse gases, the EPA's Interagency Working Group on the Social Cost of Carbon captured, in dollar terms, the social damage from one ton of carbon emissions – $36. In other words, if the EPA finalized a policy meant to eliminate 300 million tons of carbon dioxide emissions annually, the monetary value of the reduction (the "benefit" in a cost-benefit calculation) would be $36 x 300 million = $10.8 billion. The issue for the EPA would then be whether those monetized benefits would justify the costs of achieving a reduction of 300 million tons of emissions.[34]

Several questions arise from this cost-benefit exercise of the EPA. First, how can one ever be sure that the EPA, or the Interagency Working Group, or any group of deep thinkers can actually measure, in dollar terms, the economic benefits of restrictions on carbon dioxide. Second, even if the social cost of carbon can be calculated, should this cost account for the *global* damage done by emissions from the United States or only *domestic* damage? If the latter, then the cost would be significantly lower. And third, do policymakers and the humans they regulate in fact actually consider the costs and benefits of choices before making a choice?

The reality of human behavior is best understood in light of social science and cognitive psychology instead of old assumptions or hunch and guesswork. A number of modern neuroeconomists, psychologists, and behavioral economists had recently offered up empirical findings about how we make choices and arrive at decisions. These scientific observers of the human condition have concluded that humans are not necessarily rational in their behavior.[35] They do *not* deliberately weigh the costs and benefits of alternative courses of action, but instead make choices based on other influences such as altruism, fairness, teamwork, networking, and the choices of others.[36] Humans, not surprisingly, give undue weight

---

[34] Climate Change: The Social Cost of Carbon, 2015–2050, Technical Support Document (July 2015), http://www.epa.gov/climatechange; Cass Sunstein, A Good Price on U.S. Carbon Emissions – Bloomberg View, The Denver Post 19A (July 16, 2015).

[35] David Kahneman, Thinking, Fast and Slow (2011)

[36] Amos Tversky & Daniel Kahneman, The Framing of Decisions and the Psychology of Choice, 211 Science 453 (1981); Coren L. Apicella, et al., Social Networks and Cooperation in Hunter-Gatherers, 481 Nature 497 (Jan. 2012); Elinor Ostrom, Governing the Commons: The Evolution of Institutions for Collective Action (1990).

to the short term, in light of a high decisional discount rate that diminishes the value of the future in terms of its utility. Humans also seem to believe that what matters in choices is what is salient to them, particularly when making choices where our usual rules-of-thumb seem familiar and well suited to the choice.[37]

When behavioral economics guide environmental policy initiatives, it seems that historic command-and-control rules are not as effective. If people are more responsive to "desired" rather than undesired information (which is what behavioral economists have discovered), then disclosures to people about how well they are doing – for example, how energy efficient they are compared to their neighbors – may be a preferred policy to a flat mandate.[38] Indeed, behavioral economics suggest that, instead of *compelling* certain environmentally friendly behaviors, it may be better to *persuade* people while preserving their freedom of choice. Instead of laws reflecting traditional "hard" paternalism, which impose real costs on people, behavioral economists favor "soft" paternalism, which only imposes affective or psychic costs.[39]

C. Environmental Policies Fail Because They Are Built on a Skewed Worldview and on Three Flawed Models

Those who make environmental policy too often base their laws and government actions on a human worldview that skews the real human relationship to Nature, as well as on flawed models of nature and humans. This kind of thinking will cause environmental policies to fail. Conversely, if environmental policies are instead consistent with an accurate view of how humans and their surroundings interrelate, and if they correctly reflect the reality of how nature works and humans behave, then those policies will be more likely to succeed. Unfortunately, most environmental policies correspond to inaccurate and unrealistic views of nature, humans, and humans in nature. This book analyzes the most critical among environmental policy failures. Here is a short summary.

---

[37] Pedro Bardalo, Nicola Gennaioli & Andrei Shleifer, Science in Experimental Tests of the Endowment Effect, 102 Am. Econ. Rev. 47 (2012).

[38] See, e.g., Jim Tankersley, Will People Save Energy Just to be Good Citizens? Actually, Yes, The Washington Post (Oct. 27, 2014).

[39] Cass R. Sunstein, Why Nudge? The Politics of Libertarian Paternalism (Yale Univ. Press 2014); Richard H. Thaler & Cass R. Sunstein, Nudge: Improving Decisions About Health, Wealth & Happiness (2008); Matthew Adler, Well-Being and Fair Distribution: Beyond Cost-Benefit Analysis 6–8 (2011).

1.   A Skewed Worldview: Humans Apart from Nature

Virtually all governmental responses to environmental changes seem to be grounded in the assumption that "Nature" or the "Natural World" is in trouble because it is harmed by anthropomorphic actions. Most environmental policies thereby reflect the notion that humans, through their policies, need to correct the problems that the natural environment is experiencing. Humans see their role as policymakers who can "protect" the environment, cure various environmental "ailments," and bring ecosystems back to a more "natural" state. Such traditional policy responses are akin to the gardener viewing the poorly producing garden and deciding to "fix" the problems of the sick garden, while perceiving the garden as completely separate from, and exogenous to, the gardener.

This traditional perspective, which is embedded in most modern environmental policies, reflects two central themes about how humans have viewed their place in Nature. Each of these prevailing views is wrong. First, humans see themselves as *independent* and *separate* from their natural environmental surroundings.[40] Like the gardener observing a dying garden, humans (and their laws) consistently see themselves outside of and apart from nature. But humans are most assuredly not separate from or exogenous to nature.[41] Rather, humans are integrated within it, so that there is in fact only one planetary system – a human/nature SES.[42]

Second, humans have historically viewed themselves as being *superior* to Nature, because of a faith in human *exceptionalism*.[43] Our environmental policies have reflected a view that the rules governing the rest of the natural world do not apply to us, as we are an exceptional species. As a result, we posture with an attitude of superiority. We are delusional to think that we can manage natural resources and the surrounding environment.[44] We see ourselves as the stewards of Nature, able to dominate it and control it for anthropocentric ends.[45] If Nature seems damaged by us, we can reverse these human-induced changes and bring it back to a more "natural" baseline. Or, if Nature seems threatened by humans, we

---

[40] Emilio F. Moran, People and Nature 7 (2006).
[41] Cormac Cullinan, Wild Law 63 (2d ed. 2011); *Kellert, supra* note 13.
[42] *Simon Levin, supra* note 13.
[43] Jonathan Baert Wiener, Beyond the Balance of Nature, 7 Duke Envtl. L. & Policy 3–4 (1996); Evolution, Categories, and Consequences, 22 Ecology L. Q. 325, 343 (1995).
[44] William Leiss, Modern Science, Enlightenment, and the Domination of Nature: No Exit?, www.vta.edu/huma/agger/fastcapitalism (2014).
[45] Jedediah Purdy, American Nature: The Shape of Conflict Environmental Law, 36 Harvard Envtl. L. Rev. 169, 189–197 (2012).

can preserve places and objects so they remain in a more "Natural" state.[46] We become the superior gardener, better able to manage the garden than the garden itself, for our very selfish needs.

Environmental policies will fail when based on notions of human separation from, and human superiority to, Nature. If such policies continue to fail, then human actions may certainly become the main driver for global environmental change. Earth's systems could be pushed outside the stable environmental state of the Holocene era, which could lead to a condition that is no longer conducive to human development. The Earth will not be a safe operating space for humanity.[47] The garden will continue to exist, but it will not be able to support the gardener anymore.

2.   Three Flawed Models

a.   Nature as Self-Regulating, and the Regulatory State

Regulation is the most common policy tool used to control human decisions affecting the natural environment. A regulatory policy is mostly a negative strategy of simply trying to prevent some human action that appears to be disturbing some mythical natural baseline.[48] This idea of a natural baseline usually reflects the view, discredited by CAS theory, that the Earth system is a closely integrated, self-correcting system, where life regulates the planetary environment to suit itself and to keep it stable. This notion of life on this planet sees natural feedbacks and control loops as stabilizing conditions, which eventually bring about homeostasis.[49] But modern ecological science rejects this model of how life and environment interact on Earth. The better view is that the environment is far from stable. The accepted scientific wisdom is that "stationarity is dead" and that all environmental systems are dynamic and changing.[50] The Earth is well suited to life only because organisms continuously adapt to constant change.[51]

---

[46] *Craig, supra* note 20 at 31–35.

[47] *Johan Rockstrom, supra* note 15 at 472–473.

[48] A. Dan Tarlock, The Future of Environmental "Rule of Law" Litigation, 17 Pace Envtl, L. Rev. 237, 243 (2000).

[49] J. E. Lovelock, Gaia: A New Look at Life on Earth (Oxford Univ. Press 1979); Kate Ravilious, Perfect Harmony, The Guardian (April 28, 2008);

[50] P. C. D. Milly et al., Stationarity Is Dead: Whither Water Management?, 319 Science 573 (Feb. 1, 2008).

[51] Toby Tyrell, On Gaia: A Critical Investigation of the Relationship Between Life and Earth (Princeton Univ. Press 2013); *Simon Levin, supra* note 13 at 113–114.

When the prevailing (and incorrect) model of Nature assumes that the Earth's systems are self-regulating, however, then environmental policy will seek to restore Nature, particularly when humans interfere with this hypothetical natural condition. Policies responding to this flawed model of Nature tend to be negative and regulatory, in that they are designed either to halt or ban seemingly environmentally "destructive" human actions, or to mandate behavior that does not "interfere" with Nature. For example, our laws order us not to pollute air, water, or land; they mandate that we not interfere with open spaces, wilderness areas, and certain wildlife, and they command us not to remove too many trees, fish, or rangeland. These negative regulatory laws often remove human choice, and they presume that if humans leave Nature alone, since it is self-regulating, it will eventually recover on its own.[52]

b.   Seeking a Stable Equilibrium Instead of a Dynamic,
Unstable, Adaptive, and Coupled Natural and Human System

Throughout much of the modern era of reliance on environmental policies – roughly 1960 to 2010 – the end goal of most of the environmental policies was grounded in the twin objects of "stationarity" and "separateness." The concept of *stationarity* reflected a prevailing idea "that natural systems usually fluctuate within an unchanging envelope of variability."[53] Environmental and natural resources laws became preservationist because they were based on a stationarity framework that presumed that all anthropogenic change adversely affects Nature's "unchanging envelope." Human-caused interference with this envelope was therefore unnatural and harmful, needing to be reversed. Policies have sought either to preserve ecosystems and natural objects or to restore areas or resources back to some non-human-induced "natural baseline."[54] But, as noted previously, stationarity is dead, and natural systems are ever-changing, nonlinear, complex adaptive systems.[55]

The concept of *separateness* between humans and their natural environment has also been reflected in environmental policy. This policy has humans observing natural systems, places, and objects from a perspective that is outside of, and apart from, the environment that policies are intended to manipulate, or improve. It has been only relatively recently that some policymakers have come to realize that humans are not separate

[52] *Sunstein, supra* note 39 at 19–20, 55–59.
[53] *Milly, supra* note 50 at 573.
[54] *Tarlock, supra* note 48.
[55] *Glicksman, supra* note 22; *Craig, supra* note 30; *Ruhl, supra* note 23.

from their surroundings. Instead, the planet consists of "coupled" natural and human systems, or socio-ecological systems (SES), that comprise natural systems and humans, who are a part of them, and who depend on them.[56]

What policies should value are not stationarity or separateness, but a management framework that reflects the natural dynamism of ecosystems that undergo ongoing systemic changes.[57] Workable policies should acknowledge that socio-ecological systems are dependent on natural capital and ecosystem services.[58] Since the environment surrounding humans is a *complex adaptive system*, a CAS, any policy should seek to increase humans', other species', and ecosystems' adaptive capacity.[59] And because, in an SES, anthropogenic action is inevitable, especially human action that stresses natural systems, policies should seek to increase the SES's adaptive capacity and resilience to continuing, unpredictable, non-linear change.[60]

c.   Humans as Rational Choice Actors Who Obey Market-Based Rules

Standard economic theory has for centuries relied on a model of human behavior based on rational choice theory. This theory, which underscores most of our current environmental policy that is not otherwise prohibitory and regulatory, presumes that individuals act rationally when making choices. The assumption is that we act as if we are balancing costs against benefits to arrive at decisional action that maximizes personal advantage. This view of humans is sometimes termed the *homo economicus* model, where humans base their choices on their own "utility functions." Such humans ignore all social values if they do not provide

---

[56] *Simon Levin, supra* note 13

[57] Integrating Social Sciences with Ecosystem Management (H. Ken Cordell & John C. Bergstrom eds. 1999).

[58] Dieter Helm, Natural Capital: Valuing the Planet (2015); *Ruhl, supra* note 31.

[59] Intergovernmental Panel on Climate Change (IPCC), Climate Change 2014: Synthesis Report, Summary for Policymakers (AR5), SPM 3.2, Climate Change Risks Reduced by Mitigation and Adaption, SPM 3.3, Characteristics of Adaptation Pathways; Klaus J. Puettmann, Restoring the Adaptive Capacity of Forest Ecosystems, 33 J. of Sustainable Forestry S15–S27 (2014).

[60] Carl Folke et al., Resilience Thinking: Integrating Resilience, Adaptability and Transformability, 15 Ecology and Society 20 (2010); Linking Social and Ecological Systems: Management Practices and Social Mechanisms for Building Resilience (Cambridge University Press 1998) (Colding J. ed.); Council on Environmental Quality, Climate Change Resilience, www.whitehouse.gov/administration (July 25, 2015).

utility, or if they do not help *homo economicus* attain very specific goals with the least possible cost.[61]

Modern social psychologists and behavioral economists have largely undermined this economic model of humans as rational maximizers of their self-interest.[62] In reality, the rational actor is a myth. People's decisions are not determined by a careful weighing of costs and benefits, or by pure selfishness, or welfare maximization, but by emotions such as altruism, susceptibility to peer influences, and all sorts of cognitive biases.[63]

This more modern understanding of how humans behave predicts that environmental policies based on the *homo economicus* model will fail. In particular, policies built around market-based instruments should no longer be presumed to be reliable or effective in influencing behavior. Such instruments, such as taxes, incentives, subsidies, penalties, and even cap-and-trade systems, are all based on the traditional rational choice model that simply holds that humans will seek to avoid a cost, while making choices that maximize an individual's selfish welfare.[64] But a more accurate model of human decision-making, using behavioral economics, presumes that individuals are equally susceptible to other influences, such as a selfless desire to enhance collective welfare. Moreover, humans often display often a willingness to incur certain costs because of the psychic gain experienced knowing that Nature thereby benefits.[65]

D.   Have Environmental Policies Failed?

The planet's environment has been stable for the past ten thousand years – the Holocene.[66] During this period of relative stability, environmental conditions permitted the emergence and development of human civilizations. Since the Industrial Revolution, however, human actions, not natural conditions, have driven global environmental change. We are now in a new

---

[61] Jon Elster, Nuts and Bolts for the Social Sciences (Cambridge Univ. Press 1989); Gary Becker, The Economic Approach to Human Behavior (Chicago 1976); Daniel Cohen, Homo Economicus: The (host) Prophet of Modern Times (2014); T. Lawson, The Nature of Heterodox Economics, 30 Cambridge J. of Economics 483 (2006).

[62] See *Kahneman* and *Tversky, supra* notes 36.

[63] Peter Singer, The Most Good You Can Do: How Effective Altruism is Changing Ideas About Living Ethically (2015).

[64] See, e.g., William Nordhaus, The Climate Casino: Risk, Uncertainty, and Economics for a Warming World (Yale Univ. Press 2014).

[65] Science for Environmental Policy, Future Brief: Green Behavior, European Commission, Issue 4 (Oct. 2012).

[66] J. R. Petit, et al., Climate and Atmospheric History of the Past 420,000 Years from the Vostok Ice Core, 399 Nature 429 (1999).

era – the Anthropocene.[67] This is a time when human activities have so altered the Earth's regulatory capacity that we may have started to exceed planetary boundaries and assorted thresholds for human survival.[68] Countless environmental policies and decades of lawmaking designed to "protect" the environment, have not been able to reverse, or even slow, this anthropomorphic assault on natural systems and planetary boundaries.[69]

Human activities have begun to push Earth systems outside the stable environmental state of the Holocene in several critical ways. First, humans have interfered with biophysical subsystems, resulting in environmental *losses* that may adversely affect humans. Chief among these losses has been: (1) loss of biodiversity (e.g., deforestation, exhaustion of fish stock, or loss of plant species)[70]; (2) loss of natural systems (e.g., ecosystems, wetlands)[71]; (3) loss of freshwater reserves[72]; and (4) mass extinctions leading to a loss of species.[73] Second, humans have *changed* essential biophysical processes. They have caused climate change[74] and unmatched

[67] P. J. Crutzen, Geology of Mankind, 415 Nature 23 (2002).

[68] Joel Achenbach, Scientists: Human Activity Has Pushed Earth Beyond Four of Nine Planetary Boundaries, Washington Post (Jan. 15, 2015); *Johan Rockstrom, supra* note 15; W. Steffen, et al., Global Change and the Earth System: A Planet Under Pressure (2004).

[69] Chris Mooney, The World's Most Famous Climate Scientist Just Outlined an Alarming Scenario for our Planet's Future, The Washington Post (July 20, 2015); Becky Oskin, 2014 Was Earth's Hottest Year on Record, Live Science (Jan. 16, 2015); Douglas J. McCauley et al., Marine Defaunation: Animal Loss in the Global Ocean, 347 Science 6219 (Jan. 2015); M. Scheffer et al., Catastrophic Shifts in Ecosystems, 413 Nature 591 (2001).

[70] Patrick Whittle, Fading Fishermen: A Historic Industry Faces a Warming World, The Associated Press (Apr. 28, 2016); Bruce Finley, Study: Air Pollution Hurting Plant Diversity, The Denver Post 41 (Apr. 25, 2016). World Wildlife Fund Global, Deforestation, http://wwf .panda.org (Jan. 5, 2015); Keith Ridler, Half of Columbia River Sockeye Salmon Dying Due to Hot Water, Assoc. Press (July 27, 2015); Plenty More Fish in the Sea? The Economist 66 (Dec. 21, 2013); Douglas Main, Feds Close Most of Northeast to Cod Fishing, Newsweek (Nov. 13, 2014); Deforestation and its Extreme Effects on Global Warming, Scientific American (Nov. 13, 2012).

[71] Scientists Warn an Entire Eco-System is Under Threat From Climate Change, Science Daily (July 31, 2015); John Flesher, Great Lakes Only Region to Gain Wetlands, Assoc. Press, The Denver Post 10A (Jan. 6, 2014).

[72] Hilary Hanson, One-Third of the World's Largest Groundwater Sources Are in Serious Trouble: Study, www.huffingtonpost.com/2015/06/17; Earth's Freshwater Reserves Are Disappearing, www.msn.com/en-us/news.technology (Nov. 11, 2014).

[73] Gerardo Ceballos, et al., Accelerated Modern Human-Induced Species Losses: Entering the Sixth Mass Extinction, Sci. Adv.; 1:e1400253 (June 19, 2015); Ocean Life Faces Mass Extinction, Broad Study Says, New York Times A1 (Jan. 16, 2015); Elizabeth Kolbert, The Sixth Extinction (2014); A World without Bees, Time Magazine (Aug. 19, 2013).

[74] Michael Slezak, April Breaks Global Temperature Record, Marking Seven Months of New Highs, The Guardian (May 16, 2016); Peter U. Clark, et al., Consequences of Twenty-First-Century Policy for Multi-Millennial Climate and Sea-Level Change, Nature Climate Change, doi: 10.1038 (Feb. 2016); Karl Ritter, U.N. Report Concludes Human Altering Climate, Associated Press, The Denver Post 10A (Nov. 2, 2014).

sea level rise,[75] brought about by anthropogenic chemical pollution of the atmosphere.[76]

Human actions driving these losses and changes will not likely abate without some radically different approach to environmental policy, because the Earth's human population continues to grow at a relentless pace.[77] And it is not just the fact of population growth that is so troubling; what is particularly alarming is how these many humans interrelate with each other. This growing population of humans is not just overexploiting a resource, and in doing so imposing negative externalities upon a larger group that has a stake in the resource, such as the climate. Rather, what these many humans are now experiencing is what has been termed a "true" tragedy of the commons, where their actions are detracting from *their own ability* to enjoy the resource.[78]

E.   How Better to Address Earth's Environmental Issues

If the goal of environmental policy is to encourage human behavior that does not interfere with the biosphere's ability to sustain human life, then any proposed policy initiative should, at a minimum, align with accurate and scientifically realistic models of humans and Nature. Such a policy would be based on an accurate worldview of how humans do relate to, and are connected with, their natural surroundings. The policy would be built on scientifically current models of (1) how Nature works, in fact, (2) how humans should value their surroundings, and (3) how humans really behave and make decisions.

Any workable policy should ensure that legal rules or government requirements would not be designed in a regulatory vacuum, but would

---

[75] Rafi Letzter, Sea Levels May be Rising Twice as Fast as We Thought, Business Insider (Nov. 3, 2016); Andy Horowitz, New Orleans New Flood Maps: An Outline for Disaster, The New York Times (June 1, 2016) (Because of global warming, roughly 75 percent of New Orleans will be below sea level by the year 2050); Robert DeConto & David Pollard, Contribution of Antarctica to Past and Future Sea-Level Rise, 531 Nature 591 (March 2016); Seth Borenstein, Seas are Rising Faster Than Any Time in Past 2800 Years, Associated Press (Feb. 22, 2016); Oliver Milman, Sea Level Rise Over Past Century Unmatched in 6000 Years, Says Study, The Guardian (Oct. 14, 2014).

[76] J. Lelieveld, et al., The Contribution of Outdoor Air Pollution Sources to Premature Mortality on Global Scale, 525 Nature 367 (Sept. 2015); Bruce Finley, Ozone Reaching Risky Zones, The Denver Post 12A (July 29, 2015); Joby Warrick, Delaware-Sized Gas Plume Over West Illustrates the Cost of Leaking Methane, The Washington Post (Dec. 29, 2014).

[77] Allen Weisman, Countdown (2013); Steven Emmett, Ten Billion (2013); The World in 2050, www.msn/en-us/news/technology (Jan. 5, 2015).

[78] Shi-Ling Hsu, What Is a Tragedy of the Commons? Overfishing and the Campaign Spending Problem, 69 Albany L. Rev. 75 (2005).

instead conform to, and be consistent with, certain universal truths, or "theorems," that apply when constructing a realistic set of principles for guiding humans in Nature. If one is seeking to identify central truths about Nature that should serve as a kind of "constitution" for policies regulating humans in Nature, then such policies need to obey an organizing rule for Nature, and laws pertaining to nature: the Rule of Symmetry.[79] Human-based environmental policies can most easily satisfy the Rule of Symmetry by embracing principles of equivalence, unification, and conservation.

Consistent with the Equivalence Principle, laws about nature will fail if they are built on an anthropogenic view of the world. The success or failure of laws should *not* be judged, consistent with standard welfare economics, exclusively in terms of their effects on the well-being on humans.[80] Such a view presumes that humans are superior to their surroundings, when in fact humans and their natural environment are "equivalent."[81] Consistent with the Unification Principle, policies need to reflect the fact that humans and their environment are not separate, but are a unified, coupled SES.[82] And, consistent with the Conservation Principle, successful workable environmental policies would not be complicated, but simple. An environmental policy reflecting the Conservation Principle would be an example of bilateral or mirror-reflection symmetry.[83]

Environmental policies that are (1) consistent with accurate, realistic models about humans in Nature and (2) obey the Symmetry Theorem guiding humans in Nature would confer a specialized *right* and impose a symmetrical correlative *duty*:[84] (1) A "positive" right would be conferred on an integrated, equivalent, unified, holistic SES human/Nature beneficiary; and (2) an "affirmative" duty to the natural environment would be imposed on humans to fulfill the basic preconditions of human survival and sustainability on this planet.

---

[79] See generally *Livio, supra* note 1, *Wilczek supra* note 1 at 8, 11.

[80] Economic Institutions and Behavioral Economics (Peter Diamond & Hannu Vartiainen eds. 2007); Mark Sagoff, Principle and the Environment 3–9 (2004).

[81] Einstein's "Equivalence Principle" originally asserted that a gravitational field cannot be distinguished from a suitably accelerated reference frame; in other words, we cannot tell the difference between gravity and acceleration through time and space. And Einstein's theory of special relativity showed that matter and energy, thought to be separate and different, are really one and the same when one gives to matter the speed of light squared ($E=mc^2$).

[82] See note 28, *supra*.

[83] This type of symmetry occurs when there is some kind of correspondence between opposing views, such as when there is a correlative relationship between positions, which is the case when there is a right-duty relationship.

[84] This right and duty would be "correlative," because the existence of one relationship (the right) implies the existence of the other (the duty).

1.   A Positive Right to Environmental Conditions Where Planetary Boundaries Are Not Exceeded

Unlike a negative right, which is a claim on others to not interfere with the right, a positive right claims for the right-holder the assistance of others in providing the essential constituents of the right. A positive right provides something to the right-holder, while imposing on others the need to help fulfill the conditions to a successful outcome.[85] In the case of humans and Nature, their positive right would be consistent with the prevailing model of "how nature works" in that it would be a right to environmental conditions that permit natural systems to operate so that critical planetary boundaries are respected and not transgressed by human actions. While the Earth can and will adapt to any and all anthropomorphic activities, humanity needs a safe operating space with respect to Earth systems and associated biophysical thresholds. Humans may survive only when human actions do not cause these planetary boundaries to be crossed.

In order for this right to be consistent with the Equivalence and Unification Principles, it would have to be held not just by humans but also natural resources, natural systems, and environmental goods. Humans and nature exist in an interdependent relationship that is a single system – a social-ecological system. It is this combined human-Nature system that should be conferred a right to environmental conditions that restore planetary boundaries.

By making nature a right-holder, really a co-right-holder with humans, the SES right ascribes traits typically reserved for humans (i.e., the ability to be endowed with legal rights) to a "nonhuman world," thereby elevating Nature's position within a human-centric system of rules.[86] Packed within the SES right is the normative premise that humans and Nature ought *not* be considered, or treated, separately. Human and Nature act as a unified whole.

Humans would be the only sentient beings that would be aware of this right, and again, the right would be to a safe operating space for humanity with respect to Earth systems and biophysical subsystems. Nevertheless, traditional notions of human "exceptionalism" and "superiority-to-Nature" do not "entitle" only humans to this right; both humans *and* their natural surroundings have a right. This right is to a continuation of environmental

---

[85] Stanford Encyclopedia of Philosophy, Rights 2.1.8 (July 2, 2011), http://plato.stanford.edu/entries/rights; Eugene Volokh, Positive Rights, the Constitution, and Conservatives and Moderate Libertarians, The Volokh Conspiracy (May 7, 2013); *Gunnar Beck, supra* note 42.

[86] Jan Laitos, The Right of Nonuse (Oxford University Press 2012).

conditions where (1) Nature may operate as a CAS, and (2) humans may survive to participate as part of the CAS, so long as their activities do not cross planetary thresholds.[87] The right may be asserted both by humans and Nature (i.e., in the form of humans on behalf of Nature). The gardener and the garden both have a right to co-evolve.

Why should this right to environmental conditions be limited to conditions that only sustain *human survivability*, but not to the survivability of Nature? The simple answer to this quite understandable question is that human actions that affect natural systems (e.g., climate) and environmental goods (air, water) are problematic *not because Nature is being harmed*, but because humans are being, or will be, harmed. Humans are entirely dependent on Nature and natural systems, *but not vice versa*. Humans exist within larger natural systems that have limits to the anthropogenic activity they can accommodate. When these limits are exceeded, there is irreversible degradation of the life-supporting ecological processes on which humans depend.[88] But as a CAS, the natural systems and ecological processes that comprise Nature will ultimately adapt and survive; it is primarily the humans who will not be able to adapt if planetary boundaries are breached.[89] Hence, the right is devoted to ensuring the conditions necessary only for *human* survival.

Is human survival a value that can ground a legal right? For those who doubt whether a right can be based on human survival, it is best to recall that this new right would be a positive right. A strictly "human right" is, in a Kantian sense, usually a negative right.[90] It is negative in that, if the right is a justifiable claim to have something (e.g., a particular environment), then there arises a correlative duty to not take actions, or a duty to forego actions, that interfere with the right. Such negative rights simply repeat the notion, embedded in traditional negative laws, that humans are "harming" the natural environment, which usually results in humans being ordered not to take actions that perpetuate this harm. But negative laws (and negative rights) do not necessarily reflect modern thinking about how humans behave. Modern behavioral economics suggest that humans prefer to be

---

[87] S. Diaz, et al., Biodiversity Regulation of Ecosystem Services in Ecosystems and Human Well-Being: Current State and Trends 297–329 (H. Hassan, H. Scholes, & N. Nash eds. 2005).

[88] *Carl Folke, supra* note 13.

[89] Carl Folke, et al., Adaptive Governance of Social-Economic Systems, 30 Annual Review Envir. Res. 441 (2005).

[90] J. Narveson, A Question of Trust (Cambridge Univ. Press 2002); Gunnar Beck, Immanuel Kant's Theory of Rights, 19 Ratio Juris 371 (Dec. 2006); W. Hohfeld, Fundamental Legal Conceptions (Yale Univ. Press 1919).

told what TO DO, while the creation of a negative right is in effect telling humans what NOT TO DO.[91]

By contrast, an affirmative right claims for the right-holder the aid of others in ensuring that the conditions of the right are fulfilled. Since the right is held by humans *and* Nature in an SES, humans can seek the assistance of other humans to restore planetary boundaries, while Nature (or, rather, humans on behalf of Nature) can do the same. Although the purpose of the right is anthropomorphic, the beneficiary of the right is an SES that is both ecocentric and anthropocentric. Humans have more than a right to restore a safe operating space for survival; humans have a duty to other humans (and to Nature) to ensure their survival.

2.   An Affirmative Duty to Support Natural Systems So That Humans May Survive

Positive rights impose affirmative duties.[92] If an SES, made up of humans and their natural surroundings, has a positive right to be provided environmental conditions where planetary boundaries are not crossed, then the "social" – human component – of that system has an affirmative duty to provide the SES with those environmental conditions. In other words, respecting the positive right to environmental conditions that remain within planetary boundaries requires more than what environmental policies typically require – not acting in an environmentally destructive way, or not interfering with planetary systems. A positive right imposes on humans an affirmative obligation to act, to ensure that those Earth system conditions are restored.

This affirmative duty is different from the traditional negative duty to not interfere with Nature, which follows from the historically negative right granted us by most environmental laws and policies. These policies create the legal right to a justifiable claim on others to *not* do something. Such negative duties are reflected in traditional regulations that mandate "Don't Pollute," or preservation laws that say "Don't Trespass Here," or market instruments that proclaim "Don't Exceed the Cap." These historic policies are designed to halt, or prohibit, human activities that produce negative externalities. An affirmative duty, by contrast, requires us to create positive externalities. Such a duty would be manifested in laws aimed at influencing human behavior that lead individuals to make choices restoring

---

[91] *Sunstein, supra* note 39 at 19.
[92] R. M. Hare, The Language of Morals (Oxford Univ. Press 1952).

planetary boundaries – for example, laws that urge us to take mass transit, buy fuel-efficient cars, plant trees, recycle, or otherwise engage in "green" behavior.[93]

An affirmative obligation to act, instead of a negative duty to not act in particular ways, is consistent with the better and more modern view of how humans behave. Behavioral economics, not standard neoclassical economic theory, offers perhaps a more empirically accurate approach to law and policy questions about humans in the natural environment. Such policies would reflect how humans really behave, and how humans really make choices. People's decisions are determined in large part by emotions, peer influences, altruism, networking and group desires, and other cognitive biases. Environmental policies aligned with cognitive psychological and behavioral economics would not just rely on traditional "hard paternalism" – flat bans or mandates, or even market-based instruments like taxes. These policies presume that humans make decisions primarily based on individual welfare maximization. Instead, environmental policies should reflect "soft paternalism," emphasizing the need for affirmative actions that create positive externalities that benefit the family of humans in Nature.[94]

Such a policy, which imposes on humans a positive duty *to* Nature, is not only consistent with how humans really behave; it also reflects the reality that humans are not separate from Nature, but are a part of Nature. The Equivalence Principle is then satisfied. And so too are the Unification and Conservation Principles. The gardener tending to a sick garden has an affirmative obligation both to the garden and to the gardener.

---

[93] See note 65, *supra*.

[94] Tversky and Kahneman, *supra* note 36; Sunstein, *supra* note 39; *Science for Environmental Policy, supra* note 65 at 3–4.

A History and Assessment of Environmental Policies

If one observes environmental and Earth-based natural systems faltering or producing conditions that appear harmful to humans, and if it appears that humans are responsible for these troublesome alterations of our planet, then one would expect that humans would turn to laws and governmental policies to address human behaviors and choices that may be causing these worrisome planetary changes. After all, humans have traditionally created an important role for government (and its laws) in the allocation of natural resources. We have also used government, and its policies, to try to regulate and control, and even encourage, human use of Nature's raw materials.

Reliance on laws and government occurs whenever short-run private profit maximization aims and laissez faire free market assumptions (1) cause excessive consumption of stock natural resources, (2) accelerate depletion rates of renewable natural resources, and (3) produce negative environmental externalities such as pollution.[1] Part II considers the evolution of these social and environmental policies over time, and assesses whether these policies have been successful.

Chapter 2 is a taxonomy of the influences that have shaped the environmental policies discussed in Chapter 1. Chapter 2 explores the salient factors that have guided our choice of policy during several historical "eras" of resource use – and overuse – and environmental exploitation.[2] One of the themes in Chapter 2 is that environmental policy has been overwhelmingly human-centric. Government programs and legal rules addressing natural resources and environmental goals have been put in place to benefit humans, with little concern for the natural world

---

[1] Leonard Zobler, An Economic-Historical View of Natural Resource Use and Conservation, 38 Economic Geography 189, 192 (1962).

[2] See generally Jan G Laitos & Lauren Wolongevicz, Why Environmental Policies Fail, 39 William & Mary Environmental Law & Policy Review 24–39 (2014).

surrounding humans.[3] Chapter 3 reveals, not surprisingly, that our policies have not had much effect on Earth-based environmental problems. The stark lesson of Chapter 3 is that, despite decades of reliance on governmental policies and laws to control anthropogenic actions affecting our environmental surroundings, natural systems relentlessly continue to degrade with respect to human needs.

[3] Jonathan Padwe, Anthropocentrism, Oxford Bibliographies (Aug. 26, 2013).

Four Troubled Eras of Environmental Policies*

The legal response to demands for natural resources development, for preservation of certain lands and species, and for eventual "protection" of environmental goods may roughly be organized around four "eras," occurring over the past 200 years. During each of these four eras, lawmakers continually relied on certain assumptions and inaccurate models about nature, humans, and humans' place in nature (see Chapter 1). Initially, resource use (Era One) and conservation (Era Two) laws reflected anthropocentric assumptions of human superiority, exceptionalism, separateness, and no planetary boundaries. When humans began to realize that there were limits when we exploited and overused certain resources, they nonetheless continued to base their Era Three preservation laws on premises grounded in anthropocentrism and separateness. In this era of "preservation" law, humans continued to rely on a model that postulates that nature will achieve stability if protected from human interference (in fragmented islands) and left alone. The extremely complex array of Era Four environmental protection laws still were characterized by anthropomorphism and premised on human-nature separateness. But at least these laws no longer denied the realities of planetary boundaries. However, Era Four environmental policies were, and still largely are, rooted in the standard *homo economicus* model that assumes humans behave as rational welfare-maximizing actors.

A. Era One – Resource Use

Laws in Era One, the "Use" Era, arose in a 200-year period between the beginning of the seventeenth century and end of the nineteenth century. Era One laws were grounded in the anthropomorphic belief that nature

early 1600s – late 1800s

---

* An earlier and much expanded version of this chapter appeared in Jan G. Laitos & Lauren J. Wolorgevicz, Why Environmental Laws Fail, 39 William & Mary Environmental Law and Policy Review 1 (2014).

and its natural resources were meant for productive human use.[1] The general assumption was that nature was a limitless storehouse of raw materials. Land and resources were so abundant that it made little sense to conserve or ration them. This pressure to *use* this natural bounty was particularly strong in light of the perceived need in the short run to maximize profits for the private entrepreneur. Use of natural resources was seen as a way to add to the accumulation of physical, social, and economic capital. Natural resources were allocated socially, based on where they were needed, and by whom, in a free market largely free of governmental oversight or regulation.[2]

The westward expansion in the United States was driven in part by the view that the land and natural bounty of the new continent were intended to be used by humans who were both "industrious and rational."[3] Lawmakers embraced the ideology that use and exploitation of natural resources was a virtue.[4] Era One, the Age of Resource Use, was characterized by a combination of *predation* and *parasitism*. Humans saw natural and environmental goods as something to conquer, kill, or consume.

Out of this belief system in Western civilizations emerged a private property and ownership regime that helped facilitate the exploitation of nature. The core idea of private ownership rights in land and resources was already present in some European countries.[5] Private property had become an integral part of the United States' and European economy and market system by the nineteenth century.[6]

The advent of the law of property ownership encouraged the rush to exploit natural resources.[7] The ensuing charge to extract, develop, and use

---

[1] Jedediah Purdy, *American Natures: The Shape of Conflict in Environmental Law*, 36 Harv. Envtl. L. Rev. 169 (2012) (discussing how the belief that nature is intended for human productive use "justified the European claim to North America, [and] defined public debates about nature in the early republic, and persists in important aspects of private and public land-use law").

[2] Leondard Zobler, An Economic-Historical View of Natural Resource Use and Convervation 38 Economic Geography 189, 190–192 (1962).

[3] John Locke, Second Treatise on Civil Government 22 (Prometheus Books 1986) (1690).

[4] 7 Cong. Rec. 1719–1723, 1861–1869 (1878).

[5] Douglas C. North & Robert Pal Thomas, The Rise of the Western World: A New Economic History 19–24 (1973).

[6] David Feeny, *The Development of Property Rights in Land: A Comparative Study*, in Toward a Political Economy of Development: A Rational Choice Perspective 272 (Brian Barr et al. eds., 1988); Harold Demesetz, *Toward a Theory of Property Rights*, 57 Am. Econ. Rev. 347, 350–53 (1967).

[7] James Willard Hurst, Law and Conditions of Freedom in the Nineteenth Century United States 7 (1965) ("[Nineteenth century Americans] had in common a deep faith in the social benefits to flow from a rapid increase in productivity.").

natural resources depleted stock resources and frequently outpaced the regeneration of renewable resources.[8] Users were principally concerned with the individual benefits they derived from exploiting the natural world, and were unconcerned if their use and removal of these resources imposed negative externalities for a larger group of potential future users, who would thereby be denied their opportunity to benefit from the resource. Era One laws reflected a high discount rate, where future value was dis- counted in favor of present benefits. Era One's anthropomorphic ideas led resource users to predictably make choices based on their own near-term self-interest without regard for widespread future consequences.[9]

The property rights idea in the United States originated with early colonial ideals of sovereignty and resistance to tyranny that dominated American thought before and immediately after independence from the British crown.[10] Indeed, one of the foremost complaints the colonists had against the king was that he had denied them the right to cultivate land west of the Alleghenies.[11] The colonists "aligned clearing and using the land with inviolable human rights, invoking the Declaration of Independence."[12] According to one American historian, colonists linked the idea of freedom with the notion of private ownership of land and natural resources, because institutions built on such private property regimes allowed settlers the opportunity to become proprietors, which in turn gave individuals dignity.[13]

---

[8] Carol A. Dahl, International Energy Markets: Understanding Pricing, Policy, and Profits 16–37 (2004).

[9] Jan G. Laitos, The Right of Nonuse 55, 119 (2012) ("[T]he rationale for legal intervention has primarily been anthropocentric – to enhance immediate human self-interest, or to prevent harm to humans."). As a result of extensive resource use, "[f]orests and woodlands shrank, accounting for perhaps half of the net deforestation in world history... [and] [r]angelands and pasturelands became overgrazed, degrading or destroying naturally occurring grasslands along with the considerable ecological values provided when these resources are not used as a commodity." Id. (citing Sing C. Chew, World Ecological Degradation: Accumulation, Urbanization and Deforestation, 3000 B.C.–A.D. 2000 3 (2001); J. R. McNeill, Something New Under the Sun: An Environmental History of Nature Conservation in Britain 57 (2d ed. 1992); Daniel H. Cole, Pollution & Property 97 (2002)).

[10] See Purdy, supra note 1, at 173.

[11] See The Declaration of Independence para. 3 (1776).

[12] Jedediah Purdy, The Politics of Nature: Climate Change, Environmental Law, and Democracy, 119 Yale L.J. 1122, 1141 (2010).

[13] See Eric Foner, Free Soil, Free Labor, Free Men: The Ideology of the Republican Party Before the Civil War 1–72 (1970) (explaining that manual labor was elevated to a high status in the American social system and gave people a sense of personal worth); see also Drew R. McCoy, The Elusive Republic: Political Economy in Jeffersonian America 48–100, 185–208 (1980) (discussing how the American concept of freedom was coupled with ownership principles).

The idea of property was also rooted in the <u>assumption</u>, advanced by John Locke, that resource ownership evolved through individual labor.[14] That is, individuals had a natural right of private ownership to land and natural resources, but the mere passive ownership of natural assets was insufficient; resources also needed to be *used* by the owners, where labor was an obvious manifestation that the resource's potential was being released.[15] Locke's labor theory justified both the initial acquisition and subsequent ownership and use of natural resources.[16] Era One's laws mirrored the influential Lockian ideology that "the continent would become fruitful by disbursing land to private owners and promoting infrastructure to translate their labors into continental commerce."[17]

Beliefs about anthropomorphic superiority and exceptionalism contributed to the prominence of private property laws that encouraged resource use, as demonstrated by the prevailing idea that uncultivated land amounted to waste.[18] According to the dominant frontier mentality in the early and mid-nineteenth century, by settling and therefore taming the wilderness, Americans would reclaim the waste.[19] Humans operated under the assumption that they had a natural right to dominate their environment because they were morally superior beings that would bring anthropomorphic refinement and civilization to the wilderness.

In Era One, humans also assumed they were separate and detached from nature, and therefore saw land, nature, and natural objects as gifts to acquire, own, and control. Nor did humans in Era One consider the long-term consequences of their overzealous resource use. Humans did not take into account that the earth would be unable to supply natural resources or

---

[14] Laitos, *supra* note 9, at 37–38.

[15] *See id.*; *see also* Jeffrey M. Gaba, *John Locke and the Meaning of the Takings Clause*, 72 Mo. L. Rev. 525, 526 (2007) (discussing how John Locke's *Two Treaties of Government* provided a "coherent intellectual justification" for private property).

[16] Gaba, *id.*, at 533.

[17] Purdy, *supra* note 1, at 185; *see* Gaba, *id.*, at 536 (explaining that Locke's labor theory was premised on the assumption that even in the absence of government laws, there was an undeniable natural law that allowed individuals to assert their ownership rights by mixing their labor with a piece of property).

[18] *See* Andrew Jackson, President, Fourth Annual Message to Congress (Dec. 4, 1832) ("[A] portion of the waste lands owned by the States should be ceded to the United States for the purposes of general harmony and as a fund to meet the expenses of the war."); Martin van Buren, President, First Annual Message to Congress (Dec. 5, 1837) (declaring that west bound settlers moving westward left "immense wastes behind them and enlarge[d] the frontier beyond the means of the Government to afford it adequate protection...").

[19] James Buchanan, President, Second Annual Message to Congress (Dec. 6, 1858) (stating that the job of American settlers was "generally to reclaim the wilderness").

environmental goods forever, because the humans in Era One (and their laws) had no conception of inherent planetary boundaries. Rather, the singular focus was to exploit, dominate, own, and above all use natural resources consistent with Lockian theories about private property. "The right to have a legal property interest in a natural resource grant[ed] the owner dominion over it, which in effect remove[d] the privately owned resource from the realm of nature while transferring its potential utility to the human owner."[20]

As a consequence, humans became largely insulated from their connections with the rest of nature. Such isolation meant that humans were mostly oblivious to the effects their actions had, and would have, on the planet's ecosystems and natural systems. Planetary systems and boundaries were being influenced by humans, in an almost imperceptible way. But soon the consequences of this anthropomorphic exploitation of Nature would become obvious.

B.   Era Two – Conservation

Although policies and laws in Era Two, the "Conservation" Era, continued to reflect assumptions about human superiority and separateness, decision-makers finally began to comprehend that humans were exhausting natural resources. Lawmakers realized that a use-only ethic would eventually produce long-term resource shortages, because one fast-becoming-apparent planetary boundary was the earth's fixed supply of natural resources. To ensure that future generations could still use certain diminishing resources, present use needed to be tempered by a need also to conserve for future use.

Era Two may be characterized as a time of *commensalism,* when humans realized that they were being harmed by Era One predation. Humans were not too concerned about the planet, because they could not yet conceive that their actions could affect the Earth itself. So they imposed environmental policies and measures on themselves designed to conserve resources to later benefit humans. Private users would be motivated to conserve natural resources if the value of the conserved marginal physical product of a raw material was greater than the marginal cost of the labor or capital required to bring about the conservation.[21]

---

[20]   *See* LAITOS, *supra* note 9, at 87.
[21]   Zobler, *supra* note 2 at 193.

In the latter part of the nineteenth and early twentieth centuries, these conservation ideals surfaced as part of a progressive legal reform movement, which was reflected in national land policy. Conservation laws, however, continued to be anthropomorphic, motivated by what was in the best interest for humans. These laws adhered to the belief that nature was intended for productive future human use.[22] Era Two laws also continued to be grounded in incorrect belief systems about nature and humans.

As had been the case in Era One, the distribution of property interests was still a primary vehicle by which natural resources and environmental goods were exploited in Era Two.[23] But during this time lawmakers began to appreciate the importance of maintaining resources for sustainable future use. This conservation override on present use served to diminish the role of privatization and gave government a more resource managerial role.[24] Federal agencies in the United States, such as the U.S. Forest Service and the National Park Service, were established to ensure that certain resources would outlast the current generation.[25] Behind these laws was the realization that the private market should not be the sole arbitrator that controls the allocation of natural resources. Instead, government policy would regulate the rate of depletion of stock resources, and ensure the sustainability of particular renewable resources.

When stock energy resources like oil, gas, and coal began to be depleted, lawmakers initiated reform efforts to ensure that if these valuable minerals were owned by the government, then that government would control their rate of depletion.[26] When an otherwise renewable resource, like timber, was overharvested, lawmakers imposed conservation limits on timber-cutting.[27] And when cattle and sheep grazing threatened to denude the nation's grasslands, conservation legislation restricted and managed rangeland use by ranchers.[28]

---

[22] See Purdy, *supra* note 1 at 173 ("In this view, natural systems will reliably serve human ends only with expert governance at the system level: irrigation networks, silviculture, game preserves, and parks administration were early paradigms of this understanding.").

[23] See Leonard Zobler, *An Economic-Historical View of Natural Resource Use and Conservation*, 38 Econ. Geography 189, 190 (1962).

[24] Conservation laws manage over a quarter of the United States' acreage. Purdy, *supra* note 1, at 173, 189.

[25] See Organic Administration Act of 1897, ch. 2, 30 Stat. 11 (codified as amended at 16 U.S.C. §§ 473–482, 581 (2012)); An Act to Establish a Natural Park Service, Pub. L. No. 64–238, 39 Stat. 535 (codified as amended at 16 U.S.C. § 1 (2012)).

[26] The Mineral Leasing Act of 1920, 30 U.S.C. §181.

[27] The Forest Reserve Act of 1891, 26 Stat. 1095, 1103.

[28] Taylor Grazing Act, 43 U.S.C. §315-315r.

Conservation thinkers, such as Gifford Pinchot, the founder of the U.S. Forest Service, and Perkins Marsh, a leading American diplomat and philologist, and Theodore Roosevelt all advocated for government to take a more active role in regulating the use of natural resources.[29] As the nation's leading forester, Pinchot argued that without a conservation mandate, America's forests awaited a doomed fate – they would all soon be cleared. Pinchot similarly believed that the Era One's use ethic would eventually empty the mines, erode the waterbeds, and cause the rich soil to become barren. As early as 1890, the American Forestry Association presented similar arguments to Congress,[30] and by 1891 a report by the Secretary of the Interior Department urged Congress and the president to intervene and establish limits on resource use, especially the timber resource.[31]

Pinchot was not alone in advocating for resource conservation. Perkins Marsh stressed that healthy forests prevented erosion and played a vital role in soil integrity, promoting reasonably steady water flows, and benefiting people that lived downstream who depended on continuous stream flow.[32] Theodore Roosevelt sought to invoke a spirit of civic motivation by declaring that Americans owed it to themselves and to future generations to conserve natural resources.[33] "[T]he health and vitality of our people are at least as well worth conserving as their forests, waters, lands, and minerals," stated Roosevelt in a 1910 speech.[34]

But conservation laws and policies still encouraged resource use.[35] Their goal was to "manage present resources for undiminished future benefits."[36] The Mineral Leasing Act of 1920, for example, withdrew gas, coal, oil, and oil shale from the giveaway provisions of the General Mining Act

---

[29] *See generally* Gifford Pinchot, The Fight for Conservation (1910); George Perkins Marsh, Man and Nature (David Lowenthal ed., Univ. of Washington Press 2003) (1864) (advocating for the cessation of unregulated timber cutting in public forests); Theodore Roosevelt, The New Nationalism, Address given at Osawatomie, KS (Aug. 3, 1910), in Theodore Roosevelt, The New Nationalism 3 (1910).

[30] *See* 21 Cong. Rec. 2537 (1890).

[31] Dep't of the Interior, Report of the Secretary of the Interior 14 (1891) (discussing the importance of avoiding stream erosion and the danger of unregulated timbering).

[32] Jedediah Purdy, *What Has to Change for Forests to Be Saved? A Historical Example from the United States*, 19 Duke J. Comp. & Int'l L. 467, 471 (2009) ("Their experience of ecological interconnectedness as a motive for political action was among the earliest instances of a new approach to the natural world.").

[33] *See* Roosevelt, *supra* note 29.

[34] Theodore Roosevelt, The New Nationalism, Speech at Osawatomie (Aug. 31, 1910), reprinted in Theodore Roosevelt, The New Nationalism 22 (1910).

[35] Laitos, *supra* note 9, at 94.

[36] Purdy, *supra* note 1, at 190.

of 1872 that otherwise offered individuals ownership rights to these valuable energy resources. But use was still permitted, despite the withdrawal, since the Leasing Act simply placed energy developers within a leasing system instead of an ownership regime[37] Consistent with the leasing system, use of stock resources could occur, albeit in line with a theme of more regulated use.[38]

In addition to optimizing resource use, Era Two conservationists also were concerned with the "spoliation of human bodies and energies."[39] Conserving natural spaces for their aesthetic beauty and recreational uses were thought to be of benefit to citizens' physical and mental health. National forests in the United States, for instance, were to provide "a continuous supply of timber,"[40] while American national parks had the "fundamental purpose" to "*conserve* [for humans] the scenery and the natural and historic objects and wild life therein."[41]

Era Two laws, therefore, were still rooted in anthropomorphic principles about what would benefit humans. And because these laws presumed that human managers could manipulate resources and natural processes to serve human interests, they were driven by assumptions of human superiority and exceptionalism. The goal of conservation laws was not to strike a balance between humans and nature, but rather to control natural resources for human consumption and economic welfare. Humans assumed that they were superior entities that could and should control, and even adjust, natural processes so as to ensure that nature would continue to provide for both current and future humans' needs.

Most of the flawed assumptions and incorrect models of Era One largely remained in place during Era Two. Human exceptionalism and superiority justified the central tenet of Era Two, which was that humans could manipulate and control natural processes to enhance present and future human welfare. The belief that humans can, and should, control nature also contributed to the separation between humans and nature.[42] These laws were grounded in an overly simplified conception of nature and how it works.

---

[37] 30 U.S.C §§ 181, 22 (2012); John S. Lowe, Oil and Gas Law 18–26 (1995).
[38] Lowe, *id.*, at 18–26.
[39] Purdy, *supra* note 1, at 192.
[40] 16 U.S.C. § 475 (2012).
[41] *Id.* § 1. [emphasis added]
[42] See William Leiss, Modern Science, Enlightenment, and the Domination of Nature: No Exit?, Fast Capitalism 2.2 (2007), available at www.uta.edu/huma/agger/fastcapitalism/2_2/leiss.html (explaining that humans calculate the "world as prey" and separate themselves from nature in order to master it).

The human engineer in Era Two could seize control of natural processes and force particular resources to do the bidding of human masters.

Another assumption that remained in Era Two was the notion of the "rational man." The goal of these Era Two laws was to further *homo economicus*, the rational decision-maker whose economic welfare, present and past, was the epitome of societal optimality. What was different between Era One and Era Two was the growing, and correct, realization in Era Two that unchecked resource use would eventually encounter planetary limits. But even this eventual recognition of planetary limits did not produce laws that effectively limited the extraction and use of natural resources. While conservation laws did somewhat limit the use rights of private parties, they continued to authorize the exploitation of resources through public land management statutes, often at the expense of low-income, rural-agricultural communities.[43]

C. Era Three – Preservation

Laws in Era Three, the "Preservation" Era, which first appeared during the middle of the twentieth century, reflected a change in assumptions about the limits of natural resources. Lawmakers discovered, to their bewilderment, that some natural resources and iconic vistas, as well as various wildlife species and historic sites, were disappearing as a result of the resource policies of the previous two eras. As a response to this alarming reality, laws were hurriedly adopted that were designed to preserve places, such as wild rivers, ocean sanctuaries, and wilderness areas, and certain natural, objects, such as endangered plants and animals, as well as archeological ruins that evidenced our cultural heritage.[44]

This Era Three approach can be characterized as a *passive mutualism*, because humans benefited from the wild spaces that made humans feel better, and the wild spaces benefited because new environmental policies denied humans access to some spaces. Increased understanding about the limits of Earth's plentitude demonstrated an emerging central belief that was contrary to the foundation of many Era One use laws – in Era Two, policymakers realized that there were real planetary boundaries. This realization caused a shift in attitudes about nature. An Era One indifference in the face of seemingly limitless supplies of natural resources had been

---

[43] Dorceta E. Taylor, *The Rise of the American Conservation Movement: Power, Privilege, and Environmental Protection* (Duke 2016). *See* Organic Administration Act of 1897, ch. 2 30 Stat. 11 (codified as amended at 16 U.S.C. §§ 473–482, 581 (2012).

[44] *See, e.g.,* Juliet Eilperin, *Obama Will Propose Expanding Pacific Sanctuary*, Denver Post, June 17, 2014 at 14A.

replaced by an Era Three anxiety about how planetary goods and spaces would fare in the face of limitless anthropomorphic needs.

Era Three laws continued to be centered on anthropocentric values. Landscapes and natural objects were preserved because it was thought that humans would benefit from their existence.[45] And this policy reinforced the continuation of the separation between humans and nature, since preservation laws created pristine areas that were off-limits to human interference, but which allowed us to view these special places from the outside.

Even worse, however, preservation laws relied on the unrealistic model that nature should be left alone, in protected islands, because it is self-regulating. Preservation laws failed to preserve ecosystems and the larger environmental spaces enveloping specially protected lands and object. Consequently, environmental goods continued to degrade and fall below suboptimal levels.[46]

Firmly embedded in Era Three laws was the anthropocentric premise that nature, in its untouched state, provided physic, almost semireligious value to humans.[47] Part of this perceived benefit was the deeply personal and often mystical feelings humans had about nature.[48] Behind this idea was the belief that untouched nature had an almost transcendent power – experiencing the natural beauty of the outdoors could lead one toward self-enlightenment and awareness.[49] In the Wilderness Act of 1964, for example, Congress defined wilderness as a place that offered "outstanding opportunities for solitude or a primitive and unconfined type of recreation."[50] This recognition of the benefits nature provided for humans when it remained unused justified government rules demanding preserved

---

[45] *See generally* Purdy, *supra* note 1, at 173 ("[C]ertain places or qualities in the natural world elicit essential human experiences. Alone in the wilderness, or facing the dramatic vistas that Romantic aesthetics deemed sublime, people could shake off habit and custom, discover their authentic wishes and convictions, and become, in that respect, more free. Romantic epiphany has seemed a way to salvage individuality and meaning from a disenchanted and pervasively managed world.").

[46] *See* Don Hinrichsen et al., Consequence of Overuse and Pollution, XXVI Population Reports, ch. 4 (Info. Program ed., 1998); William Mckibben, The End of Nature 51 (2006).

[47] Purdy, *supra* note 1, at 169–73 (describing the "aesthetic and spiritual value[s] of nature").

[48] *See, e.g.*, Wallace Stegner, *Why We Need Wilderness*, Mother Earth News, Aug./Sept/ 2004 at 64, 65.

[49] Purdy, *supra* note 1, at 199–200 (2012); *see also* Dan Tarlock, *Is a Substantive, Non-positivits United States Environmental Law Possible?*, 1 Mich. J. Envtl. & Admin. L. 159, 191 (2012) ("The early preservation movement saw landscapes as awe inspiring natural areas, endowed with rights, which spiritually uplifted and sustained us with their physical beauty, compelling us to maintain their natural state.").

[50] 16 U.S.C § 1131(c) (2012).

special lands found in national forests, national parks, national refuges, and wild rivers.[51]

Humans also realized that they cared deeply about preserving wildlands, wildlife, and endangered species and their habitats, partly because of an emotional, noneconomic appreciation of the benefits that follow from humans being closely interconnected with their natural environment.[52] John Muir, an American naturalist and the founder of the Sierra Club, described the connection with nature that he discovered in his first summer exploring the Sierra Nevada:

> Never before had I seen so glorious a landscape, so boundless an affluence of sublime mountain beauty ... I shouted and gesticulated in a wild burst of ecstasy ... [T]he whole body seems to feel beauty when exposed to it as it feels the camp-fire or sunshine, entering not by the eyes alone, but equally through all one's flesh like radiant heat, making a passionate ecstatic pleasurable glow not explainable.[53]

Not only did nature in its pristine state provide a spiritual and aesthetic benefit to humans; people also were concerned that unchecked exploitation of natural resources and environmental goods adversely affected human health and welfare.[54] What seemed most troubling in Era Three were activities adversely impacting the "quality of the *human* environment."[55] What seemed less troubling were human actions that degraded natural environmental systems necessary for the continuation of the biosphere.[56]

---

[51] *See, e.g.,* Wild and Scenic Rivers Act, 16 U.S.C. §§ 1271, 1281 (a) (2012) ("It is ... the policy of the United States that certain selected rivers of the Nation which, with their immediate environments, possess outstandingly remarkable scenic, recreational, geologic, fish and wildlife, historic, cultural, or other similar values, shall be preserved in free-flowing condition, and that they and their immediate environments shall be protected for the benefit and enjoyment of present and future generations."); National Forest Management Act of 1976, 16 U.S.C. §§ 1600–1614; Colorado v. New Mexico, 467, U.S. 310, 314 (1984) (discussing the importance of in stream flow in relation to water users' needs for a continuous supply).

[52] Dan Tarlock, *The Nonequilibrium Paradigm in Ecology and the Partial Unraveling of Environmental Law,* 27 Loy. L.A. L. Rev. 1121, 1126–27 (1994). John Muir, My First Summer in the Sierra 175 (1911).

[53] MUIR, *id.,* 169, at 175.

[54] *See* Richard J. Lazarus, The Making of Environmental Law 59 (2004).

[55] *See* 42 U.S.C. § 4332(2)(c)(2012) (establishing that under the National Environmental Policy Act, an environmental impact statement must be prepared if a proposed action might impact the human environment) (emphasis added).

[56] Gunther Handl, *Human Rights and Protection of the Environment: A Mildly "Revisionist" View, in* Human Rights, Sustainable Development and the Environment 117 (Antonio Trindafe ed., 1992) (explaining that preservationist statutes and regulations were focused

This anthropocentric emphasis was particularly apparent in laws designed to address overuse of open access resources, such as air and water.[57] In addition, many of the preservation laws of Era Three emphasized the need for publically owned lands to be protected from development because of the "anthropocentric virtues of wild lands."[58] For instance, the purpose of the National Wilderness Preservation System was to designate certain federally owned areas as

> "wilderness areas," [which] shall be administered for the use and enjoyment of the American people in such manner as will leave them unimpaired for future use and enjoyment as wilderness, and so as to provide for the protection of these areas, the preservation of their wilderness character, and for the gathering and dissemination of information regarding their use and enjoyment as wilderness.[59]

By "secur[ing] ... the enduring resource of wilderness" for human benefit,[60] Congress sought to ensure that natural resources and objects would provide value to present and future generations of Americans.

Era Three laws were not only shaped by anthropocentric ideals; their preservation emphasis was also grounded in the belief that, if left alone in a natural state, nature would eventually self-correct and reach some kind of co-friendly balance with humans. In other words, by preserving nature and preventing "the imprint of man's work,"[61] humans would allow the natural world to revert back to a condition that was considered desirable and beneficial for human welfare and enjoyment. But the reality of nature is that it is not ever in balance, but rather is asymmetrically dynamic and changing as a "complex adaptive system."[62] Ecosystems do not exist in a constant state of equilibrium, but rather are influenced by various

---

on the harmful effects resource use decisions had on humans, instead of the deleterious impacts they had on the natural environment itself).

[57] Resources such as air, sunlight, and wind, are open access goods because they are not subject to private ownership the same way specific tracts of land, for example, can be. That is, they are open to the public and considered common property because it is not practical for users to exclude others.

[58] Sandra Zellmer, *A Preservation Paradox: Political Prestidigation and an Enduring Resource of Wildness*, Envtl. L. 1015, 1040 (2004); Wilderness Act of 1964, 16 U.S.C. § 1131(b)–(c) (2012); LAZARUS, *supra* note 171, at 93.

[59] § 1131(c).

[60] *Id.*

[61] § 1131(c).

[62] *See* C.S. Holling, et al., Discoveries for Sustainable Futures, in Panarchy: Understanding Transformations in Human and Natural Systems 68–69 (Lance H. Gunderson & C.S. Holling, eds. 2002).

changing intertwined natural processes. By preserving focused, localized areas, environmental spaces, and natural objects, Era Three laws may have denied to nature the essential components of diversity and heterogeneity, which are vital to a healthy ecosystem.

D.   Era Four – Protection

Era Four, the "Protection" Era, began in the latter half of the twentieth century and continues to this day. In Era Four, environmental policies protected environmental goods, primarily air and water, as well as soil and subsurface waters.[63] The catalyst for environmental protection laws can still be characterized as anthropocentric, and premised on assumptions about an inherent separateness between humans and nature. Humans in Era Four recognized that while we were polluting and poisoning natural resources and environmental goods, we were also contaminating natural systems in a way that was harming us.[64] The environmental protection policies of Era Four assumed that humans could be regulated to rein in this anthropomorphic penchant to poison our surroundings, by managing the human interface with the natural environment. These Era Four policies reflected an increasing role of government in the allocation of natural resources and raw materials. Government rules and laws were supplanting market forces and the private profit motives of Era One.

By Era Four, it became even more obvious that there were indeed planetary boundaries. Although we began to suspect the presence of these limits to resource use in Era Two, in Era Four planetary boundaries are undeniable. The role of humans in transgressing Earth's limits and producing perhaps unalterable changes in planetary systems is also becoming less debatable. Laws in Era Four, nonetheless, seem to have fully embraced a model of human behavior based on resource economics and *homo economicus*. This model presumes that humans are best regulated if they are told *what not to do*, or if their actions are punished that adversely affect environmental goods. Consistent with this model, laws would impose on humans the costs of their environmentally harmful actions, so that humans *do not* engage in the behaviors that produce the harm. But, as noted in Chapter 1, humans are equally motivated (or more efficiently

---

[63] *See* 42 U.S.C § 7409(b) (2012); 33 U.S.C § 1251(a)(2).
[64] *See generally* Holmes Rolston III, *Is there an Ecological Ethic?*, 85 Ethics 98 (1975) (discussing the idea that humans were not the only natural organisms that deserved to be protected).

action vs. inaction

motivated) by laws encouraging them *to do* something.[65] Era Four's more negative laws, grounded in the "rational man" wishing to avoid costs, have proven to be less successful than laws based on a more nuanced and realistic model of human behavior.

Era Four's environmental protection laws by and large continued the tradition of previous eras by having the central purpose of these laws the promotion of human welfare.[66] Lawmakers only contemplated laws that placed limits on human consumption, when the idea of preserving or protecting natural resources and ecological systems was beneficial to humans.[67] Nevertheless, throughout Era Four people more and more questioned the soundness of purely anthropocentric laws.[68] Humans began to realize that both humans *and nature* were being negatively impacted by environmental pollution.[69] This recognition represents a departure from the common understanding in Era Three, which was solely centered on the impact environmental degradation and contamination had on humans. By contrast, in Era Four, an environmental ethic emerged in the public discourse that voiced concern about the threats to Earth itself.[70]

Despite this growing recognition that nature and natural objects have intrinsic value, not derivative of human welfare, Era Four's protection law continue to be dominated by anthropocentric ideals. For instance, the focus of the American Clean Air Act is to prevent atmospheric pollution for human health and welfare, not because of the greenhouse gases that may result in climate change that disable the natural systems necessary for Earth's biosphere.[71] And the parent statute of Era Four – the National Environmental Policy Act of 1969 – requires an environmental impact

still anthro pocentric

---

[65] If environmental policies shift from ordering us not to take certain actions to urging us to take certain actions, we will be in an era characterized by "active mutualism." Then, Nature would be benefited by humans engaging in affirmative acts that help the planet, like planting trees where there has been deforestation.

[66] John Passmore, Attitudes in Nature, In Nature and Conduct 259 (R.S. Peters ed. 1975).

[67] *See* John O'Neill, *The Varieties of Intrinsic Value*, Monist 119–38 (1992) (explaining that nature and natural resources had derivative values, not intrinsic values in of themselves).

[68] Laitos, *supra* note 9, at 203.

[69] *See generally* Purdy, *supra* note 12, at 1160 ("[A]n 'ecological' awareness of natural and human phenomena as pervasively interconnected [arose].").

[70] "Environmental ethics ... sought to replace [the] spiritualism and deism [of preservationist laws] with hard ethical imperatives." Dan Tarlock, *supra* note 50, at 191. However, it is debatable whether this effort gained any momentum outside of the academic sphere.

[71] 42 U.S.C.§ 4332(2)(c) (2012); *see also* Utility Air Regulatory Group v. EPA, 573 U.S. __ (2014) (the Clean Air Act does not compel a definition of "air pollutant" that includes greenhouse gases).

assessment only when actions might affect the quality of "the *human environment*."[72]

The anthropocentric assumption of human separateness and superiority also continue to be present in Era Four. Separation is reflected in environmental ethics that simultaneously elevate nature to a morally superior position while perceiving humans as a taint upon the pristine and perfectly balanced conditions of the natural world.[73] However, during Era Four humans still occupy a dominant position in the natural world. This dominance is reflected in part by the tendency to assign to humans the duty to serve as stewards to, and self-righteous protectors of, nature.[74] Era Four's laws seek to manage natural forces by reining in human tendencies to treat environmental sinks as garbage dumps for our economic progress. Such laws still are grounded in notions of human independence from and superiority to the rest of nature.

Another hallmark of Era Four's protection laws is the desire to achieve environmental goals in more economically efficient ways.[75] Many environmental protection laws are consistent with the principles developed by resource economists, who have argued that we need to utilize economic models to control human exploitation and consumption of natural resources. Legal protections of ecosystem services are based on human-centric economic values, where the assumption has been that restrictions of environmental goods as waste dumps will provide measurable long-term economic benefits to humans. These advantages are thought to offset the short-term disadvantages of forgoing or limiting development by making pollution more costly.

Era Four's laws reflected this assumption by telling polluters not to pollute environmental goods, or face stiff penalties and cleanup costs.[76]

---

[72] § 7409(b)(emphasis added); *see also* Purdy, *supra* note 12, at 1160 (discussing that "concern with the public-health effects of pollution" still formed the basis for environmental protection laws).

[73] Jonathan Baert Wiener, Law and the New Ecology: Evolution, Categories, and Consequences, 22 Ecology L.Q. 325, 343 (1995).

[74] Jedediah Purdy, *American Nature: The Shape of Conflict in Environmental Law*, 36 Harvard Envt'l. L. Rev. 169, 189–197 (2012).

[75] Alyson C. Flournoy, *The Case for the National Environmental Legacy Act xix, in* Beyond Environmental Law (A. Flournoy & D. Driesen eds. 2010); Daniel H. Cole & Peter Z. Grossman, *When Is Command-and-Control Efficient? Institutions, Technology, and the Comparative Efficiency of Alternative Regulatory Regimes for Environmental Protection*, 1999 Wis. L. Rev. 887 (1999).

[76] *See e.g.,* The Comprehensive Environmental Response, Compensation and Liability Act of 1980 42 U.S.C § 9601 (2012) (requiring cleanup of abandoned hazardous waste sites, where those responsible for the land contamination may be jointly severally and strictly liable for all cleanup costs).

Era Four's laws were also modeled on the presumed behavior of *homo economicus*, who prefers to make choices in markets where supplies are limited. To mimic this behavior, economists advanced systems that allocated transferable private property rights in pollution emissions.[77] Title IV of the 1990 Clean Air Act Amendment is a leading example of a trading program that created markets that allocated waste discharge costs to regulated firms that had the lowest costs of control.[78]

Era Four's assumptions on protecting environmental goods continue to rely on a model of human behavior grounded in the assumption that humans are driven by a self-interested need to maximize one's own welfare, in particular one's economic welfare.[79] Federal and state laws attempted to make resource use as a pollution receptacle less economically viable; other laws restricted the availability of natural resources and even environmental goods by putting a limit on how much human use would be tolerated; some laws penalized resource developers and users with taxes or flat bans.[80] These laws are consistent with the prevailing standard economic model that humans need to be told how to behave, and need to be directed on *what not to do*. Otherwise, humans would instinctively exploit resources and goods to benefit themselves and blindly maximize their own welfare in accordance with the *homo economicus* model.[81]

---

[77] *See* J. H. Dales, Pollution, Property and Taxes: An Essay in Policy Making and Economics 107 (1968).

[78] 42 U.S.C. §7651 ("It is the intent of this subchapter to effectuate such reductions [of sulfur dioxide emissions] by requiring compliance by affected sources with prescribed emission limitations by specified deadlines, which limitations may be met through alternative methods of compliance provided by an emission allocation and transfer system.")

[79] Boris N. Mamlyuk, *Analyzing the Polluter Pays Principle Through Law and Economics*, 18 Southeastern Envtl. L.J. 39, 70 (2009) (explaining that the core values of the homo economicus model are individualism and self-interest). See generally, Guido Calabresi, *The Future of Law and Economics* (Yale 2016).

[80] *See, e.g.*, Archeological Resources Protection Act, 16 U.S.C § 470ee (2012) providing that "[n]o person may excavate, remove, damage, or otherwise alter or deface any archeological resources locate on public lands or Indian lands"); 16 U.S.C. §§ 1271, 1281 (a) (2012) (imposing a flat prohibition on resource use proposals that may hinder the scenic value of some rivers or have a negative aesthetic effect on people wishing to view and recreate on these rivers); Colorado Parks and Outdoor Recreation, Colo. Rev. Stat. § 33-10-101 (declaring that the state's policy was to protect, preserve, enhance, and manage outdoor recreation areas "for the use, benefit, and enjoyment of the people of this state and visitors of this state"); *see also* Rio Declaration on Environment and Development, P 16, U.N. Doc.A/CONF.151/26 (Aug. 12, 1992) (illustrating the polluter pays principle, which requires a polluting private party or nation to bear the cost of their pollution as a method of abating and allocating harm to the environment.)

[81] *See generally* Village of Euclid v. Ambler Realty Co., 272 U.S. 365, 397 (1926) (the state police power includes the ability to enact zoning regulations that restrict private land use decisions by property owners in order to promote citizen health, safety, and welfare).

3

An Assessment: Environmental Policies Have Failed

Chapter 2 summarized the array of policies that have been tried, for decades, if not centuries, either to manage our natural surroundings or to control human behavior affecting environmental conditions. These policies have been implemented for anthropocentric reasons, not for eco-centric purposes, in order to maintain or restore conditions that have enabled human development. The catalyst for many of these environmental laws has been a growing realization that humans in the twentieth and twenty-first centuries may be experiencing the end of the Holocene era – a 10,000-year period during which the planet's environment has been unusually stable, permitting human civilizations to arise and *homo sapiens* as a species to dominate. These laws and policies have in large part been a response to the recognition that a new era has arrived – the Anthropocene – where human actions have become the main driver of environmental change on this planet.[1] Governments have realized that human activities have reached levels that are damaging to Earth's systems and are negatively altering the planetary systems that keep Earth in the conducive-to-humans Holocene state. Environmental policies have sought, and largely failed, to halt or alter the human behaviors that have pushed planetary systems outside the stable Holocene state. This failure of environmental policies has a consequence that may be catastrophic for human survival.

The central question for this chapter is this: Is the Earth more or less conducive to human survival and development in light of all these laws and policies? The consensus among the international scientific community is that, despite a plethora of environmental laws and policies, human activities have so damaged Earth-based systems that the planet will soon not be a "safe operating space for humanity."[2] One respected group of

[1] P. J. Crutzen, Geology of Mankind, 415 Nature 23 (2002); Jeremy Davies, The Birth of the Anthropocene (2016); Will Steffen, et al., The Anthropocene: Conceptual and Historical Perspectives, 369 Philosophical Transactions of the Royal Society A: 1036 (2011).
[2] Johan Rockstrom, et al., A Safe Operating Space for Humanity, 476 Nature 282 (Aug 2011); W. Steffen, et al., Global Change and the Earth System: A Planet Under Pressure (2004); John

59

international researchers has proposed that, to understand how humans have created detrimental environmental change, we need to consider the status of critical "planetary boundaries." These boundaries define the safe operating space for humans with respect to Earth's systems and associated biophysical subsystems or processes.[3]

If these boundaries, or thresholds, are crossed by human activities, then the scientists believe the Earth could experience environmental change unacceptable to human life. This large group of international scientists and researchers has concluded that several of these thresholds, such as climate change and biodiversity loss, "have already transgressed their boundaries." These scientists fear that humanity "may soon be approaching the boundaries for critical thresholds," such as global freshwater, ocean pollution, and land uses, that are destructive of ecosystems and natural capital.[4] The growing consensus seems to be that humans have become a substantial, if not dominant, driver of important global systems. These impacts are not neutral; they are negative impacts on the functioning of these systems that human societies depend on for their survival.[5] If this group of researchers is correct, then not only is the relatively stable Holocene era finished, but so too may be the days when the Earth provides a safe operating space for humanity.[6]

Another group of researchers from around the world has likewise warned of imminent and irreversible changes to the Earth's biosphere resulting from human population growth and extensive environmental destruction.[7] Instead of raising concerns about human activities crossing critical planetary boundaries, this group of scientists and ecologists is arguing that human influences are causing global ecological systems to shift abruptly and irreversibly from one state, conducive to human life, to

A. Dearing, et al., Safe and Just Operating Spaces for Regional Social-Ecological Systems, 28 Science Digest 227 (2014).

[3] Nine Earth-systems processes define planetary boundaries: climate change; biodiversity loss; interference with nitrogen and phosphorous cycles; ozone depletion; ocean acidification; global freshwater depletion; land use change; chemical pollution; and atmospheric aerosol loading. *Rockstrom, id.*

[4] Will Steffen, et al., The Anthropocene: Are Humans Now Overwhelming the Great Forces of Nature? 36 Ambio 614 (2007); *Rockstrom, id.*

[5] Will Steffen, et al., Planetary Boundaries: Guiding Human Development on a Changing Planet, 347 Science Issue 6223 (2015).

[6] See Peter F, Sale, Our Dying Planet: An Ecologist's View of the Crisis We Face (2012); M. Scheffer, et al., Catastrophic Shifts in Ecosystems, 413 Nature 591 (2001); *Steffen, supra* note 1.

[7] Anthony Barnosky et al., Approaching a State Shift in Earth's Biosphere, 486 Nature 52 (June 7, 2012).

another state, incompatible with human existence. The evidence seems to suggest that humans are forcing a planetary-scale "state shift" or "tipping point," resulting in ecological changes that lead to a reduction in biodiversity and a severe negative impact on much of what humans depend on to sustain quality of life.[8] So extensive and pervasive have human activities been that this global state shift could occur within just a few generations.[9]

There are three important messages that emerge from these studies about humans and their natural surroundings on this planet. First, all of these bleak and disheartening warnings are being raised *despite the presence of* the numerous environmental policies and environmental laws and statutes recounted in Chapter 2. All these policies have been intended to prevent the very environmental catastrophe that is now looming. The only logical conclusion one can derive is that environmental policies and laws have failed to do their job. They have not been able to provide humans with a "safe operating space." They have been unable to halt a future "global state shift or tripping point" in the Earth's biosphere. Second, these changes are not the result of non-anthropogenic, "natural" forces; human anthropogenic actions are responsible for the dismantling of the Earth's ecosystems. We are in a new era – the Anthropocene – in which human actions have become the primary cause of global environmental change.[10] Human behaviors, driven by a desire to provide for peoples' most basic needs, are damaging, or outright destroying, Earth's natural capital and ecosystem services. For example, take the case of coral reefs, a natural capital ecosystem that provide numerous benefits to humans. These "rainforests of the seas" protect shores and coastlines, provide food, and are integral to the well-being of the oceans. But due to anthropogenic activity, such as coastal development, ocean acidification, global climate change, and inland pollution, coral reefs are dying around the world.[11] Or take the case of the wetlands, a natural capital performing ecosystem services for humans. America's coastal wetlands have shrunk by almost 400,000 acres between

[8] Paris Vasilakopoulos & C. Tara Marshall, Resilience and Tipping Points of an Exploited Fish Population Over Six Decades, Global Change Biology (2015), doi:10.1111/geb.12845; Bradley J. Cardinale, et al., Biodiversity Loss and Its Impact on Humanity, 486 Nature 59 (June 7, 2012).

[9] Kelly Fang, Report Warns Earth May Be Approaching an Environmental Tipping Point, Daily Californian (June 11, 2012).

[10] *Rockstrom, supra* note 2.

[11] Brady Dennis, Death of Coral Reefs Could be Devasting to Humans, Washington Post (Nov. 10, 2016); Anup Shah, Coral Reefs, Global Issues, www.globalissues.org (March 3, 2013), Bruce Einhorn & James Paton, A Fight in Australia Pits Coal v. Coral, Bloomberg News (Apr. 3, 2015).

2010 and 2014.[12] Humans are largely responsible for this loss of wetlands.[13] Humans are also responsible for the depletion of another form of natural capital, groundwater.[14]

Our anthropogenic influence on our natural environment is particularly alarming in light of our increasing population size and growing per capita impacts on ecosystems and natural capital.[15] There are roughly 7 billion people on the planet. By 2050, the United Nations predicts the number may be close to 9.6 billion, a leap of more than 30 percent.[16] More people will predictably have more impacts on Earth's systems and resources, contributing to the likelihood that regardless of environmental laws, entire global ecosystems may suffer a catastrophic tipping point.[17] As one commentator aptly put it, "for every step taken forward in protecting the environment, for example, reducing pollution emitted per automobile, three-steps are taken backwards by exponentially increasing number of cars demanded by an ever-expanding population worldwide."[18]

This unprecedented increase in overall human population means that there will be an increase in negative impacts on global environmental systems as a result of the aggregation of large numbers of relatively small-scale *individual* actions. In other words, it is not just an increase in large industrial or institutional activities that are impacting global systems, but a phenomenal increase in individual actions, which when grouped together significantly impair Earth-based environmental systems.[19] For example, a major reason for persistent pollution of water bodies is the contribution of pollutants from "non-point" sources, such as individual agricultural and

[12] John Flesher, Great Lakes Only Region to Gain Wetlands, The Denver Post 10A (Jan. 6, 2014).

[13] Suzanne Goldenberg, Lost Louisiana: The Race to Reclaim Vanished Land Back From the Sea, The Guardian (Oct. 14, 2014).

[14] Eli Fenichel, et al., Measuring the Value of Groundwater and Other Forms of Natural Capital, 13 Proceedings of the National Academy of Sciences No. 9 2383 (2016) (in order for humans to achieve sustainability, they must ensure that natural capital, such as groundwater, forests, and fish populations, does not decline over time).

[15] Paul Ehrlich, Peter Kareiva, & Gretchen Daily, Securing Natural Capital and Expanding Equity to Rescale Civilization, 486 Nature 68 (June 7, 2012).

[16] Zoe Schlanger, The World in 2050, Newsweek (Jan. 5, 2015)

[17] Stepehn Emmott, Ten Billion (2013); Alan Weisman, Countdown (2013).

[18] Robert Hardaway, It's the Population Stupid. The Real Cause of Environmental Degradation, http://politixtopix.com (May 5, 2014).

[19] See, e.g., Hope M. Babcock, Assuming Personal Responsibility for Improving the Environment: Moving Toward a New Environmental Norm, 33 Harv. Envtl. L. Rev. 117 (2009).

urban contributors.[20] Similarly, many areas in the United States are "non-attainment" for national air quality standards – those standards for the most dangerous and ubiquitous air pollutants – due to individual acts of air pollution.[21] Indeed, one can persuasively make the case that separate decisions of millions (billions?) of individuals on this planet are the central cause of the greenhouse gas emissions contributing to climate change.[22]

It is particularly difficult for environmental policy to manage or control the impacts of individual or atomized small-scale activities. The regulation of dispersed sources is administratively expensive and often politically impossible.[23] To control emissions from mobile sources, it is far easier to regulate the automobile manufacturer than the automobile driver; similarly, the chemical factory's effluent flow into a river can be regulated, while an individual farmer's decision to apply fertilizer on agricultural field often escapes legal oversight.[24]

The third message that arises from the researchers' warnings about planetary boundaries and tipping points is that, while the Earth's systems and biosphere will eventually adapt to anthropogenic activities, humans may not be able to adapt in time to survive as a species.[25] In other words what is being "damaged" and "harmed" by human action are not the ecosystems and natural resources that are seemingly being most affected by human-caused pollution and resource-exploitative behavior. Earth-based systems will eventually respond to human activities because they are all complex adaptive systems that always have been able to eventually alter

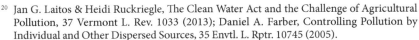

[20] Jan G. Laitos & Heidi Ruckriegle, The Clean Water Act and the Challenge of Agricultural Pollution, 37 Vermont L. Rev. 1033 (2013); Daniel A. Farber, Controlling Pollution by Individual and Other Dispersed Sources, 35 Envtl. L. Rptr. 10745 (2005).

[21] Jason N. Czarnezki, Everyday Environmentalism: Law, Nature, & Individual Behavior (2011); Michael P. Vandenbergh, The Individual as Polluter, 35 Envtl. L. Rptr. 10723 (2005); Michael P. Vandenbergh, From Smokestack to SUV: The Individual as Regulated Entitiy in the New Era of Environmental Law, 57 Vand. L. Rev. 515 (2004).

[22] Climate Change 2014, Mitigation of Climate Change, Intergovernmental Panel on Climate Change, Working Group 3 (IPCC WG3) at 24, 86–87 (emissions of methane from rice cultivation or livestock manure); Michael P. Vandenbergh, The One Percent Problem, 111 Columbia L. Rev. 1385, 1389 (2011); Michael Vandenbergh, et al, Individual Carbon Emissions: The Low Hanging Fruit, 55 UCLA L. Rev. 1701 (2008).

[23] David E. Adelman, Environmental Federalism: When Numbers Matter More Than Size, 32 UCLA J. Envtl. L. & Policy 238 (2014).

[24] Katrina Fischer Kuh, When Government Intrudes: Regulating Individual Behaviors That Harm the Environment, 61 Duke L.J. 1111 (2012); Katrina Fischer Kuh, Capturing Individual Harms, 35 Harv. Envtl. L. Rev. 155 (2011).

[25] Rockstrom, supra note 2.

their "state" to accommodate exogenous change.[26] What is at risk is the ability of *humans* to develop and live on a planet (a quite different planet from the current one) that has adapted to these human-induced changes to create a biosphere which may be inhospitable to human survival.[27]

What follows in Chapter 3 is a summary and description of the chief examples of the failure of environmental policy to halt the human dismantling of Earth-based systems. Anthropogenic actions, unchecked by environmental laws, have resulted in: (1) climate change and global warming; (2) extinctions and loss of biodiversity; (3) air pollution; (4) human exploitation, degradation, and depletion of natural resources; and (5) alteration of natural cycles and ecosystems.

A.   Climate

Humans are accelerating the rate they are adding greenhouse gases, such as carbon dioxide, to the Earth's atmosphere.[28] Planetary systems have responded to this anthropogenic environmental change in two related ways. First, the overall climate is changing. Second, surface temperatures are increasing, causing global warming.

1.   Climate Change

As unprecedented amounts of greenhouse gases are pumped by humans into the air,[29] the Earth's climate changes in ways that affect both natural

---

[26] S. A. Levin, Ecosystems and the Biosphere as Complex Adaptive Systems, 1 Ecosystems 431 (1998).

[27] Peter U. Clark, et al., Consequences of Twenty-First Century Policy for Multi-Millenial Climate and Sea-Level Change, Nature and Climate Change (Feb. 8, 2016) (projected impacts of anthropogenic climate change will have profound consequences for the survival of human societies for the next ten millennia); Lizzie Wade, Earth in 10,000 Years, The Atlantic (Sept. 7, 2015) (humans are not guaranteed to survive in the new world that will emerge if climate change continues); Marissa Fessenden, Here's What Our Future World Might Look Like, Smithsonian.com (Sept. 3, 2015) (humans and other animals may not "make it" in a world with extremely warm temperatures).

[28] Alex Kirby, Global Climate: New Records Focus on Earth's Sensitivity, Boulder Daily Camera 4C (Jan. 1, 2014) (if the current rate of CO_2 increase of 2 ppm per year continues, CO_2 levels could reach 600 ppm by the end of the century, levels not seen for 24 million years).

[29] World in "Uncharted Territory" as Greenhouse Gases Hit New High: UN, Agence France-Presse (Nov. 9, 2015); *IPCC WG3, supra* note 22 at 42. The primary greenhouse gases in the Earth's atmosphere are carbon dioxide, water vapor, methane, fluorinated gases, nitrous oxide, and ozone.

systems and the humans who rely on these systems. The general scientific consensus is that climate change is causing rainfall to shift, heat waves to grow more intense, storm systems to become extreme, water supplies to become strained, plants and animals to move to cooler areas, and certain species to go extinct.[30] These changes may produce marine crises, when aquatic life begins to die off. Such changes may spell the demise of the Earth's natural capital, as ecosystems are put at risk.[31]

Perhaps the most dramatic effect of climate change on natural systems appears to be what has been called "The Big Melt." Melting glaciers and ice sheets in Antarctica and Greenland are pouring water into the sea – 130 billion tons of ice per year, threatening to push sea levels up 10 feet (3 meters) worldwide in a century.[32] There has already been a 20 cm rise in global sea levels since the twentieth century, which is unmatched in 6,000 years.[33] Some scientists fear that major ice loss from both Antarctica and Greenland will flood populated sea-level cities that would be submerged by rising oceans, accelerate ice melt in the Arctic, remove glaciers in Europe and North America, and thaw carbon-rich permafrost.[34] Melting ice from Greenland and the Antarctic could also change the circulation of the oceans at both poles. This freshwater influx could decrease

[30] Tony Barboza, Climate Change is Felt Globally and Risks are Rising, U.N. Panel Says, Los Angeles Times (Mar. 31, 2014). See also Ian Sample, Collapsing Greenland Glacier Could Raise Sea Levels by Half a Metre, Say Scientists, The Guardian (Nov. 12, 2015); Mary Beth Griggs, What Would Happen If We Burned All the Fossil Fuels on Earth? http://www.msn .com/en-us/news (Sept. 11, 2015).

[31] Scientists Warn an Entire Eco-system is Under Threat From Climate Change, Science News (University of York, July 31, 2015).

[32] Luis Henao & Seth Borenstein, The Big Melt: Antarctica's Retreating Ice May Re-shape Earth, Associated Press (Feb. 27, 2015); Chris Mooney, Study Suggests Key Glacier Is Melting, The Denver Post 12A (Mar. 17, 2015). See also Ian Sample, Collapsing Greenland Glacier Could Raise Sea Levels by Half a Metre, Say Scientists, The Guardian (Nov. 12, 2015); Mary Berth Griggs, What Would Happen If We Burned All the Fossil Fuels on Earth? www.msn.com/en-us/news (Sept. 11, 2015).

[33] Seth Borenstein, Seas Are Rising Way Faster Than at Any Time in Past 2800 Years, Associated Press (Feb. 22, 2016); Oliver Milman, Sea Level Rise Over Past Century Unmatched in 6000 Years, Says Study, The Guardian (Oct. 14, 2014); Roberto Schmidt, Sea-Level Rise Accelerating, Say Scientists, AFO (May 11, 2015).

[34] Antarctic Glacier Thinning More Rapidly Than Thought: Study, NASA, www.msn.com/ en-us (Oct. 25, 2016); Chris Arsenault, Rising Seas to Displace Millions of Americans if Warming Unchecked, www.msn.com/en-us/news (Oct. 12, 2015); Denise Balibouse, Vast Alpine Glacier Could Almost Vanish by 2100 Due to Warming, www.msn.com/en-us (Oct. 17, 2015); Chris Mooney, North of Normal: Record Heat in the Arctic Could Cause the Melting of Major Glaciers in Greenland, and the Thawing of Carbon-Rich Permafrost, The Washington Post (Feb. 19, 2016).

saltiness of the oceans and possibly block the ocean's overturning circulation (in the northern hemisphere, this circulation means warm water travels northward and then colder, denser water sinks and travels south again).[35]

All of these effects on natural systems of course have consequences for humans, who depend on the systems. When oceans grow more acidic (caused by high levels of carbon dioxide in the atmosphere), marine life is harmed, which is a source of food for billions of people.[36] Rising temperatures will likely depress crop yields, making it more difficult for farmers to grow enough food to meet the demands of the world's growing population.[37] And perhaps most devastating of all for humans, climate change will produce, and has already caused, unforgiving long-term droughts.[38] Some scientists predict that in the United States, the Southwest and Central Plains states could experience a true "mega-drought," worse than the one that doomed the Pueblo civilization in the last millennium.[39]

Scientists studying climate change have derived three bleak conclusions from their extensive research. First, it appears now certain that *humans, not natural processes, are responsible* for this altering of the Earth's climate system.[40] Second, we may be seriously *underestimating* the problem of carbon dioxide and other greenhouse gases that we are emitting. The Earth, it appears, is less resilient and more sensitive to these human additions of gases into the atmosphere.[41] Third, the consequences of climate change

---

[35] Michael Slezak, "The Blob": How Marine Heatwaves are Causing Unprecedented Climate Chaos, The Guardian (Aug. 14, 2016);] Chris Mooney, The World's Most Famous Climate Scientist Just Outlined an Alarming Scenario For Our Planet's Future, The Washington Post (July 25, 2015).

[36] Scott C. Doney, The Growing Human Footprint on Coastal and Open-Ocean Biochemistry, 328 Science 1512 (2010).

[37] Doyle Rice, Report: Effects of Climate Change Seen Everywhere, www.usatoday.com (Dec. 16, 2015).

[38] Chris Mooney, Climate Change: Wild Weather a Sign. Scientists Say Recent Droughts, Rainfall, Stem From Warming, The Washington Post (March 12, 2016); Climate Change Intensifies California Drought, Scientists Say, New York Times, www.msn.com/en-us/ 8/20/2015; Jim Tankersley, Could Drought Slow America's Most Vibrant Economy? The Washington Post (May 20, 2015).

[39] Mark Fischetti, U.S. Droughts Will Be the Worst in 1,000 years, Scientific American (Aug. 22, 2015); Worst Megadroughts in 1,000 Years Threaten US, Live Science, www.msn.com/ en-us/2/12/2015.

[40] Karl Ritter, U.N. Report Concludes that Humans Altering Climate, The Denver Post 10A (Nov. 2, 2014); Man-Made Warming Becomes Main Cause of Glacier Retreat, Study Says, Reuters, www.msn.com/science-technology/8/14/2014.

[41] Alex Kirby, Global Climate: New Records Focus on Earth's Sensitivity, Boulder Daily Camera 4C (Jan. 1, 2014).

may be not only devastating, but *irreversible*, if carbon emissions are not aggressively cut by the end of the century.[42]

2.   Global Warming

Anthropogenic climate changes has many consequences, but one persistent, dramatic, and incontrovertible trend is that the planet is getting hotter. This global warming manifests itself in several ways. Most notable, of course, is that the Earth's surface temperatures are rising, to the point where global heat records are broken yearly, seasonally, and monthly.[43] These "records" go back to 1880, when the National Oceanic and Atmospheric Administration first began to keep temperature records. These are high temperatures for both global *land* and global *ocean* surfaces, so these are not anomalies experienced in only certain locations on Earth. The planet is obviously getting warmer, and it is doing so because of rising levels of greenhouse gases, such as carbon dioxide.[44]

One effect of these higher surface temperatures is that the sea ice that blankets the Arctic Ocean is becoming smaller in area. Indeed, the normal yearly peak of this ice, occurring in February, every year seems to be at a record low.[45] Arctic sea ice has declined almost 5 percent per decade.

[42] Chelsea Harvey, These Are the Impacts of Climate Change We Will Never Be Able to Fix, Business Insider (Feb. 14, 2015).

[43] Seth Borenstein, Hot. Hot. Hot.: Third Straight Year of Record Temperatures, Associated Press (Jan. 19, 2017); Seth Borenstein, Study: Earth is the Warmest it has been in 120,000 years, The Associated Press (Sept. 28, 2016); Michael Slezak, April Breaks Global Temperature Record, Marking Seven Months of New Highs, The Guardian (May 16, 2016); Doyle Rice, Animation Shows How Global Warming is Spiraling Out of Control, USA Today (May 10, 2016); Seth Borenstein, 2015 Was Hottest on Earth by a Wide Margin, Associated Press (Jan. 20, 2016); Kurtis Alexander, Planet's Heat Record Shattered – and 2016 Likely to Be Even Warmer, San Francisco Chronicle (Jan. 2016); Seth Borenstein, Winter Warmer-Land: US Breaks Record for Hottest Winter, Associated Press (March 8, 2016); Seth Borenstein, Beyond Record Hot, February Was "Astronomical" and "Strange," Associated Press (March 17, 2016); 2015 Hottest Year to Date, Could Top 2014 Record, Climate Central (Apr. 19, 2015); Seth Borenstein, On the Hot Spot: 2014 Was Earth's Warmest, Driven by Ocean Temps, The Denver Post 15A (Jan. 17, 2015); This Winter Was Warmest on Record, www.msn.com/en-us/3/21/15; Seth Borenstein, Feeling the Heat: Earth Has Hottest Month on Record, Associated Press (Aug. 20, 2015); Seth Borenstein, Another Month, Another Global Heat Record – By Far, Associated Press (July 20, 2015).

[44] Gregg Zoroya and Doyle Rice, Global Warming Worsens With Record Temps, and Widespread Coral Bleaching, USA Today (May 16, 2016) (a benchmark reading of carbon dioxide from the Mauna Loa Volcano in Hawaii reached an all-time monthly average high of 407 parts per million in April of 2016); Brian K. Sullivan, Earth on Track for Back-to-Back Records for Highest Temperatures, Bloomberg (Aug. 23, 2015).

[45] Oliver Morin, Hottest Arctic Year on Record Triggers Massive Ice Melt, AFP (Dec. 15, 2016); Suzanne Goldenberg, Arctic Sea Ice Extent Breaks Record Low for Winter, The

Changes in sea ice area have been linked to changes in weather patterns over North America, Europe, and Asia; loss of sea ice also affects habitat for animals like polar bear and walrus. Not only is Arctic ice retreating; global warming helps melt glaciers in Greenland, thin the ice cap in Scandinavian countries, shrink snow cover in northern Europe, and unfreeze the tundra in Alaska and Canada.[46]

The surface of the planet is not the only location affected by global warming. There has been a dramatic warming of the deep oceans as well. While some of the heat from human-caused global warming goes into melting sea ice and heating of the surface, the bulk goes into the oceans. Unfortunately, while the deep seas can absorb much of this heat, and thereby take some of the warming off the Earth's surface, it will not do so forever.[47] There is a limit to how much anthropogenic-caused heat even the deep oceans can take in.

Global warming has both ecological and economic effects. Warming waters promote toxic algae blooms, which threaten marine life and the communities that rely on the sea or lakes to survive.[48] Global warming will also harm the economies of three-quarters of the nations of the world – those counties south of the United States. High temperatures will harm agriculture there, reduce industrial production, and shrink worldwide income by 23 percent by the century's end.[49]

Are humans really responsible for this global warming? The consensus among scientists is that at least three out of four very hot days can be linked directly to human's effect on climate.[50] If climate change worsens around mid-century, the percentage of extremely hot days attributable to human influence could push 95 percent.[51] Humans are the central culprits. And global warming has *not* hit some plateau. In 2013 there were reports that the Earth was experiencing a slowdown in the increase of global surface

Guardian (March 28, 2016); Seth Borenstein, Earth Is a Warmer Place since 1997 Talks (in Kyoto), Associated Press (Nov. 30, 2015) (Arctic Sea Ice has shrunk 820,000 square miles since 1997); Arctic Sea Hits Low Winter Peak, www.msn.com/en-us/3/21/15.

[46] Joby Warrick, An Arctic Cap Sliding Into Sea, The Washington Post (Jan. 25, 2015).

[47] Paul J. Glecker, et al., Industrial-Era Global Ocean Heat Doubles in Recent Decades, Nature Climate Change (Jan. 18, 2016); Larry O'Hanlon, Deep Oceans Warming at Alarming Rate, Discovery News (July 11, 2013).

[48] Ryan Schvessler, This Could Explain all Those Strange Happenings in Alaska's Waters, The Washington Post (Feb. 16, 2016); Angela Fritz, This Year's Disgusting, Green Algae Bloom in Lake Erie Was the Most Severe on Record, The Washington Post (Nov. 12, 2015).

[49] Seth Borenstein, Global Warming Chills Poor Nations, Associated Press (Oct. 22, 2015).

[50] Study Blames Man for 75 Percent of Very Hot Days, The Denver Post, 14A (Apr. 28, 2015).

[51] E. M. Fischer & R. Knutti, Anthropogenic Contribution to Global Occurrence of Heavy-Precipitation and High-Temperature Extremes, 5 Nature Climate Change 560 (2015).

temperature – a "hiatus."[52] It turns out this so-called hiatus was caused by "data biases," and in fact global warming trends are actually *higher* than reported.[53]

When the world's countries met in late <u>2015</u> to negotiate a climate change agreement, <u>the consensus was that the world's temperature should not climb much more than 1.5 degrees Celsius above preindustrial levels.</u> There had already been an average increase of .85 degrees Celsius in global warming over the past 130 years, and the fear was that if greenhouse gas emissions continued growing on current trends, there would be a likely global temperature increase of 3.1–4.8 degrees Celsius by 2100. Such an increase was thought to be inconsistent with human survival.[54] Nonetheless, the individual pledges that nations made at the <u>Paris Agreement</u> are estimated to still put the world on course for at least 3 degrees Cesius of warming. The world cannot seem to wean itself from using the Earth's atmosphere as a carbon dumping ground.[55]

B.   Loss of Biodiversity and Extinctions

Relentless and pervasive anthropogenic climate change causes more than melting ice, rising sea levels, and global warming. Scientists believe that climate change was responsible for biotic transitions and megafaunal population extinctions prior to the Pleistocene/Holocene boundary.[56] Similarly, the climate change and global warming that the Earth is now experiencing warm both the atmosphere and the ocean, altering ecosystems and threatening the web of all living species. Researchers fear that many species will not be able to adapt to these altered environmental conditions, particularly marine life in the oceans and marine ecosystems such as coral reefs, whose environment has become much warmer and more acidic.[57]

Human activities threaten the existence of species in a multitude of ways, apart from our pollution of the atmosphere. Pesticides seem responsible

---

[52]   The Missing Heat, The Week (Aug. 30, 2013).

[53]   Thomas Karl, et al., Possible Artifacts of Data Biases in the Recent Global Surface Warming Hiatus, 348 Science 1469 (2015).

[54]   *IPCC, WG3, supra note* 22 at 430–431.

[55]   Climate Change: Hopelessness and Determination, The Economist 16 (Dec. 19, 2015).

[56]   Alan Cooper, et al., Abrupt Warming Events Drove Late Pleistocene Holarctic Megafaunal Turnover, Science Magazine (July 23, 2015).

[57]   Michael Slezak, Most Coral Dead in Central Section of Great Barrier Reef, The Guardian (May 29, 2016); Carl Zimmer, Warming Oceans Putting Marine Life in a "Blender," The New York Times (Sept. 3, 2015); Al Gore, Without a Trace, The New York Times Book Review (Feb. 10, 2014); *Shah, supra* note 11.

for an enormous "die-off" of honeybees. Local bee populations often do the pollination essential to the agriculture ecosystem.[58] U.S. populations of feral honeybees have fallen to a fraction of their levels in 1985, threatening global food supply.[59] Excessive non-sustainable logging has led to wide-spread deforestation. The absence of trees on the land increases the runoff of sediments and nutrients, impeding the survivability of ecosystems and species habitat that rely on fertile soil.[60] Both overfishing and global warming also have decimated fish stocks.[61]

All of this human-caused loss of biodiversity has led some commentators and scientists to conclude that we are close to experiencing a "Sixth Mass Extinction," where almost half of all living species on Earth could disappear by the end of the century. And humans will be the cause.[62] Studies predict that between one in six[63] to one in thirteen species,[64] could become extinct by the end of the century. Scientists use "climate extinction models" to predict the scale of extinctions. It is feared that the latest generation of such models are more accurate, and they produce more dire estimates.[65]

---

[58] Alan Bjerga, US Bee Colonies Continue to Decline, Bloomberg News (May 15, 2016); Steve Ellis, Honeybees Are Dying and Our Food Supply Will Go with Them, U.S. News & World Report (Nov. 14, 2015).

[59] John Schwartz, Decline of Species That Pollinate Poses a Threat to Food Supply, New York Times (Feb. 26, 2016); Bruce Finley, Abuzz Over Bees: Insect Population Falls 38% in Colorado, The Denver Post 1A (July 29, 2015) (noting there has been a 42 percent national die-off); Bryan Walsh, A World without Bees, Time Magazine (Aug. 19, 2013).

[60] Plenty More Fish in the Sea?, The Economist 66 (Dec. 21, 2013).

[61] Chelsea Harvey, Why We've Been Hugely Underestimating the Overfishing of the Oceans, The Washington Post (Jan. 24, 2016); Half of Marine Life Wiped Out in 40 Years: World Wildlife Fund Report, www.ndtv.com/world-news (Sept. 17, 2015); Douglas Main, Feds Close Most of Northeast to Cod Fishing, Newsweek (Nov. 14, 2014); Keith Ridler, Half of Columbia Sockeye Salmon Dying Due to Hot Water, www.msn.com/en-us/7/27/15.

[62] Elizabeth Kolbert, The Sixth Extinction (2014); Anthony Barnosky, Dodging Extinction: Power, Food, Money, and the Future of Life on Earth (2014); Erin Brodwin, Earth is on the Edge of a Sixth Extinction, Business Insider (Apr. 27, 2015). Since the origin of life 3.8 billion years ago, our planet has experienced five mass extinction events. These have been caused by volcanic action, non-anthropogenic climate change, and even asteroids. The last mass extinction occurred 66 million years ago, when a six-mile-wide asteroid is thought to have collided with the Earth, ending the Cretaceous period.

[63] Carl Zimmer, Study Finds Global Warming as Threat to 1 in 6 Species, New York Times (May 1, 2015).

[64] Study: 1 in 13 Species Heading Toward Extinction, The Denver Post, 20A (May 1, 2015).

[65] The World Wildlife Fund estimates that population sizes of vertebrate species – mammals, birds, reptiles, and fish – have declined by 52 percent over the last 10 years. Living Planet Report 2014, www.worldwildlife.org. See also Alejandro Estrada et al., Impending Extinction Crisis of the World's Primates, Why Primates Matter, 3 Science Advances e1600946 (Jan. 18, 2017).

What is particularly disheartening is that estimates of species loss reveal an exceptionally rapid loss of biodiversity over the last few centuries, indicating that a sixth mass extinction is already under way.[66] Even more discouraging is that there is agreement that these species losses are entirely human-induced, and not at all typical of the pre-human background rate of normal extinctions.[67] And there is agreement that biodiversity loss is a major driver of ecosystem damage.[68]

Since humans seem to be completely responsible for a looming sixth global extinction, humans have the power to make anthropomorphic changes to prevent this catastrophe.[69] They should start by taking a hard look at failed environmental policies that have *not* deterred humans from making choices leading to another mass extinction.

C.   Exploitation of the Atmosphere

Ever since the Industrial Revolution of the nineteenth century, humans have chosen to use, extract, and develop environmental goods. Certain environmental sinks, like the atmosphere and oceans, have been exploited as a convenient place to put our garbage, emissions, and effluent because they are free, and not subject to the normal rules of property ownership, since users cannot be excluded from them.[70] Because these enormous environmental sinks are free to use, unrestricted access to them has been essential to the world's post-nineteenth-century economic growth.[71]

For centuries, humans have used the atmosphere as a convenient, and cost-free, receptacle for all of our gaseous wastes. Since we have been burning carbon-based matter, in the form of trees and vegetation, coal, oil, and gas, it is not surprising that we have been loading the air with a particularly potent greenhouse gas – carbon dioxide. Despite decades of

---

[66] Gerardo Ceballos, et al., Accelerated Modern-Induced Species Losses: Entering the Sixth Mass Extinction, Sci. Adv. (June 19, 2015).

[67] *Id.*

[68] Bruce Finley, Study: Air Pollution Hurting Plant Diversity, The Denver Post 4a (Apr. 25, 2016)("The problem with reducing plant diversity is that plants serve as ecological buffers against calamities such as droughts."); David U. Hooper, et al., A Global Synthesis Reveals Biodiversity Loss as a Major Driver of Ecosystem Change, 486 Nature 105 (2012); Stuart H. M. Butchart, et al., Global Biodiversity: Indications of Recent Declines, 328 Science 1164 (2010).

[69] Tony Barnosky, Dodging Extinction: Power, Food, Money, and the Future of Life on Earth (2015).

[70] See, e.g., Garrett Hardin, Tragedy of the Commons, 162 Science 1243 (1968).

[71] J. W. Hurst, Law and Conditions of Freedom in the 19th Century United States 7 (1965); Jan G. Laitos, The Right of Nonuse 55, 119 (2012).

environmental policies designed to curb air pollution, global emissions from fossil fuel burning have not leveled off; rather, they have steadily and relentlessly increased since measurements began in 1958.[72] Carbon dioxide emissions have risen more than 120 parts per million since preindustrial times, where half of that rise has occurred since 1980.[73] In addition to carbon dioxide, we have continued to emit the equally potent greenhouse gases of ozone and methane.[74] And we have used the atmosphere to dump heavy metals (cadmium, copper, and zinc) and toxic pollutants (mercury and lead) produced by industrial activities.[75]

What makes "air" pollution particularly difficult to control or regulate is that the Earth's atmosphere is a perfect example of a "commons," or an open space not owned privately. Since no one's gaseous wastes can easily be excluded from this commons, there is an incentive to not only use it; there is often a race to use it before some other possible user exploits it. In the case of the atmosphere, even if one nation, such as the United States, unilaterally decides to stop using this commons as an emissions garbage dump, that one nation will then be adversely affected by other nations who choose to continue to use the air as an environmental sink. For example, China's legendary air pollution blows eastward across the Pacific Ocean, where it winds up eventually (just days later) in the United States.[76] To solve the problem of air pollution, then, environmental policy will require some global solution.

The international fossil fuel trade exemplifies the interlinked futility of any reduction in fossil fuel burning by just a handful of countries. If U.S. environmental policy reduces the gases blamed for climate change domestically by forbidding coal burning in America, such a policy will have little effect on overall global air pollution if the United States does not simultaneously halt the export of American coal to other parts of the world. The United States can curb carbon dioxide emissions from within its borders, but if U.S. coal exports (or exports of diesel and oil) continue to fossil fuel–burning countries like China, global levels of greenhouse gases

---

[72] Justin Worland, Global Air Pollution Is on the Rise Despite Decades of Efforts to Stop It, Time (May 12, 2016).

[73] Record Global Carbon Dioxide Concentrations Surpass 400 Parts Per Million in March 2015, Science Daily (May 7, 2015).

[74] Bruce Finley, Ozone Reaching Risky Levels, The Denver Post 12 A (July 29, 2015); Joby Warwick, Delaware-Sized Gas Plume Over West Illustrates the Cost of Leaking Methane, The Washington Post (Dec. 29, 2014).

[75] Agnieszka Galuszka, et al., Assessing the Anthropocene With Geochemical Methods, in A Stratigraphical Basis for the Anthropocene 255, 258 (C. N. Waters, et al., eds 2014).

[76] John Schoen, China's Unwelcome Export to the U.S.: Air Pollution, CNBC (Jan 21, 2014).

will not change.[77] And because of international atmospheric transport of air pollution, the United States will still experience domestically the effects of greenhouse gases produced in China.

And what exactly are the "effects" of air pollution? As noted earlier, it appears quite certain that anthropogenic emissions into the atmosphere are causing climate change and global warming.[78] When these changes contribute to the melting of the Greenland Ice Sheet, then not only is there a rise in sea level; there is evidence that there has also been a weakening of the Atlantic meridional overturning circulation (AMOC) in the oceans.[79] Without the AMOC, the seas begin to stagnate. Air pollution also can produce "acid rain," which can devastate forests and lakes hundreds of miles downwind.[80] And, apart from environmental consequences, policymakers need to remember that air pollution also kills humans, millions of them, every year.[81]

D.   Depletion and Degradation of Natural Resources

The natural resource demands of humanity are so great that the Earth may soon not have sufficient area to provide for this insatiable need. The day is soon coming when human demands on the Earth will exceed the planet's ability to supply it.[82] Already certain metals are in short supply, fresh water is becoming more scarce, deforestation has become the norm, and our oceans are becoming overwhelmed with plastics.

The Earth only has a finite supply of commodity metals, and when they are gone, there simply is no more. Take the case of zinc. From Africa to Ireland, mines that have produced the metal for decades are now tapped

---

[77] Dina Cappiello, U.S. Exports Pollution, Offsets Advances, The Denver Post 15A (Dec. 9, 2014); Dina Cappiello, Dirty Fuels Shifted Abroad, The Denver Post 1A (July 28, 2014).

[78] See Sections A1 and A2 of Chapter 3.

[79] Gabriel Samuels, Scientists Warn of "Global Emergency" Over Jet Stream, The Independent (July 1, 2016); Ryan Cooper, Why Climate Change is the Public Policy Problem From Hell, This Week (March 25, 2015); Stefan Rahmstorf, et al., Exceptional Twentieth Century Slowdown in Atlantic Ocean Overturning Circulation, Nature Climate Change (Mar 23, 2015).

[80] John Metcalfe, Acid Rain Has Turned Canadian Lakes into a Kind of Jelly, www.msn.com/en-us/11/19/2014.

[81] Millions Die from Air Pollution, Mainly in China, India, AFI, http://msn.com/en-us (Feb. 12, 2016); J Lelieveld, et al., The Contribution of Outdoor Air Pollution to Premature Mortality on a Global Scale, 525 Nature 367 (Sept. 2015); Dan Levin, Study Links Polluted Air in China to 1.6 Million Deaths a Year, The New York Times (Aug. 13, 2015).

[82] Justin Worland, How Humans Used Up a Year of Natural Resources in Under Nine Months, Time (Aug. 15, 2015).

out. When these big zinc mines go "off stream," there is no supply to replace what used to be produced from them. Zinc producers are being driven to increasingly remote locations, such as northern Greenland. As supplies shrink and prices rise, geologists may be able to discover additional deposits, in even more inaccessible locations, like the bottom of the ocean. But eventually even those will be extracted.[83]

Sheer population growth is straining freshwater supplies and creating freshwater shortages. In many parts of the world, particularly in the dry mid-latitudes, far more water is used than is available on an annual renewable basis. Precipitation, snowmelt, and surface waters cannot supply the competing human demands for freshwater. When surface water is insufficient, we turn to nonrenewable groundwater. More than two billion people rely on groundwater as their primary source.[84] Unfortunately for humans, the Earth's biggest groundwater basins are being depleted far quicker than previously believed. Of the thirty-seven largest aquifers on the planet, twenty-one have exceeded their sustainability "tipping points." They lose more water every year than is being naturally replenished through rainfall and snowmelt.[85]

Since the mid-nineteenth century, worldwide deforestation has sharply accelerated, precipitated by growing human population and industrialization. Approximately one-half of the Earth's mature tropical forests have now been cleared – before humans, the Earth had 5.6 trillion trees, and now there are 3 trillion trees. Forest protection policies have largely failed, and the thinking is that by the year 2030, with 15 billion trees being cut down each year by humans, almost 90 percent of the planet's forests will have been removed.[86] There are only two large tracts of intact forest left on Earth – the Amazon and the Congo. The rest of the wooded areas

---

[83] Joe Deaux & Matt Craze, In a World Filled with Gluts, One Metal Is Suddenly Hard to Find, Bloomberg News (Apr. 9, 2015).

[84] B.Lynn Ingram and Frances Malamud-Roam, The West Without Water: What Past Floods, Doughts, and Other Clues Tell Us About Tomorrow (2015); Earth's Freshwater Reserves Are Disappearing, Business Insider (Nov. 11, 2014); Charles J. Vorosmarty & Dork Sahagian, Anthropogenic Disturbance of the Terrestrial Water Cycle, 50 BioScience 753 (2000).

[85] 6 Locations Where Groundwater is Vanishing, www.usatoday.com (Dec. 10, 2015); Pumped Beyond Limits, Many U.S. Aquifers in Decline, www.desertsun.com (Dec. 12, 2015); Ian James, California in Overdraft: Dry Wells and Sinking Ground as State Struggles with Groundwater Crisis, USA Today News (Dec. 11, 2015); Hilary Hanson, One-Third of the World's Largest Groundwater Sources are in Serious Trouble: Study, The Huffington Post (June 17, 2015); Freshwater: Supply Concerns Continue, and Uncertainties Complicate Planning, GAO-14-430 (May 20, 2014).

[86] Chelsea Harvey, Humans Have Destroyed 7% of Earth's Pristine Forest Landscapes Just Since 2000, The Washington Post (Jan. 14, 2017); Seth Borenstein, Concerns Taking Root Over Trim in Number of Trees, The Denver Post 15A (Sept. 3, 2015); Deforestation, www .eoearth.org/151673/4/8/2015.

on Earth are fragmented by everything from roads to cultivated fields.[87] Deforestation does not just remove habitat and reduce biodiversity; cutting and burning trees also adds more global warming pollution to the atmosphere than all the cars and trucks in the world combined.[88]

Although humans cannot ever extract or deplete the water from the Earth's oceans – our most basic natural resource – we can poison and contaminate it. One study has calculated that 8 million tons of plastic trash makes its way from land to the oceans each year. Since environmental policy seems incapable of slowing this trend, that number is set to double by 2025. There are some 270,000 tons of microplastics floating on the surface of the world's oceans and there is even more plastic trash on the ocean bottom.[89] Scientists have even calculated that, thanks to humans, there are more than 5 trillion pieces of plastic floating in the ocean waters of the world.[90] Marine biologists who have gathered data from the world's largest ocean, the Pacific, have concluded that there is an "endless layer" of plastic garbage there.[91] Indeed, by 2050 there may be more plastic than fish in the world's oceans.[92]

E.   Alteration of Natural Cycles and Ecosystems

When one considers how humans impact global systems, the most obvious, of course, is how we impact global climate systems. However, humans are also altering critical biogeochemical cycles, such as the nitrogen cycle. More nitrogen is now being converted into reactive forms, by fertilizer production and fossil fuel combustion, resulting in substantial increases in the flow of nitrogen through waterways into lakes and oceans. These flows cause eutrophication of territorial and aquatic systems and acidification of ecosystems.[93]

---

[87] Jenn Gidman, Earth Has Just Two Giant Forests Left, Newser (Mar. 25, 2015).

[88] Deforestation and Its Extreme Effect on Global Warming, Scientific American (Nov. 13, 2012).

[89] Jenna R. Jambeck et al., Plastic Waste Inputs from Land into the Ocean, 347 Science 768 (Feb. 2015); Douglas Main, 8 Million Tons of Trash Added to Ocean from Land Each Year, Newsweek (Feb. 12, 2015).

[90] Jenna R. Jambeck et al., Plastic Waste Inputs From Land Into the Ocean, 347 Science, Issue 6223 (Feb. 13, 2015); Oliver Milman, Full Scale of Plastic in the World's Oceans Revealed for First Time, The Guardian (Dec. 10, 2014).

[91] Olga R. Rodriguez, Scientists Study "Endless Layer" of Plastic Garbage in Pacific, The Denver Post 14A (Aug. 24, 2015).

[92] Sarah Kaplan, By 2050, There Will Be More Plastic Than Fish in the World's Oceans, Study Says, The Washington Post (Jan. 20, 2016).

[93] Nicolas Gruber & James Galloway, An Earth-System Perspective of the Global Nitrogen Cycle, 451 Nature 293 (2008).

Humans have also had global-level impacts on terrestrial and ocean eco-systems. It has been estimated that one-third of the terrestrial biosphere has been transformed into "anthromes" – human-modified or -dominated ecosystems. One of the most pervasive, but least recognized, ways that humans are marring the coherence and functioning of the natural world is by building an endless number of roads. Roads fragment natural habitats and alter natural ecosystems.[94] Global warming, caused by humans, is also altering ocean ecosystems on a scale not seen for millions of years. Marine species will try to shift away from the waters near the equator and move into new ecosystems near the poles. No one really knows what this species movement will do to old, and new, marine habitats.[95]

This bleak recounting of the state of Anthropocene Era certainly sug-gests that our environmental policies have not worked, and are not work-ing. Planetary boundaries are being exceeded and environmental "tipping points" are being reached. There is certainly no indication that the world's population is about to change its ways, to address a very foreboding future. Indeed, major international companies, especially energy supply compa-nies, predict that global development and economic growth are so criti-cal that it is "highly unlikely" that governments will adopt environmental policies to prevent climate change.[96] Even Pope Francis concurs. In his first papal letter dedicated to the environment, he wrote, "[W]hatever is fragile, like the environment, is defenseless before the interests of the deified mar-ket, which becomes the only rule."[97]

One central question, then, becomes: Why have decades of environ-mental policies failed to significantly affect what appears to be a headlong race by humanity to its eventual doom? How and why have all these laws and policies not worked very well? And a second question is: Can anything be done to prevent an outcome that will deny humans their "safe operating space" on this planet? The remainder of this book is devoted to answering those two key questions.

---

[94] Pierre Ibisch et al., A Global Map of Roadless Areas and Their Conservation Status, 354 Science 1423 (Dec. 2016); Erle C. Ellis, Anthropogenic Transformation of the Terrestrial Biosphere, 369 Philosophical Transactions of the Royal Society A: 1010 (2011); Jonathan A. Foley, et al., Global Consequences of Land Use, 309 Science 570 (2005).

[95] Carl Zimmer, Global Warming Alters Arctic Food Chain, Scientists Say, with Unforeseeable Results, New York Times (Nov. 23, 2016); Carl Zimmer, Warming Oceans Putting Marine Life "In a Blender," New York Times (Sept. 3, 2015).

[96] Exxon: "Highly Unlikely" World Will Limit Fossil Fuels, The Denver Post 14A (Apr. 1, 2014).

[97] Rosie Scammel, Pope Francis Challenges Humanity to Fight Global Warming in Historic Encyclical, Religious News Service (June 18, 2015).

III

Why Environmental Policies Fail I

Faulty Assumptions Behind Environmental Rules

It should be obvious, based on the sad contents of Chapters 2 and 3, that our environmental policies are not working very well, nor have they worked well in the past. But a description recounting *how* environmental systems are being anthropogenically changed,[1] and the *ways* that planetary boundaries are being exceeded,[2] is not an explanation of *why* these changes are occurring. The central question is this: Why are the systems essential to human existence faltering, despite the presence of so many governmental policies and legal rules seeking to restore environmental health to the Holocene-era Earth?

Part III provides one explanation for these failed environmental policies: they have been built on incorrect, flawed, or incomplete assumptions about both humans and their environmental surroundings. Part IV examines a second reason for these unsuccessful policies: limitations, defects, and unrealistic premises built into each of the environmental policies most commonly deployed and proposed in the United States and elsewhere. Part V posits an even more fundamental explanation for laws and rules addressing the environment that have not worked particularly well: a failure to reflect the often overlooked requirements of "symmetry" that infuse all of Nature, including its anthropomorphic components.

In Part III, Chapter 4 discusses the "false" worldview too often embraced by humans, including policymakers, toward Nature. We have wrongly believed we are somehow separated from our environmental surroundings. We have also presumed that we are a blessed exceptional species that is vastly superior to other species and to Earth systems, natural

---

[1] Amy Larkin, Environmental Debt (2013); Robert Verchick, Facing Catastrophe (2010); James G. Speth, Red Sky at Morning: America and the Crisis of the Global Environment (2004).
[2] Will Steffen et al., Planetary Boundaries: Guiding Human Development on a Changing Planet, 347 Science #6223 (Feb. 13, 2015).

objects, and environmental goods. Because of this false assumption, we have unleashed policies designed to master and control Earth systems. But these systems have proven to be far more complicated and complex than we realized. We have failed to master Earth systems, and now find these systems are turning on us.

Chapter 5 introduces the first of three flawed models that have traditionally grounded environmental rules. The chapter is a reminder that environmental policy has long been grounded in a model of Nature that assumes a "stationarity" state, where natural processes operate in a linear, predictable, self-regulating fashion to seek an equilibrium where life flourishes. This model is wrong; Nature is a nonlinear, ever-changing "complex adaptive system" that thrives on change and disturbances.[3]

Chapter 6 considers a second faulty model – a model of how humans should value Nature. Traditionally, environmental policy has valued Nature because it supports human life, and because it is capable of being mastered by human will. But in reality "Nature" is a symmetrical synthesis of integrated anthropocentric "social" systems and ecocentric biological systems, deemed a Social Ecological System – an SES. Policy needs to value the integrated SES. Policy should not focus on natural systems and environmental goods and ecosystem services as exogenous resources apart from humans, which humans can costlessly exploit.[4] And, as will be noted in Part V, environmental policy needs to reflect the basic symmetries that comprise the social-ecological SES.

Chapter 7 reviews the third flawed model influential to policymakers – the model of how humans behave. One prominent model of human behavior has been advanced by neoclassical economists, primarily resource, welfare, and environmental economists. They have assumed that humans should be viewed consistent with the *homo economicus* model. According to this model, people are seen as self-interested welfare-maximizing market actors operating according to price signals and cost-benefit calculations to rationally optimize their individual position.[5] These selfish individual actions should then eventually lead to a stable equilibrium state

---

[3] R. Lewin, Complexity: Life at the Edge of Chaos (2d ed. 1999); M.N. Waldrop, Science at the Edge of Order and Chaos (1992).

[4] Social-Ecological Systems in Transition (S. Sakai & C. Umetsu eds. 2014); Forest Isbell, Ecosystem Services, Oxford Bibliographies (Feb. 25, 2014).

[5] Guido Calabresi, The Future of Law and Economics (Yale 2016); Roger Perman, Environmental Economics, Oxford Bibliographies (Sept. 29, 2015); Ari Rabl, Joseph Spadaro, & Mike Holland, How Much is Clean Air Worth? Calculating the Benefits of Pollution Control (Cambridge 2014).

(the economist's version of the biologist's "stationarity" state, discussed in Chapter 5). Another influence on public policy has come from environmental historians, who have written about a legacy of humans seeking total anthropogenic domination over their environmental surroundings.[6]

Chapter 7 points out how a countervailing group of researchers, called behavioral economists, have engaged in scientific observations of people, which yield a view of human behavior quite contrary to the *homo eonomicus* and humans-as-masters-of-Nature models.[7] This model is characterized by altruism, nonrational decisions, more collective goals, and mirror-image symmetrical anthropogenic tendencies. This model suggests an entirely new set of policy paradigms that might be more effective at influencing human choices.

[6] Stephen Mosley, Environmental History, Oxford Bibliographies (Sept. 29, 2015).
[7] See, e.g., Richard Thaler, Misbehaving: The Making of Behavioral Economics (2015); Yannis Papadogiannis, The Rise and Fall of Homo Economicus (2014); Daniel Kahneman, Thinking Fast & Slow (2011); Richard Thaler & Cass Sunstein, Nudge: Improving Decisions About Health, Wealth, and Happiness (2009); Elinor Ostrom, Governing the Commons: The Evolution of Institutions for Collective Action (1990).

4

A False Worldview

Most industrial cultures seem to have embraced two worldviews that now dominate our environmental policies, as well as our personal decisions about the Earth. The economies, political systems, and laws of most of the world's industrial societies appear to be premised on the twin beliefs that humans are both *separate from* and *superior to* their surrounding natural world. These two beliefs, in turn, have incentivized humans to use and exploit environmental goods and natural resources as quickly as possible.[1] Both premises are false, however, and environmental policy grounded in this worldview is destined to fail.

A. Human Separation from Environmental Surroundings

1. *The Disconnect*

Although the reality is that humans in the modern industrial world are entirely dependent on the Earth for survival, food, and well-being, most of us are increasingly disconnected from this reality. Instead of human beings feeling a part of a whole, "we now experience ourselves, our thoughts and feelings, as something separated from the rest – a kind of optical delusion of our consciousness."[2] How did a widespread belief come about that humans are somehow separate from, and not dependent on, the Earth and its natural resources and systems? What caused this disconnect?

One may be able to trace back the source of the disconnect to a much earlier time, when humans were more integrated into their environmental surroundings. Modern humans emerged during the Pleistocene Epoch, tens of thousands of years ago. Our ancestors were hunter-gatherers who eked out a tenuous existence, which was harsh and threatening to this new

---

[1] Cormac Cullinan, Do Humans Have Standing to Deny Trees Rights? 11 Barry L. Rev. 11, 15 (2008).

[2] Albert Einstein, quoted in Earth Jurisprudence – Earth Law, www.gaiafoundation.org/earth-centered-law.

species.[3] Resource stress was frequent, and these struggling human populations needed to constantly alter their behavior and adapt to changing
conditions. This instability meant that larger, more organized and cooperative societies could not arise. But our close connection to our surroundings meant that humans were quite aware of their interconnection with the
Earth. Their survival depended entirely on nature's ecosystem services and
benefits that provided the conditions of life.[4]

Because the climate was variable, nomadic hunter-gatherers needed to
adapt frequently to new conditions. They lived in scattered small groups.
They could not enjoy a level of resource reliability and population organization necessary to create stable, complex social institutions.[5] It appears
that hunter-gatherers emphasized resource sharing between and within
groups. Competition for scarce, and unreliable, natural resources was
maladaptive to survival.[6]

Then, about 10,000–11,000 years ago, the climate became much less
variable, and the Holocene Era began. With climate more stable, agriculture subsistence systems began to emerge over a large fraction of the Earth's
surface.[7] The rise of organized, human-controlled agricultural production
marks a critical transition point in human social evolution and the beginning of the human-Nature disconnect. Humans could begin to form social
institutions, such as civilizations and cities, that previously would have
been impossible because of dramatically changing climate conditions.
But with climate stability came (1) resource reliability, (2) domestication
of wildlife, and (3) agriculture.[8] The greater efficiency of agriculture also
meant that agricultural populations competed with, and eventually overwhelmed, hunter-gatherer populations. And while the hunter-gatherer
economy was connected to Nature, the new agricultural lifestyle was more
separated from its environmental surroundings.[9]

---

[3] Brian Hayden, Research and Development in the Stone Age: Technological Transitions
Among Hunter-Gatherers, 22 Current Anthropology 519 (1981).
[4] Peter J. Richerson & Robert Boyd, Built for Speed: Pleistocene Climate Variation and the
Origin of Human Culture, in 13 Perspectives in Ethology 1 (Francois Tonneau & Nicolas S.
Thompson eds. 2000).
[5] Peter J. Richerson & Robert Boyd, Institutional Evolution in the Holocene: The Rise
of Complex Societies, in the Origin of Human Social Institutions 197, 199–204 (W.
G. Runcimaned 2001).
[6] *Hayden, supra* note 3 at 527, 542.
[7] Bruce D. Smith, The Emergence of Agriculture 19–20 (1995).
[8] Harvey Weiss, Beyond the Younger Dryas: Collapse as an Adaptation to Abrupt Climate
Change in Ancient West Asia and the Eastern Mediterranean, in Environmental Disaster and
the Archaeology of Human Response 75 (Garth Bowden & Richard M. Reycraft eds. 2000).
[9] Paul Shepard, Nature and Madness (1982).

Climate stability in the Holocene not only helped encourage agriculture as an alternative to hunting and gathering; it also was a catalyst to human cooperation, coordination, and division of labor. As agriculture and plant-intensive resource strategies became dominant, human population densities rose, and more complex social organization developed.[10] Humans no longer lived in small, atomized egalitarian groups where resources were shared. Instead, new social institutions evolved, such as fixed communities, and eventually cities. In those locations with high human densities, natural resources were allocated initially by barter and trade, and eventually by money.[11]

To those humans engaged in creating the first civilizations (and cities), natural resources needed for survival and agriculture seemed plentiful.[12] These humans had little understanding of, and only limited control over, Nature's production processes. There did appear to be an unlimited stock of untouched natural resources, awaiting humans to use and develop for human survival and growth. With a seemingly endless supply of natural resources on this Earth, forests were burned to enlarge grazing areas,[13] turf was stripped to remove peat,[14] and soils were exhausted.[15] The human discount rate was high – we were far more interested in resource use in the present rather than conserving or preserving natural resources for future generations. Instead of feeling a connection to Nature's store of goods and services, we began to feel a separation; the benefits of our environmental surroundings were just "there," apart from humans, ready to be exploited by us.

Modern ecopsychologists also argue that as humans became even more civilized and enlightened, we became even more obsessed with other humans, and the human condition. Conversely, we then became even less connected to our environmental surroundings. The beginnings of language and literacy led to the rise of rationalism, which was based in turn

---

[10] Richard Manning, Against the Grain: How Agriculture Has Hijacked Civilization (2004).
[11] Leonard Zobler, An Economic-Historical View of Natural Resources Use and Conservation, 38 Econ. Geography 189, 191 (1962).
[12] Peter A. Corning, The Synergism Hypothesis: A Theory of Progressive Evolution (1983).
[13] *Hayden, supra* note 3 at 519.
[14] Coralie M. Mills et al., Neolithic Land-Use and Environmental Degradation: A Study From the Western Isles of Scotland, 78 Antiquity 886, 892 (2003).
[15] Leendert P. Kooijmans, Archaeological Approaches to the Long-Term History of the Landscape, in Exploitation and Over-Exploitation in Societies Past and Present 63, 73 (Brigitta Benzing & Bernd Herman eds. 2003).

on the notion that humans, and their intellect, were not just quite differ-ent from the way nature is, but separate from natural systems.[16] During the Enlightenment of the seventeenth century, humans felt comfortable with feelings of domination over Nature. One controlling image of the Enlightenment was human transformation of the desert wilderness to the cultivated garden.[17]

Rationalism eventually was replaced by industrialism and urbanism, where people largely lived indoors in cities. Our human interactions were not with environmental goods or natural systems, but with other people and human institutions. The twin forces of industrialization and urbanization combined with a shift away from a land-based economy to split humans from their connection to the Earth.[18] This physical separa-tion from our environmental surroundings led to a further psychological alienation and disconnection.[19]

Another dynamic accelerating the separation was the rise of the con-cept of Self. A fundamental principle of the new postindustrial disci-pline of economics is that individuals (i.e., humans) make choices to maximize their own selfish welfare. Individuals are seen as rational decision-makers who choose actions regarding natural resources with the aim of furthering individual self-interests. To benefit these selfish individual interests, humans engaged in resource use did not take into account the actions of other humans, or the effect their own actions would have on other humans and Earth systems.[20] Humans interested only in benefiting themselves had too limited a view to incorporate in their decisional calculus impacts on environmental goods or natural resources.[21] Those were exogenous to humans, originating outside of the human condition.

---

[16] L. White, The Historical Roots of Our Ecological Crisis, 155 Science 1203 (1967). See generally D. D. Winter, Ecological Psychology: Healing the Split Between Planet and Self (1996); E. O. Wilson, Sociobiology (1975).

[17] C. Merchant, Reinvesting Eden: Western Culture as a Recovery Narrative, in Uncommon Ground: Rethinking the Human Place in Nature 132–159 (W. Cronon ed. 1996).

[18] W. Cronon, The Trouble With Wilderness, The New York Times Magazine 42–43 (Aug, 13, 1995); A. Franklin, Animals and Modern Culture: Sociology of Human-Animal Relations in Modernity (1999).

[19] E. A. Bragg, Towards Ecological Self: Deep Ecology Meets Constructionist Self Theory, 16 Journal of Environmental Psychology 93–108 (1996).

[20] David Rindos, The Origins of Agriculture: An Evolutionary Perspective (1981).

[21] J. Hillman, A Psyche the Size of Earth: A Psychological Forward, in Ecopsychology: Restoring the Earth, Healing the Mind (T. Roszak, M.E. Gomes, & A. D. Kannes eds. 1995).

2.   Reconnecting

Although humans in the modern industrialized and urbanized world seem increasingly disconnected from the Earth and its natural resources and systems, the reality is that humans are not, and cannot be, so disconnected. The Earth and its resources and systems are the source of life for all organisms (including humans) in the biosphere. Humans are dependent on Earth for all the conditions that make life possible – food, air, water, heat, climate, soil, ecosystems, fuel, and natural systems like photosynthesis and the hydrologic cycle. Many humans at this point may not have daily personal contact with these Earth-based resources and systems, as did the hunter-gatherers of the Pleistocene, but our current physical and psychological separation does not mean that humanity is not fully interconnected with Nature.

How, then, should we seek to bring about a worldview, a much more accurate one, which recognizes our connection to the Earth, to Nature? Ecopsychologists have long debated that interesting question.[22] They are largely in agreement that people need to stop putting borders between themselves and Nature, and to remove human-perceived barriers to our environmental surroundings. The consensus is that an individual's level of concern for these surroundings is related to the sense of connectedness the individual feels with Nature. In order for environmental policy to be effective, then, such policy should first seek to reconnect humans to their Earth.[23] Two standard, traditional, policies have been urged as tools to bring about this reconnection.

First, humans can simply declare that the Earth is the primary whole, and humans are only a part of this larger holistic natural reality. We can go one step further and call for an Earth Jurisprudence that recognizes that "the well-being of the integral world community is primary, and that human well-being is derivative."[24] Such jurisprudence could devolve into positive law, an Earth Law, which requires the human community to

---

[22] P. W. Schultz et al., Implicit Connections With Nature, 24 J. of Environmental Psychology 31 (2004); P. W. Schultz, Inclusion within Nature, in *Psychology of Sustainable Development* 61–95 (P. Schmuck & P. W. Schultz eds. 2002).

[23] C. Frantz, et al., There is No "I" in Nature: The Influence of Self-Awareness on Connectedness to Nature, 25 Journal of Environmental Psychology 427–436 (2005); Cronon; *supra* note 18; P. W. Schultz, Empathizing with Nature: The Effects of Perspective Taking Concern for Environmental Issues, 56 Journal of Social Issues 391–406 (2000).

[24] Thomas Berry, quoted in Earth Jurisprudence – Earth Law, www.gaiafoundation.org/earth-centered-law.

comply with laws that acknowledge that the good of the whole (the Earth) takes precedence over the good of the separate elements of the whole (such as humans). Or, as discussed in Section B of this chapter, we can grant legally enforceable rights to Nature, or natural resources.[25] Giving legal rights to Nature may presume that the Earth has an intrinsic right to be, and to exist, but such rights do not reconnect humans to Nature. To the contrary, an "Earth law" or "Rights of Nature" approach only furthers the separation because it creates a duality where humans have one set of rights (e.g., private property rights in natural resources) and Nature has counter-vailing rights (e.g., rights to be left alone).

Second, we maintain and preserve special places in our surround-ings, which stand out as being "natural," or "without human imprint," or "wild."[26] Preservation laws in the United States accomplish this goal with statutes and ordinances that create wilderness areas, national parks and monuments, wild rivers, landscape conservation areas, conservation ease-ments, and dedicated open space. These are special places where, in theory, humans can visit and experience a refuge from human actions that inter-fere with environmental beauty and natural processes. These special places are areas that people can go to to experience raw "Nature" and become reinvigorated.[27]

But these wild places do not reconnect humans with their environmen-tal surroundings. Nor do these locations alert us psychologically to the fact that humans are entirely dependent on the Earth for our survival. Instead, these "special places" only serve to reinforce the separation between Nature and humans. These places are "special" because they are perceived to be unusual and rare locations absent from any human interference. A person visiting such a place thinks that true Nature is unique and special, while the rest of the "non–natural" Earth is dominated by humans – creating a human/Nature duality. In reality, throughout all of the Earth (even in these special places), humans affect the Earth, and the Earth affects humans. Humans and Nature are interconnected, not separate. It is misleading and unrealistic to presume that true Nature can only be experienced and observed by traveling to some protected and preserved "special" natural environments that are separate from humans.

[25] See, e.g., Jan Laitos, The Right of Nonuse (Oxford Univ. Press 2012).
[26] H. W. Schroeder, Experiencing Nature in Special Places. Surveys in the North-central Region, 100 Journal of Forestry 8–14 (2002).
[27] Mary Reynolds Thompson, Reclaiming the Wild Soul: How Earth's Landscapes Restore Us to Wholeness (2014).

Despite calls for a class of "Earth Law," and the creation of protected special "natural" locations, humans in western and developed countries continue to perceive themselves to be separate from Nature. When researchers from three different studies examined people's perceptions of their connection or separation from Nature, they uncovered a cognitive dissonance: while the majority of the participants in the studies considered themselves "part of nature" (76.9 percent), this majority also described "natural environments" to be limited to "special places" absent any human interference.[28] Although the participants rationally understood that humans are a part of nature, they simultaneously believed that true Nature ("natural places") only existed when the location was independent and free from human contact and interference. In other words, Nature seemed to exist only in isolated, separate, and probably legally preserved special places, in which humans are not allowed.[29]

For policymakers, this dissonance means that environmental policies should not underestimate this stubborn tendency toward a disconnect between humans their environmental surroundings. While it seems apparent that the level of connectedness an individual feels toward the Earth will affect the level of success for policy decisions about the Earth and Earth systems,[30] the connection that an individual feels toward the Earth and Nature may be complex and contradictory.[31] What environmental policies should reflect and reinforce is our essential human connectedness to Nature, leading to an anthropogenic feeling of a human community within Nature.[32]

Such a policy would do well to remember the land philosophy of the American Plains Indians, the Lakota Native American Tribes of the Teton, Sioux, and Oglala. The Lakota did not live in a world of total ecological harmony or mystical participation with all living beings. Rather, their

---

[28] Melinda Merrick & Emily Price, The Distinction between Humans and Nature: Human Perception of Connectedness to Nature and Elements of the Natural and Unnatural, 15 Human Ecology Review 1 (2008).

[29] Unless they could *walk* into the special place, with no mechanical or artificial help, such as in American Wilderness Areas. See, e.g., 16 U.S.C. § 1133(c).

[30] *Schroeder, supra* note 26, *Schultz, supra* note 23.

[31] *Merrick & Price, supra* note 28 at 10.

[32] Rachel Salcido & Karrigan Bork, Ditching Our Innocence: The Clean Water Act in the Age of the Anthropocene, 46 Envir. L. 415 (2016) ("Many of our environmental statutes and regulations are based on the outmoded view of humans as something outside of nature."). F. S. Mayer & C. M. Frantz, The Connectedness to Nature Scale: A Measure of Individuals' Feeling in Community With Nature, 24 Journal of Environmental Psychology 503–515 (2004); N. Evernden, The Social Creation of Nature (1992).

Native indigenous "policies" sought *balance* in their world, through *reciprocity* between humans and sacred Nature.[33] We shall see in Part IV of this book, how important it is for environmental policies to be characterized by the symmetrical qualities of balance and reciprocity.

B.   Human Exceptionalism

Modern humans not only hold the belief that we are separate from, and not dependent on, Earth. They also presume that our species is superior to all other life forms. This superiority, making us an "exceptional" species, permits us to believe that we have the right and the power to transform our natural surroundings to suit us.[34] This transformative right and power is historically characterized by environmental policies that (1) seek to manage and alter environmental conditions in order to (2) benefit human interests in the near term. In other words, human superiority is manifested in laws and actions that attempt to alter the natural landscape so that short-term human interests are furthered. Humans are confident that they are sufficiently intelligent, and entitled, to exploit natural resources and environmental goods, while simultaneously disregarding the effects of this anthropocentric arrogance on Earth systems and ecological reality.[35]

1.   Managing Nature for Anthropomorphic Ends

A good example of this display of human arrogance is the saga of California's drought, being played out against a backdrop of developers and residents presuming that the state could somehow sustain endless growth.[36] For well over a century, California experienced unprecedented population and economic growth. Before 1860, California's population was below 300,000 residents. By 1960, however, 15.7 million lived there, and by the second decade of the twenty-first century, 40 million resided in California. The states' economy likewise grew, fueled by high-tech firms, aerospace, agriculture, the entertainment industry, and tourism. California's $2.2 trillion economy ranks as the seventh largest in the world.

[33] Mitauye Oyasin & Raymond A. Bucko, Lakota, in Encyclopedia of Religion and Nature 983 (B. Taylor ed. 2005).
[34] *Cullinan, supra* note 1.
[35] "Short-term human interests, fueled by an insatiable drive to accumulate ... power, have been enshrined in law in total disregard for the well-being of the larger Earth community"; in *Earth Jurisprudence – Earth Law, supra* note 2.
[36] Adam Nagourney, Jack Healy, & Nelson D. Schwartz, California Drought Tests History of Endless Growth, New York Times (Apr. 4, 2015).

The assumption has long been, in California and elsewhere, that humans can actually "manage" Nature – that the natural capital, ecosystems, and environmental goods could be manipulated so as to endlessly absorb and sustain all of this unchecked growth. The belief has been that with enough technology, planning, and human exceptionalism, the carrying capacity of the natural systems of the State of California could be expanded to accommodate all these people (40 million and counting), and all their demands on ecosystem services and natural resources.

Take the example of Palm Springs, a lush city with golf courses and trees and green lawns, *located in the middle of the desert*. Our innate superiority seemed capable of permitting the growth of this anomalous green city in the sand. The thinking was that humans could, and should, imprint natural resources with anthropocentric features, like gushing fountains of water amid an arid, parched landscape.

This disconnect between human notions of exceptional capabilities and the Earth's very real planetary boundaries would have to manifest itself eventually. And it appears that the disconnect is becoming apparent in the state's lack of water, caused by a combination of drought and accelerating demands for more water to satisfy endless growth.[37] What makes matters worse is that California's mega-drought is likely caused in part by humans – by greenhouse gas emissions that have been accumulating in the atmosphere during the same period that California's economic growth went exponential.[38] Despite perceived and presumed human exceptionalism, it seems that anthropogenic warming is now accounting for a fair amount of the unprecedented drought in the American Southwest.[39] This reality certainly should call to question our assumptions about human capabilities to alter and transform Earth's capacity to sustain endless economic and population growth.

2.   Anthropomorphizing Nature

Human exceptionalism also carries with it the belief that we can imbue in Nature certain anthropogenic attributes and thereby make Nature, the Earth, and natural systems less "natural" and *more like us*. For example,

---

[37] Darryl Fears, Study Finds California its Driest in 500 Years, The Washington Post (Sept. 15, 2015).

[38] Darryl Fears, Global Warming Worsened the California Drought, Scientists Say, The Washington Post (Aug. 20, 2015).

[39] A. Park Williams, et al., Contribution of Anthropogenic Warming to California Drought During 2012–2014, Earth's Future (American Geophysical Union, Aug. 31, 2015).

if we can make Nature a "legal right holder," we can then ascribe traits typically reserved for humans (i.e., the ability to possess and assert legal rights) to natural resources[40] and to nonhuman environmental goods and objects.[41] These efforts elevate Nature's position within our socially constructed system of rules, and thereby move Nature close to being more human.

There are several ways for environmental policies to anthropomorphize Nature as a matter of positive law. One approach is to grant to Nature legal rights to protect natural resources and objects from human actions that degrade or destroy them.[42] A second approach is to impose on humans a legal and ethical duty to protect "the natural world."[43] A third option is to have humans consider the environmental impacts and implications of their actions before engaging in these actions.[44] These recommendations have actually made their way into legally binding rules in some countries. For example, both Ecuador and Bolivia have Natural laws that grant "nature … the right to exist."[45] Argentina's Congress has adopted legislation forbidding on its glaciers all "activities that may affect their natural condition."[46]

All these various forms of human exceptionalism are related to the equally flawed belief about human separation from Nature. The notion that humans are somehow superior to Nature separates us from our environmental surroundings, and an assumption of human separation from Nature permits us to presume we are superior, potential masters of natural systems and objects. But neither assumption is correct, and our worldview

---

[40] See, e.g., *Laitos, The Right of Nonuse, supra* note 25. Boulder County, Colorado, USA, has sought to establish legal rights for naturally functioning ecosystems and native species.

[41] Brian Sullivan, Instant Evolution: Some Espouse Fauna/Flora Fast Track to Personhood as Means of Legal Protection, ABA Journal 71 (Feb., 2014), commenting on a Boulder County, Colorado, Planning Commission proposal that acknowledges "the rights of all naturally occurring ecosystems and their native species populations to exist and flourish").

[42] See, e.g., The Rights of Nature: The Case for a Universal Declaration of the Rights of Mother Earth (2011); Does Nature Have Rights? Transforming Grassroots Organizing to Protect People and the Planet (2010); Cormac Cullinan, Wild Law: A Manifesto for Earth Justice (2003).

[43] Holmes Rolston, III, Conserving Natural Value (1994); Holmes Rolston, III, Environmental Ethics: Duties to and Values in the Natural World (1987).

[44] Peter D. Burdon, Earth Jurisprudence: Private Property and the Environment (2015); Judith Koons, Earth Jurisprudence: The Moral Value of Nature, 25 Pace Envtl. L. Rev. 263 (2008).

[45] http://blogs.nature.com/news/thegreatbeyond/2008/ecuador; Cecilia Jamasmie, New Bolivian Law Poses Serious Challenges for Mining Companies, www.mining.com/new-bolivian-law.

[46] Leonardo Rodriguez, New Law on Minimum Standards for Protection of Glaciers, Marval, O' Farrell & Mairal, Monthly Rep. (Oct. 2010).

of our place vis-à-vis nature is inaccurate. In the Anthropocene Era we may be the only species with the ability to produce climate change and to breach planetary boundaries that produce a safe living space for humanity.[47] However, that brand of destructive exceptionalism simply means we can destroy our habitat. It does not mean that we can master the Earth and its systems. Nor are humans ever truly "separated" from their environmental surroundings, except perhaps psychologically.[48] Environmental policies built on the twin beliefs of anthropogenic separation and superiority are bound to fail, because the resulting worldview is just not realistic.

[47] J. Rockström, J. W. Steffen, K. Noone, et al., A Safe Operating Place for Humanity, 461 Nature 472 (2009).
[48] See notes 21–23, *supra*.

5

Failed Model #1: How Nature Works

In order for environmental policy to be effective, it obviously needs to be consistent with an accurate, realistic, and science-based model of the Earth's environment – specifically, a model providing a credible explanation of how life and environment interact on Earth. If the policies are aimed at an Earth model that is flawed, or incompatible with how Nature really "works," then the policies will fail. Conversely, environmental policies that reflect, and are premised on, a science-based, reality-driven, Earth systems model will be more likely to succeed in ordering human actions that play a role in affecting the functioning of these natural systems. Unfortunately, for much of the environmental law era of the late twentieth and into the twenty-first century, both policymakers and many scientific researchers embraced an Earth model that has increasingly come to be seen as not consistent with scientific evidence and reality. For environmental policies to work, they need to conform to how Nature in fact works. More recent, and more science-based, hypotheses about life, environment, and planetary functions should instead become the foundation for more effective environmental policies.

A. The Standard, but Flawed, Earth System Model

For many decades, environmental policymakers have pictured the Earth system as a closely integrated, self-regulating, complex system whose projects were selected to optimize conditions for life.[1] Pursuant to this model, living organisms (life) adapted to the surrounding environment, and in doing so both shaped that environment and helped keep it stable for the continuation of life. In other words, life itself was not a fortuitous product of a habitable Earth; instead, life played a critical role in creating the environment that permitted life to flourish on this planet. This living system

---

[1] Simon Levin, et al., Social-Ecological Systems as Complex Adaptive Systems: Modeling and Policy Implications, 18 Environmental and Development Economics 111, 114 (2013).

automatically controlled global temperature, atmospheric content, ocean salinity, and climate so that life itself maintained conditions suitable for its own survival. Consistent with this standard model, all of the Earth's living organisms have worked to achieve a state of *equilibrium*, ensuring that if one variable (e.g., global temperatures) is misaligned for life's purposes, the "Earth living system" will eventually *self-regulate* to re-optimize that variable for life to persist.[2]

For environmental policymakers, the implications of this model are obvious. Since, if left alone, Earth systems would self-regulate to bring about conditions that would achieve a natural equilibrium, laws should seek to minimize or eliminate the destructive impact of human actions on this Earth living system. Humans were perceived to be the one variable that Earth systems could not accommodate. Therefore, environmental laws were designed to bring us back to a state that was more "natural" and less anthropomorphic. Ecosystems changed by human design needed to be "restored" so that they returned to a condition prior to being affected by human influences. Places not yet disturbed by humans needed to be "preserved" so that they again could play their role in the living Earth system. Humans needed to be commanded and controlled by negative laws so that their decisions would not interfere with the marvelous way that life (i.e., life prior to humans) kept the natural environment stable and comfortable for all life, including human.[3]

This standard model for Earth systems roughly had four central features. Although these features were, and have been, challenged by Earth scientists and ecological researchers,[4] they have proved to be durable, and influential, especially among nonscientific environmental policymakers.[5] First, the model asserts that living organisms and their inorganic surroundings have evolved together to become a single living being – an Earth living system. Second, it posits that living organisms modify and shape their nonliving environment so that both of them evolve together as

---

[2] J. E. Lovelock, Gaia: A New Look at Life on Earth (Oxford Univ. Press 1979).

[3] Alexander Lautensach, Environmental Ethics and the Gaia Theory, www.eoearth.org/ Sept. 10, 2011; R. Wallace & B. Norton, Policy Implications of Gaian Theory, 6 Ecological Economics 103 (1992).

[4] C. Folke, et al., Resilience Thinking: Integrating Resilience, Adaptability and Transformability, 15 Ecology and Society 20 (2010); S. A. Levin, Ecosystems and the Biosphere as Complex Adaptive Systems, 1 Ecosystems 431 (1998). The most devastating critique of this standard model, discussed in Section B of this chapter, is Toby Tyrrell, On Gaia: A Critical Investigation of the Relationship between Life and Earth (Princeton Univ. Press 2013). See also Richard Dawkins, The Eternal Phenotype (1982).

[5] Scientists on Gaia (Stephen Schneider & Penelope Boston ed., MIT Press 1991).

a unity. Third, the Earth living system is self-regulating, in that it automatically and predictably adjusts and readjusts conditions so that life can exist. Fourth, changes in the biosphere are brought about through a Natural, unthinking condition of living organisms that maintain appropriate condition for life through homeostasis.[6]

1.   Earth as a Single Living System

A central tenet of the standard model for Nature is that the Earth should be considered a vast living system in its own right. Both living things and their nonliving surroundings are now, and should be considered by policy to be, a single living system. This system greatly affects the chemical composition and biospheric conditions of the Earth's surface and its subsurface waters. Without humans, and their extensive anthropogenic effects on their surroundings, this Earth living system maintains environmental conditions consistent with life's survival. The analogy has been that the Earth was like an individual living organism, such as a human, a bird, or a whale, that self-regulates all its internal systems to keep the organism alive.[7]

2.   Life Makes Earth an Appropriate Place for Life

Another interesting assumption that stems from the standard model is that life itself is not the fortunate by-product of an Earth that was independently compatible with the emergence of life, but rather that living organisms actively have shaped their surrounding environment so that environment would be, and remain, conducive to life. In other words, life maintains conditions for its own survival.[8] Many scientists took issue with this claim that the Earth's biota has substantial influence over aspects of the abiotic world.[9] The dominance of life as an influential actor in the overall dynamics of the Earth's operating systems seemed self-serving at best, or at worst teleological. Nonetheless, environmental policy reflected the anthropocentric assumption that life (especially human life) shapes its environment less so than the environment shapes life. Life was not to be

---

[6] S. Schneider, A Goddess of the Earth? The Debate of the Gaia Hypothesis – An Editorial, 8 Climate Change 1 (1986).

[7] Kate Ravilious, Perfect Harmony, The Guardian (April 27, 2008); *Lautensach, supra* note 3.

[8] *Lovelock, supra* note 2.

[9] James W Kirchner, The Gaia Hypothesis: Can It Be Tested? 27 Reviews of Geophysics 223 (1989).

considered a passive ingredient in the mix of Earth systems, but a central catalyst. Life was thought to influence the physical and chemical characteristics of the planet, to the point where it was argued that life was an active control system.[10]

3. Earth as a Self-Regulating System That Automatically Achieves Equilibrium

Another central theme to the standard model is the notion of "Nature as a self-regulating system." Nature is thought to be both like a living organism and a closed-loop self-regulating system. This self-regulation takes place automatically, where the living system that is Earth maintains conditions that are perfect for life; if one natural cycle becomes misaligned, other natural cycles work to bring it back to a state of equilibrium, which in turn optimizes the conditions for life.[11] The natural balance achieved by this process is what early Holocene-era humans encountered when they first gained a toehold as a viable competing species. And, according to the standard model, it is excessive "unnatural" human behavior during the current Anthropocene era that is adversely affecting virtually all of Earth's systems. Damaged Earth systems then disrupt the equilibrium state that would otherwise be present, but for anthropogenic change. For policymakers, relying on the standard model, the goal then is to restore the equilibrium, so Earth can again self-regulate.[12]

4. Living Organisms Maintain Conditions Conducive to Life through Homeostatis

According to the standard model, environmental policymakers should either *preserve* places "untouched by man" or *restore* ecosystems to a pre-human condition. Earth's natural cycles will then, if unimpaired by humans, work together in a coordinated way to support life and the biosphere. The interplay between unaffected biota and its surrounding environment is homeostatic, characterized by "stationarity" and stabilizing negative feedback loops. These feedback loops are linear, following predictable cause-and-effect cycles as they maintain equilibrium and balance. For example, carbon dioxide spewed into the atmosphere by volcanoes is

[10] *Scientists on Gaia, supra* note 5.
[11] James Lovelock, The Ages of Gaia: A Biography of Our Living Earth (1995).
[12] James Lovelock, The Revenge of Gaia: Earth's Climate Crisis and the Fate of Humanity (2007).

kept in check by tiny organisms in the ocean. When they die, they release a gas. If carbon dioxide levels become too high, these organisms lock up more carbon dioxide in their shells and release more gas when they die – producing atmospheric clouds that reflect back sunlight and help the Earth cool. If carbon dioxide levels become too low, these organisms reduce their activity.[13] Such cybernetic feedback systems operate unconsciously by the biota, leading to a broad stabilization of conditions in homeostasis.

B.   A Better Model – Nature as a Complex Adaptive System

The standard model for Nature saw it as a system that was linear and predictable, where the normal rules of cause-and-effect applied. This model was received favorably by policymakers, because a predictable system could be understood, projected, and ultimately controlled and managed by humans. But the standard model described in Part I appears not to be accurate. Indeed, it is likely inconsistent with the scientific reality of how Nature really works. Nature's systems are often nonlinear and unpredictable, and are in fact far more difficult to manage than previously thought. Nature is best perceived as being characterized by apparently complex behaviors that emerge as a result of nonlinear spatiotemporal interactions among a large number of component systems and subsystems at different levels of organization.[14] Nature on Earth is best understood as a "complex adaptive system."[15]

A complex adaptive system (CAS) is a truly *complex* system, not just a complicated one. There is no separation between the CAS and its environment; rather, the CAS is closely linked with and *connected* to all the other related systems that comprise the mega-system that we call Nature. A CAS tends to alter its structures and behaviors as responses to interactions with (1) other parts of the system and (2) the environment. Such a system is most fit and *resilient* at the transition from order to chaos, characterized by "bounded instability," where it is stable and unstable at the same time. Change for a CAS is healthy and constant, where change needs to be seen in terms of a *co-evolution* with all other related systems, rather than as an adaptation to an environment that is separate and distinct. Contrary to the standard model's version of Nature, a CAS is in a state *far from*

---

[13] *Ravilious, supra* note 7.

[14] *S. A. Levin, supra* note 4; Wendell Jones, Complex Adaptive Systems – Beyond Intractability (Guy Burgess & Heidi Burgess eds., Oct. 2003).

[15] John H. Miller & Scott E. Page, Complex Adaptive Systems: An Introduction to Computational Models of Social Life 9–10 (2007).

equilibrium – it is unstable, chaotic, nonlinear, and unpredictable. The hallmarks of a CAS are therefore complexity, connectivity, resilience, co-evolution, and edge-of-chaos nonequilibrium. These features are entirely contrary to the standard model explaining Nature, which has long influenced environmental policymakers.

1.   Complexity

A CAS acts consistent with complexity theory, which is a theory based on multiple relationships, the notion of "emergence," patterns, and interactions. Complexity results from the interrelationships and interconnectivity of the agents within a system, and between the system and its environment. A CAS responds to changes in ways that are not simply complicated, but rather in ways that are "complex." In complicated systems, the parts of the system (the "agents") and their connections are equally important. But in truly complex systems, like a CAS, the individual agents themselves are not important; only the connections between the agents are critical. Complicated systems are linear and determined, producing controllable and predictable outcomes. By contrast, a CAS produces creative, nonlinear, complex, and "emergent" outcomes.[16]

2.   Connectivity

In a CAS, all the agents that make up the CAS are connected in some way. The interconnectivity is so pronounced that an action by one part within the CAS will influence all other related parts, but not in a uniform manner. Connectivity can contribute to systemic risk, through the contagious spread of disturbances. For environmental policymakers addressing the Earth as a CAS, it is important to realize that, although there is interconnectivity, there is no planning or managing in a CAS; there is only constant reorganizing where the goal is to discover a good fit with surrounding conditions. Connectivity also comes with modularity, or compartmentalization, by which the system's components may be separated and then recombined.[17] Modularity prevents harmful properties from spreading

---

[16] *Jones, supra* note 14; S. A. Levin, Fragile Dominion: Complexity and the Commons (1999). The idea of *emergence* is an important component of complexity theory. A CAS is emergent because application of traditional analytical tools cannot explain the behavior of the CAS. The whole (i.e., the Earth) cannot be explained by a study of the individual agents that comprise the whole.

[17] *Simon, supra* note 1 at 114.

through a system and provides building blocks for reorganization within the system when there is change.[18] In ecosystems, modularity prevents diseases, invasive species, and even forest fires from spreading in a way that threatens the survivability of the ecosystem.[19]

3.   Resilience and Adaptive Capacity

In 1973, theoretical ecologist C. S. Holling introduced the idea that successful natural systems exhibited a quality that could be described as "resilient."[20] A natural system such as the Earth has the capacity to be resilient because, as a CAS, it has been able to tolerate disturbances without changing its basic structural identity.[21] The Earth as a CAS has "the capacity of a system to experience shocks while retaining essentially the same function, structure, feedbacks and therefore identity."[22] A CAS such as the Earth manifests two features of resilience that should be noted by environmental policymakers. First, *engineering* resilience refers to the time required for a system like a CAS to recover – to reorganize after a change or disturbance.[23] Second, *ecological* resilience is the magnitude of disturbance a system can absorb without having its fundamental structure altered.[24]

Environmental policymakers should try to preserve the resilience of the Earth's CAS services, including ecosystem services such as pollination.[25] Policies cannot ever achieve a state of resilience against all kinds of uncertainties, especially uncertainties about the effects of human-driven actions that affect the Earth's complex adaptive systems. Patterns of human behavior can over time become unprecedented disturbances to ecological

---

[18] *Id.* at 116.
[19] R. M. May, S. A. Levin, & G. Sugihara, Complex Systems: Ecology for Bankers, 451 Nature 893 (2008).
[20] C. S. Holling, Resilience and Stability of Ecological Systems, 4 Ann. Rev. Ecology & Systematics 1 (1973).
[21] Lance Gunderson, Ecological Resilience – In Theory and Application, 31 Ann. Rev. Ecology & Systematics 425 (2000).
[22] Brian Walker, et al., A Handful of Heuristics and Some Propositions for Understanding Resilience in Social-Ecological Systems, Ecology & Society (June 2006).
[23] C. S. Holling & Lance H. Gunderson, Resilience and Adaptive Cycles, in Panarchy: Understanding Transformations in Human and Natural Systems 27–28 (L. Gunderson & C. S. Hollings eds. 2002).
[24] C. Folke, et al., Resilience Thinking: Integrating Resilience, Adaptability and Transformability, 15 Ecology & Society 20 (2010); J. B. Ruhl, General Design Principles for Resilience and Adaptive Capacity in Legal Systems – With Applications to Climate Change Adaptation, 89 North Carolina L. Rev. 1373, 1376 (2011).
[25] *Levin, supra* note 4.

systems. Nonetheless, we can, for example, seek to protect resilience in our fish stocks when we create artificial markets regulating fish harvesting,[26] and we can manage river flooding by building dikes that may increase short-run resilience against small yearly floods.[27]

In addition to resilience, a CAS also has the quality of "adaptive capacity." This capacity refers to how a complex system senses threats to its survivability and responds by changing resilience strategies without changing fundamental attributes of the system.[28] For environmental policymakers addressing a CAS, such as Earth's natural systems, policies should reflect the tensions that exist between the benefits of adapting to current environments and the need to maintain sufficient variation to respond to new and future environmental challenges.[29] Adaptive capacity implies that the CAS is sufficiently robust to make changes in resilience while simultaneously keeping the basic identity and integrity of the system intact. Policymakers do not want to optimize a CAS so that it adapts to a particular set of *known* disturbances, when that success could potentially decrease resilience to *unknown* disturbances.[30]

4.   Co-Evolution

Under the standard model for how Nature works, there is a two-way interaction between life and its surrounding environment, where life is the dominant property because it creates interactions that tend to improve living conditions on Earth. When Nature is viewed as a CAS, then living organisms and their abiotic environmental surroundings are seen as equals, where co-evolution better describes how both life and its environment affect each other. With co-evolution, there is no emergent property. Co-evolution is neutral with regards to predicting how life agents affect their environment. For example, biological processes such as oxygen production by photosynthesis shape the Earth's environment. Conversely, that environment influences life through the evolution of organisms to fit their

---

[26] J. M. Arderies, et al., Panaceas, Uncertainty, and the Robust Control Framework, in Sustainability Science, 104 Proceedings of the National Academy of Sciences 15194 (2007).

[27] M. A. Palmer, et al., Climate Change and the World's River Basins: Anticipating Management Options, 6 Frontiers in Ecology and the Environment 81 (2008).

[28] *Gunderson, supra* note 21 at 435.

[29] J. Norberg, et al., Phenotypic Diversity and Ecosystem Functioning in Changing Environments: A Theoretical Framework, 98 Proceedings of the National Academy of Sciences 11376 (2001).

[30] *Walker, supra* note 22, *Ruhl, supra* note 24 at 1389; Fiona Miller, et al., Resilience and Vulnerability: Complementary or Conflicting Concepts?, Ecology & Society (Sept. 2010).

environments.[31] Interactions between life and environmental surroundings do not necessarily improve living conditions.[32]

In a CAS characterized by co-evolution, all systems exist within their own environment, and they are also part of that environment. As their environment changes, they need to change to ensure that they can continue to exist in the environment. But because they are part of their environment, when they change, they also change their environment. And since the environment has now changed, they need to change again, as part of a continuing complex adapting system. Unlike the standard model, which posits that life agents adapt to a separate and distinct environment, with a CAS, change becomes a co-evolution with all other related systems.[33]

5.   Anti-Equilibrium and Variety at the Edge of Chaos

The standard model for how Nature works presumed that, without human interference, Earth-based systems would automatically achieve equilibrium. Indeed, Nature was viewed as a closed-loop, self-regulating system that maintained conditions perfect for life. However, when Nature is pictured as a CAS, just the opposite is true. Natural systems within a CAS *push away from* equilibrium. All the parts, or agents, of a CAS tend to alter their structures or behaviors as responses to other agents and to the general surrounding environment. Since they have to continue to respond to change caused by their coupled landscapes, these agents are not evolving, but co-evolving. Resilience and survivability is highest at the transition from equilibrium to chaos, what has been called "the edge of chaos."[34]

The edge of chaos is a zone between equilibrium-order and complete disorder and chaos. When a CAS is at the edge of chaos, it is characterized by "bounded instability," in that it is simultaneously stable and unstable. Stability is present because the CAS manifests patterns and short-term predictability. It is also unstable in the long term, where the system's future is both uncertain and unpredictable. A CAS in bounded instability, or at the edge of chaos, is a system that is far from equilibrium.[35] It is instead in

---

[31] Stephen Schneider & Randi Londer, The Co-evolution of Economic and Ecological Systems, 18 J. of Evolutionary Economics 1 (2008).

[32] See, e.g., *Tyrrell, supra* note 4.

[33] Peter Fryer, What Are Complex Adaptive Systems? in A Brief Description of Complex Adaptive Systems and Complexity Theory, www.trojanmice.com/articles.

[34] S. Kauffman, The Origins of Order: Self Organization and Selection in Evolution (Oxford Univ. Press 1993).

[35] P. Anderson, Complexity Theory and Organization Science, 10 Organization Science 216 (1999).

a paradoxical state, somewhere between stability and instability, order and disorder, calm and chaos.[36]

Indeed, modern science now realizes that environmental policies seeking to achieve equilibrium for Earth's systems fail because such stable systems are inconsistent with a CAS model, and because they do not have the internal dynamics to permit rapid response to environmental changes. In truth, a system at equilibrium will die.[37] A system at the edge of chaos, where there is a maximum variety and creativity, will survive. Maintaining diversity and heterogeneity sustains the CAS's capacity to compensate for losses of particular components such as species in ecosystems.[38] Environmental policies seeking to restore or preserve some steady-state mythical "natural baseline" are doomed – such a baseline never existed, and cannot now be achieved.[39]

C.   Nature as a Social-Ecological System

Scientific reality reveals that Nature does not operate like a predictable, linear, self-regulating system that seeks a condition of equilibrium so that life can exist. Instead, Nature operates like a CAS, where the system's response to disturbances is not determined, and where system responses are adaptive and nonlinear. Environmental policies will usually fail if they presume that Nature and various Earth systems act like the former "natural baseline" or "stationarity" model. Such policies should presume that Nature works more like a CAS – unpredictable, hovering at the edge of chaos, where life and living organisms are not dominant properties.

But realizing that Nature works like a CAS is only the first change in thinking that needs to take place for environmental policy to have some effect. What also needs to change is how humans perceive not only their place on this Earth but also how the rest of their environmental surroundings play a role in human survival. Humans in general and environmental policymakers in particular need to understand that humans are not apart from their environmental surroundings, but are an integral part of

---

[36] Serena Chan, Complex Adaptive Systems, MIT ESD. 83 Research Seminar in Engineering Systems (Nov 6, 2001).

[37] G. Nicolis & I. Prigogine, Self-Organization in Nonequilibrium Systems: From Dissipative Structures to Order through Fluctuations (1977).

[38] S. A. Levin, Towards a Science of Ecological Management, 3 Conservation Ecology 6 (1999).

[39] P. C. D. Milly, et al., Stationarity Is Dead: Whither Water Management, 319 Science 573 (Feb. 2008) (arguing that policies should not be based on the idea of "stationarity" – where natural systems fluctuate within an unchanging baseline envelope of variability).

them. Nature, in other words, is not something outside of humans. Nature includes humans. The Earth, Nature, and humans – the dominant species that lives on the Earth and in Nature – are all part of one unified system, a social-ecological system (an SES). This SES is being disturbed and dramatically changed in the Anthropocene Era by anthropogenic actions. The SES will, because it works like a CAS, adapt, evolve, and survive in some form. It is less clear whether the human component of the SES will be so fortunate.

1.   Viewing Nature as a Unified Social-Ecological System

For millennia, humans have viewed their environmental surroundings as exogenous – outside of or external to the human condition. Humans realized that they were affected by these surroundings, and that they were dependent on natural resources and climate for survival, but they presumed that these environmental systems were somehow separate from humans. When humans became more technologically sophisticated in the nineteenth and twentieth centuries, they believed they could manage and control these exogenous features of this planet, to better exploit for human benefit.[40] Environmental policies became grounded in the belief that humans were in effect puppeteers, able to master and manipulate natural resources and earth systems to anthropocentric ends. Environmental laws were either designed to help humans *use* the store of goods and services that the Earth provided or to *restore* and *preserve* this "Natural" bounty, after we realized that our predatory practices seemed to be degrading our surroundings.

By the twenty-first century, humans finally came to the realization that the Earth was not comprised of two separate entities – humans and everything else. Rather, Earth, and Nature, were interlinked systems of people and ecosystems. An integrated anthropogenic-ecocentric whole is the SES.[41] The premise behind the idea of social-ecological systems is that there are no natural systems without people, nor are there human-based social systems without natural systems. An SES is interdependent and constantly co-evolving, like a CAS.[42]

[40] See Chapter 2.
[41] Brian H. Walker, et al., Exploring Resilience in Social-Ecological Systems Through Comparative Studies and Theory Development, 11 Ecology and Society #12 (2006).
[42] *Levin, supra* note 1 at 113–114; The Economics of Non–Convex Ecosystems (P. Dasgupta & K.-G. Maler eds. 2004); B. H. Walker, et al., A Handful of Heuristics and Some Propositions

The idea of an SES emphasizes a humans-in-the-natural-environment perspective, instead of humans outside the environment. There is consistent interplay between humans and natural systems in an SES. The Earth's ecosystems, from local areas to the biosphere as a whole, provide the biophysical foundation and ecosystem services for anthropomorphic social and economic development. Conversely, ecosystems have been shaped by human actions throughout the advent of homo sapiens as an Earth species. Human actions directly alter the capacity of ecosystems to sustain societal growth and development.[43]

SES theory is, or should be, enormously important to environmental policymakers. Most environmental policies have focused on investigating processes within the social-human domain only, treating ecosystems as a fixed given. Such policies wrongly assume that if the social-legal system performs adaptively, or if it is well organized internally, it will be able to manage ecosystems and environmental goods in a sustainable fashion. But the ability to cope with changes and adaptions in the social dimension may be at the expense of changes in the capacity of ecosystems sustain the adaption. Polices are best directed at the holistic SES, not just the ecological or social components. And environmental policies should seek to manage and achieve resilience in the SES.[44]

2.   When Humans Affect the SES

Another critical error by environmental policymakers is that anthropogenic action somehow "harms" or "threatens" natural systems or conditions. The policy goal is therefore to "protect" or "restore" natural environmental conditions from the ravages of destructive human action.[45] The underlying assumption is that "Nature has been unjustly violated by mankind."[46] But the scientific reality is to the contrary – natural systems

---

for Understanding Resilience in Social Ecological Systems, 11 Ecology Law and Society #13 (2006).

[43] N. Adel, et al., Collapse and Reorganization in Social–Ecological Systems: Questions, Some Ideas, and Policy Implications, 11 Ecology and Society #17 (2006).

[44] L. Lebel, et al., Governance and the Capacity to Manage Resilience in Regional Social-Ecological Systems, 11 Ecology and Society #19 (2006); M. A. Janssen, Toward a Network Perspective of the Study of Resilience in Social-Ecological Systems, 11 Ecology and Society #15 (2006).

[45] See, e.g., Thomas Lovejoy, Mitigation and Adaptation for Ecosystem Protection, 39 Envtl. L. Rep. (Envtl. Law Inst.) 10,072 (2009); Richard J. Hobbs & Viki A. Cramer, Restoration Ecology: Interventionist Approaches for Restoring and Maintaining Ecosystem Function in the Face of Rapid Environmental Change, 33 Ann. Rev. Env't & Resources 39 (2008).

[46] Ted Nordhaus & Michael Shellenberger, Break Through: From the Death of Environmentalism to the Politics of Possibility 8 (2007).

and Earth-based environmental processes are a CAS, which means they will eventually *adapt* to whatever humans do to alter "natural" conditions. The Earth may not be the same place that it was before humans, but it will remain. The same cannot be said for humans. Their anthropogenic changes might eventually make the Earth uninhabitable for them as a species.[47]

There seems to be no question that anthropogenic actions are affecting the Earth SES. Scientists are increasingly convinced that in the coming decades the Earth could cease to be a "safe operating space" for human beings.[48] Note that this conclusion is *not* that the Earth's natural systems might disappear, or cease working, only that these system's (the Earth's SES) may not work well for humanity anymore. For humans to survive, and thrive, researchers believe that the so-called planetary boundaries cannot be crossed. Human life will be compromised if too many of these essential planetary boundaries are exceeded. These boundaries set theoretical limits on changes to the surrounding environment, such as ozone depletion, ocean acidification, and freshwater use. Beyond each planetary boundary is a zone of uncertainty, where it may be too late for policymakers to make a difference.[49]

What the science is showing is that human activities – economic growth, overpopulation, and consumption patterns – are destabilizing the global environment and Earth systems for humans. Already it appears that four planetary boundaries have been crossed, which means that planetary conditions may be soon changed to a point where the Earth may become an unfamiliar, and less hospitable, platform for homo sapien life.[50] If environmental policies do not take into account the reality of how Nature works, then what is threatened is not the Earth, but the "social" in the Earth-based social-ecological system.

---

[47] *Nordhaus & Shellenberger, id.* ("Global warming threatens human civilization so fundamentally that it cannot be understood as a straightforward pollution problem, but instead as an existential one."); Ramsus Heltberg, Paul Siegel, & Steen Lau Jorgensen, Addressing Human Vulnerability to Climate Change: Toward a "No Regrets" Approach, 19 Global Envtl. Change 89 (2009).

[48] Joel Achenbach, Scientists: Earth Could Become Unsafe for Humanity in the Coming Decades, The Washington Post (Jan. 16, 2015)

[49] Stockholm Resilience Center, The Nine Planetary Boundaries, www.stockholmresilience .org/21/research-programmes (2014).

[50] Will Steffen, et al., Planetary Boundaries: Guiding Human Development on a Changing Planet, 347 Science #6223 (Feb. 13, 2015) (the boundaries already crossed are deforestation, carbon dioxide levels in the atmosphere, extinction rates, and the flow of nitrogen and phosphorous [from fertilizer] into the oceans).

6

Failed Model #2: How to Value Nature

In the previous chapter, it became obvious that traditional environmental policy has failed in part because this policy has embraced a model for how Nature works that is not scientifically accurate. Natural systems do *not* seek a stable equilibrium, sometimes termed "stationarity."[1] And the Earth system is *not* a closely integrated, linear, predictable, self-regulating system that always tends to maintain the conditions for life on the planet within an "unchanging envelope of variability."[2] Researchers, scientists, biologists, and ecologists instead believe that ecological systems are unpredictable, nonlinear, complex adaptive systems.[3] As a result of this conclusion about the workings of Nature, it has become apparent that environmental policies that do not account for complex adaptive system characteristics will lead to undesirable ecological outcomes.[4] The stationarity concept therefore should no longer serve as a central, default assumption in natural resource or environmental planning.

Unfortunately, most environmental and natural resources laws have been grounded in the now-discredited stationarity framework. These laws have tended to be preservationist – valuing "natural" Earth-based systems because of their seemingly uncanny, inevitably unerring ability to achieve a natural baseline equilibrium supportive of life. The resulting policy paradigm has been either (1) to seek to return places or ecosystems to a previous, less anthropocentrically degraded, more "natural" state, or (2) to preserve sites and systems that have not yet been anthropogenically

---

[1] P. C. D. Milly, et al., Stationarity Is Dead: Whither Water Management?, 319 Science 573, 573 (2008).
[2] *Id.*
[3] S. A. Levin, Ecosystems and the Biosphere as Complex Adaptive Systems, 1 Ecosytems 431 (1998); Linking Social and Ecological Systems: Management Practices and Social Mechanisms for Building Resilience (F. Berkes & C. Folke eds.) (Cambridge University Press 1998).
[4] Simon Levin, et al., Social-Ecological Systems as Complex Adaptive Systems: Modeling and Policy Implications, 19 Environment and Development Economics 111, 114 (Cambridge Univ. Press 2012).

contaminated.[5] Consistent with this view, Nature has been valued because of its mythical ability to always achieve life-supporting balance and homeostasis.[6] Part of this historic policy paradigm has also been based on the assumption that anthropogenic change is not only unnatural but harmful to the "normal" functioning of ecosystems.[7] Humans are to be feared, and their actions mitigated. Purely eco-centric, human-free, *natural* conditions are to be valued.

If scientific reality rejects the old stationarity model for Nature, replacing it with a more accurate CAS model, then just how should policymakers value Nature? The short answer is that Nature should not be valued because of the benefits that flow from imaginary nonhuman "natural" states and baselines. The truth is that there is now no meaningful distinction between "natural" and "anthropogenic." As one leading scholar maintains, "naturalness is a human conception."[8] What should be valued by policymakers is not some fictional equilibrium or stationarity condition found in purely natural, non-anthropogenic systems; what should be valued are those systems that accurately describe the interlinked reality of a planet that is comprised of *both* humans and their environmental surroundings. The Earth that we live on, and which is experiencing the dramatic changes set out in Chapter 3, is a *social-ecological system* – an SES. This SES is a coupled human-environmental system that is the constantly changing result of human-environmental interactions.[9] What policymakers need to value is the Earth as an SES.

Policymakers should change their approach to environmental decision-making in two ways. First, they need to conclude that the stationarity model outlined in Chapter 5 should no longer serve as the default assumption in resource/environmental planning. Second, they need to replace the stationarity model with an SES model, which assumes that Earth-based social-ecological systems respect symmetry, in that they include the interconnected actions of humans *and* natural systems. The natural systems of an SES that humans depend on, and constantly affect, are ecosystems

[5] Robin Kundis Craig, "Stationarity Is Dead" – Long Live Transformation: Five Principles for Climate Change Adaption Law, 34 Harvard Envtl. L. Rev. 9, 31–33 (2010).
[6] See, e.g., Daniel B. Botkin, Discordant Harmonies: A New Ecology for the Twenty-First Century 8–13 (1990).
[7] Ted Nordhaus & Michael Shellenberger, Break Through: From the Death of Environmentalism to the Policies of Possibility 24–26 (2007).
[8] J. B. Ruhl, The Pardy-Ruhl Dialogue on Ecosystem Management, Part IV: Narrowing and Sharpening the Questions, 24 Pace Envtl. L. Rev. 25, 31 (2007).
[9] Elinor Ostrom, Marco A. Janssen, & John M. Anderies, Going Beyond Panaceas, 104 Proc. Nat'l Acad. Sci. 15, 176 (2007).

characterized by biodiversity and natural goods. Natural resources and ecosystems in turn provide natural capital and ecosystem services to humans. These natural systems, along with human social systems, operate jointly as complex adaptive systems (CAS). This Earth-based SES should be valued for two central and critical qualities, which work together as a symmetrical property: *ecological resilience* and *adaptive capacity*. For environmental policy to succeed, then, it must address, and ultimately value, an Earth-based SES model, characterized by ecological resilience and adaptive capacity.

Such a policy paradigm would be in line with hard scientific reality, not anthropocentric wishful thinking. Much environmental policy has adhered to outmoded anthropocentric assumptions about "nature" being separate from humans, and subject to our human power to manage natural resources and systems for our exclusive benefit.[10] We have lately sought to "freeze" ecosystems and environmental goods in some hypothetical pre-human state because we have presumed that misguided anthropogenic changes have proved to be "harmful" to the natural world. These changes seem to have interfered with "natural baselines" and nature's self-regulating ability to achieve stationarity. Policies reflecting these assumptions have taken the form of mitigation, restoration, and preservation laws, seeking to restrain destructive human actions, repair human-damaged ecosystems, and save natural places and objects.[11] But when policymakers reject the stationarity model and accompanying preservation laws and replace that model with a more scientifically accurate Earth-based SES model, then a new legal policy paradigm emerges. This policy is called adaptive management, and it is grounded in SES theory, notions of continuing unpredictable, nonlinear CAS change, ecological resilience, and adaptive capacity.

A.   How Humans Should View, and Value, Nature

For centuries it was thought that one of Earth's species – homo sapiens – live on the Earth separate from and independent of Earth-based systems. This species presumed it could exploit and benefit from the natural resources and systems that also happen to occupy the Earth.[12] Instead, the

---

[10] See Chapter 4.

[11] *Craig, supra* note 5 at 34.

[12] See Emilio F. Moran, People and Nature: An Introduction to Human Ecological Relations 7–8 (2006) ("The Nature-culture dichotomy has been central to western thinking ... The Cartesian dichotomy between humans and nature is a peculiar notion in Western society.").

Earth consists of natural systems *and* the humans who depend on them, interconnected in social-ecological systems. The Earth-based SES has certain characteristics, such as behaving like a complex adaptive system (CAS), that should be reflected in environmental policies. And this SES-CAS in turn has two critical features that are relevant for management models: (1) ecological resilience and (2) adaptive capacity. The SES and its two critical features, resilience and adaptive capacity, manifest the central quality of symmetry.

1.   Nature as a Social-Ecological System

Coupled natural and human systems, termed social-ecological systems, make up the biosphere. Human system agents' collective behavior creates feedback that influence natural systems, which in turn affect the macroscopic properties of the human agents, which then change natural systems again. The interlinked nature of the human and natural systems means there is really a unified system, an SES, which is the entity that should be valued by environmental and natural resources policy.[13] Earth-based SES are also complex adaptive systems, possessing the nonlinear, unpredictable, varying, heterogeneous qualities described previously in Chapter 5.[14] Environmental policies that do not account for CAS characteristics of the Earth's SES will result in undesirable social-ecological outcomes.[15] Successful management strategies should consider Earth an SES and a CAS locked in a co-evolving relationship, characterized by resilience and adaptive capacity.[16]

The SES has two central components, engaged in a symmetrical relationship with each other. The "social system" in a broad sense covers all kinds of relationships between people. These relationships, and the distinctly human behaviors that drive them, will be the subject of Chapter 7. The "ecological systems" in the SES include the dynamic environmental goods, systems, and services that surround humans on this Earth. It

---

[13] Emilio F. Moran, Environmental Social Science: Human-Environment Interactions and Sustainability 2 (2010); F. Berkes, J. Colding, & C. Folke, Navigating Social-Ecological Systems: Building Resilience for Complexity and Change (Cambridge Univ. Press 2003); A. Agraul, Sustainable Governance of Common-Pool Resources: Context, Methods, & Politics, 32 Annual Review of Anthropology 243 (2003).

[14] See also *Berkes & Folke, supra* note 3.

[15] M. Scheffer, Critical Transitions in Nature and Society (2009).

[16] Social-Ecological Resilience and Law (Ahjond Garmestani & Craig Allen eds. 2014); Adapting Institutions: Governance, Complexity, and Social-Ecological Resilience (E. Boyd & C. Folke eds. 2012); *Berkes, Colding, & Folke supra* note 13.

is important that policymakers understand the nature of these environmental surroundings, so that they are valued correctly and accurately in environmental policy. For too long humans and their policies valued Nature for its separate utilitarian worth to humans.[17] To be successful, environmental policy must first determine how humans *should* view and understand human environmental surroundings, and how best to optimize policy initiatives that work consistent with the realistic functioning of these surroundings.

The natural environment surrounding humans consists of *ecosystems*. An ecosystem is not a single living organism or even a group of living things, but rather is a larger "system" of biotic and abiotic resources that interrelate with each other in a varied, nonlinear, unpredictable fashion. There is no stable equilibrium model of ecosystems; there is instead a dynamic unstable model of ecosystems as complex adaptive systems.[18] Since they are a CAS, ecosystems require large-scale, flexible management scopes and authorities. Policy regarding the environmental surroundings of humans should not be fragmented or specialized by living species, or categorized by specific natural resource. The policy should be broad-scale "ecosystem management."[19] Its goal would be to maintain variable populations, biodiversity, ecosystem representation, and ecological processes such as natural disturbance regimes, evolutionary potential protection, and human interactions.[20]

Beyond ecosystem management, environmental policy should be designed to facilitate the delivery of certain service functions provided by humans' environmental surroundings. The services of ecological systems and the natural capital stocks that produce them are critical to the functioning of the Earth's life support systems – the SES. *Natural capital*, such as forests and wetlands, is what Nature provides humans for free. Natural capital is the foundation that ensures the survival of humans and the planet's biosphere.[21] *Ecosystem services* are ecological life support systems, such

---

[17] Gilbert F. LaFreniere, The Decline of Nature: Environmental History and the Western Worldview 341 (2008).

[18] Kurt Jax, Ecosystem Functioning (2010).

[19] The Laws of Nature: Reflections on the Evolution of Ecosystem Management & Policy (K. Robbins ed. 2012); Managing Forest Ecosystems: The Challenge of Climate Change (F. Bravo, V. Le May, & R. Kamdl eds. 2008); Integrating Social Sciences With Ecosystem Management (H. Ken Cordell & John C. Begstrom eds. 1999).

[20] R. David Simpson & Norman L. Christensen, Ecosystem Function and Human Activities: Reconciling Economics and Ecology (2012); Alanna J. Cortner & Margaret Ann Moote, The Politics of Ecosystem Management (1999); R. Edward Grumbine, What Is Ecosystem Management?, 8 Conservation Biology 27 (Mar. 1994).

[21] Dieter Helm, Natural Capital: Valuing the Planet (2015).

as carbon storage and photosynthesis. Many of these services, and much natural capital, have been traditionally viewed by policymakers as "free" benefits to humans, or "public goods." Without a formal market, these assets from our surroundings are often overlooked in public policy and individual decision-making.[22]

When natural capital and ecosystem services are undervalued, they become increasingly susceptible to development pressures and conversion. Environmental policy needs to ensure that natural capital and ecosystem services have value, and are valued.[23] An ecosystem services policy framework can support both conservation and economic development activities.[24] And environmental policy that seeks to strengthen ecosystem services not easily traded in markets can benefit both the human population and natural capital components of the Earth's SES.[25]

2. Social-Ecological Systems with Ecological Resilience

The concept of resilience refers to a system's ability to continue to function when intrinsic and extrinsic disturbances occur. It is one of the properties that make up the Earth-based SES. Resilience is actually achieved either when a system is resistant to change or when it is able to successfully reorganize after change. If the system is an "ecosystem," or an SES, then resilience is an important quality of those systems because, both are complex adaptive systems that are constantly subject to change.[26] The Earth-based SES's resilience is defined by its capacity to maintain a high level of consistency of behavioral structure (its functions, feedbacks, and capacities) in

---

[22] Gretchen Daily, Nature's Services: Societal Dependence on Natural Ecosystems (1997).

[23] Payments for Ecosystem Services: Legal and Institutional Frameworks (T. Grieber ed. 2009); S. Wunder, S. Engel, & S. Pagiola, Taking Stock: A Comparative Analysis of Payments for Environmental Services Programs in Developed and Developing Countries, 65 Ecological Economics 834 (2008); Robert Costanza, et al., The Value of the World's Ecosystem Services and Natural Capital, 387 Nature 254 (May 15, 1997).

[24] H. Tallis, P Kaeiva, M. Marvier, & A. Chang, An Ecosystem Services Framework to Support Both Practical Conservation and Ecnomic Development, 105 *Proceedings of the National Academy of Sciences of the United States* 9457 (2008).

[25] Heran Zheng & Guosheng Wang, Achieving Ecological Restoration by Working With Local People: A Chinese Scholar Seeks Win-Win Paths, 19 Ecology and Society 35 (2014); J. B. Ruhl, Steven Kraft, & Christopher Cant, The Law and Policy of Ecosystem Services (2007).

[26] Michael Unger, The Social Ecology of Resilience: A Handbook of Theory and Practice (2012); *Levin, supra* note 3; C. S. Holling, Resilience and Stability in Ecological Systems, 4 Annual Review of Ecology & Systematics 1 (1973). See also W. Neil Adger, et al., Socio-Ecological Resilience to Coastal Disasters, 309 Science 1036 (2005); Stella Hurtley, Editor's Choice: Ecology: Resistance and Resilience, 293 Science 1731 (2001).

the face of relentless dynamic change.[27] For example, humanity has for the last 10,000 years lived in a relatively stable climate during an era referred to as the Holocene. Profound anthropogenic actions have affected this stability domain, producing change in the Earth's SES. The central question during the Earth's current, anthropocentric period – the Anthropocene – is how resilient the Earth-based SES is in the face of these human influences.[28]

The nature of the Earth-based SES's resilience is important to policy-makers, because environmental policy measures designed to address this transition from the Holocene to the Anthropocene need to be consistent with the SES's capacity to face anthropogenic change. Environmental policy needs to accommodate the SES's *engineering* and *ecological* resilience. The former refers to the time required for a system to recover from a disturbance, and the latter describes the magnitude of disturbance a system can absorb without having its central behavioral nature altered.[29] One central difficulty with current environmental policy strategies is that they have focused primarily on ecological resilience, presuming that human actions have been the external drivers of ecosystem dynamics, which have been anthropogenically disturbed and harmed. Environmental policies and laws have sought to control these human actions to protect the Earth's ecological resilience.[30]

Unfortunately, such policies continue to separate the "social" and "ecological" components of the Earth-based SES, and treat them independently. These policies reflect concern about how anthropogenic actions are adversely affecting the ecological resilience of the ecological half of the SES. But, of course, natural ecosystems and the social systems that use them and depend on them are inextricably linked. The feedback loops among them, as interdependent social-ecological systems, determine their overall dynamics and ultimate resilience. Earth-based SES resilience concerns

---

[27] Brian Walker, et al., A Handful of Heuristics and Some Propositions for Understanding Resilience in Social-Ecological Systems, 11 Ecology & Society #13 (June 2006).

[28] E. Steffen, P. J. Crutzen, & J. R. McNeill, The Anthropocene: Are Humans Now Overwhelming the Great Forces of Nature?, 36 Ambio 614 (2007).

[29] Lance H. Gunderson, Ecological Resilience – In Theory and Application, 31 Ann. Rev. Ecology & Systematics 425, 426–427 (2000); C. S. Holling & Lance H. Gunderson, Resilience and Adaptive Cycles, in Panarchy: Understanding Transformations in Human and Natural Systems 27–28 (L. Gunderson & C. S. Holling eds. 2002); J. B. Ruhl, General Design Principles for Resilience and Adaptive Capacity in Legal Systems – With Applications to Climate Change Adaption, 89 North Carolina L. Rev. 1373, 1376–1377 (2011).

[30] See, e.g., F. S. Brand & K. Jax, Focusing the Meaning(s) of Resilience: Resilience as a Descriptive Concept and Boundary Object, 12 Ecology and Society #23 (2007); *Simon Levin, supra* note 4 at 115 ("we would like preserve the … resilience of valuable ecosystem services like pollination").

people and nature as symmetrical *interdependent* systems. Policies that separate the social and the ecological, or that presume they are independent of each other, are irrational and are bound to fail.[31] What effective environmental policies need to do is to protect and restore the resilience of the Earth-based SES.

For example, resilience of human behavioral patterns among Earth's "social" populations is in itself a serious impediment for preventing loss of Earth system resilience. Environmental policies will fail if they simply concentrate on bolstering the ecological resilience of Earth-based ecosystems (like coral reefs, or forests), while ignoring the importance of social systems, such as the tendency of humans to make miscalculations in their decisions (e.g., by stubbornly denying the reality and consequences of climate change).[32] This critical "social" component of the Earth-based SES, which is symmetrically linked to "ecological systems," is explored more thoroughly in Chapter 7.

To improve Earth's SES resilience, policymakers need to focus equally on *social* change. For instance, the U.S. Council on Environmental Quality (CEQ) has recognized the need to take into account social resilience when it comes to climate change. Implementing President Obama's Executive Order on Climate Change,[33] the CEQ offered up a plan to improve "the nation's ... resilience" to better prepare American states, communities, and cities for climate impacts.[34] This American plan reflects the notion that it is not just ecosystem resilience but overall SES resilience that will contribute to Earth system resilience, which in turn will help the Earth remain in the human-friendly Holocene state.[35]

3.   Social-Ecological Systems with Adaptive Capacity

While the resilience of the SES refers to its ability to absorb impacts and continue to function, its "adaptive capacity" refers to the ability of the SES

---

[31] Carl Folk, et al., Resilience Thinking: Integrating Resilience, Adaptability and Transformability, 15 Ecology and Society #20 (2010); *Berkes, Colding, & Folke, supra* note 13.

[32] Richard Thaler, Misbehaving: The Making of Behavioral Economics (2015).

[33] Executive Order, 13 653 (Nov. 1, 2013).

[34] Council on Environmental Quality, Climate Change Resilience, www.whitehouse.gov/administration/eop/ceq/iniatives/resilience.

[35] Brian Walker & David Salt, Resilience Thinking: Sustaining Ecosystems and People in a Changing World (2006); *Carl Folke, supra* note 31; B. Walker, et al., Resilience Management in Social-Ecological Systems: A Working Hypothesis for a Participatory Approach, 6 Conservation Ecology 14 (2002); L. Lebel, et al., Governance and the Capacity to Manage Resilience in Regional Social-Ecological Systems, 11 Ecology & Society #19 (2006).

to change in order to adjust to new conditions.[36] Adaptive capacity implies system robustness to changes in resilience, where the goal of the adaptation is to keep the basic identity of the system intact.[37] Adaptive capacity also maintains certain processes despite changing internal demands and external forces on the SES.[38] Ecosystem resilience and adaptive capacity are linked symmetrically: when resilience is affected, adaptive capacity determines whether the underlying system remains. If adaptive capacity is diminished, resilience will be compromised.

The Earth-based SES benefits from an adaptive capacity because it permits the system to identify imminent changes to components of the SES and to respond by rebalancing resilience strategies. This SES has survived relatively intact for thousands of years because it has secured the benefits of adapting to changed conditions while simultaneously maintaining sufficient variation to respond to new environmental challenges.[39] For example, when disease or limited food resources put selective pressures on changing environments in the biosphere, adaptive processes like species mutation occur to permit continued sexual reproduction. Similarly, when there are losses of particular components of the SES, such as particular populations or species in ecosystems, the system's diversity and heterogeneity sustains its adaptive capacity to compensate for these losses.[40]

For environmental policymakers, the fact that the Earth-based SES is characterized by adaptive capacity means that environmental and natural resources laws need to restore and *increase* the continuing capacity of the SES to adjust to conditions that are transforming the SES. Consider changed anthropogenic conditions – in the form of deforestation – that are transforming forest ecosystems. To save the resilience of ecosystems in face of this relentless human drive to destroy them, what is needed is policy that seeks to restore the adaptive capacity of these forest ecosystems.[41] Instead of simply mitigating anthropomorphic behavior (e.g., relentless

---

[36] *Craig, supra* note 5 at 22.

[37] *Gunderson, supra* note 29 at 428.

[38] B. H. Walker, C. S. Holling, S. R. Carpenter, & A. Kingzig, Resilience, Adaptability and Transformability in Social-Ecological Systems, 9 Ecology & Society #5 (2004). See also S. R. Carpenter & W. A. Brock, Adaptive Capacity and Traps, 13 Ecology & Society #40 (2008).

[39] J. Norberg, et al., Phenotypic Diversity and Ecosystem Functioning in Changing Environments: A Theoretical Framework, 98 Proceedings of the National Academy of Sciences 11376 (2001).

[40] S. A. Levin, Fragile Dominion: Complexity and the Commons (1999); *Levin et al., supra* note 4 at 115.

[41] Klaus J. Puettmann, Restoring the Adaptive Capacity of Forest Ecosystems, 33 Journal of Sustainable Forestry 15 (2014).

clearcutting of forests), laws should also seek to bolster the inherent adaptive capacity of trees and forest ecosystems to respond to human-based socioeconomic forces.[42]

Or consider climate change, which is transforming the Earth-based SES by producing extreme climate variability, global warming, altered ecosystem behavior, and threats to human viability in some parts of the world.[43] A new and more workable paradigm for environmental policy might be to try to increase the adaptive capacity of the Earth-based SES. Indeed, the Intergovernmental Panel on Climate Change has suggested that mitigation efforts to reduce greenhouse gas emissions should *not* be the only approach that should be taken to reduce the risks of climate change. Rather, "[b]uilding adaptive capacity is crucial … at all levels of governance."[44]

4.   *The Essential Property of the Earth-Based SES: Symmetry*

The word *symmetry* derives from ancient Greek terms "sym" and "metria." When combined, they mean "the same measure."[45] In other words, even though the parts of something may seem dissimilar, when combined with the other parts, they become that "something," which is the whole of its components. The Earth-based SES exhibits symmetry because it is comprised of parts – the "social" and the "ecological systems." The social and the ecological systems are the "same measure" because they become parallel parts of the Earth-based SES. When policymakers view the Earth, they should value its symmetry as an SES, not as a separated dichotomy where humans are somehow independent and apart from their environmental surroundings. We will see in Part IV that one of the main reasons for the failure of traditional environmental policies is their refusal to consider the Earth, and Nature, as a symmetrical SES.

A more modern definition of symmetry posits that something is symmetrical when it exhibits immunity to change. Mathematician Herman Weyl (1885–1955) believed that a system was symmetrical "if there is something you can do to it so that after you have finished doing it, it looks

---

[42] Marcus Linder, et al., Climate Change Impacts Adaptive Capacity, and Vulnerability of European Forest Ecosystems, 259 Forest Ecology and Management 698 (2010).

[43] Rasmus Heltberg, Paul Bennet Siegel, & Steen Lau Jorgensen, Addressing Human Vulnerability to Climate Change: Toward a "No Regrets" Approach, 19 Global Envtl. Change 89, 90 (2009).

[44] Climate Change 2014: Synthesis Report Summary for Policymakers, Intergovernmental Panel on Climate Change, Fifth Assessment Report at 19.

[45] Herman Weyl, Symmetry 3 (1952).

the same as before."[46] This meaning of symmetry is remarkably similar to the concept of an SES's ecological resistance, which is the ability of a system to reorganize and retain its essential characteristics, despite the presence of disturbances.[47] And an SES's adaptive capacity, linked to resilience, is a system's ability to respond to rebalancing resilience strategies.[48] So symmetry helps define the Earth-based SES itself, as well as its two connected features: resilience and adaptive capacity.

B. Adaptive Management

Environmental policy has traditionally been grounded in misguided assumptions about how Nature should be valued by humans. As noted in Chapter 4, humans have tended to presume they are separate from their surroundings and capable of managing and using (without cost) environmental goods and systems for anthropogenic ends. In Chapter 5, we saw how humans have embraced a view of Nature based on a stationarity concept, according to which Nature, if left alone, will inevitably return to a self-regulating, linear, equilibrium state conducive to life. Traditional environmental policy has followed from these assumptions. Policymakers have attempted to recapture ecosystems and environmental goods and natural systems so that they replicate some prior, pre-anthropomorphic state when all was well on planet Earth because "natural" baselines ruled. Laws have sought to undo harmful anthropogenic change by *mitigation* regimes that reduce human impacts on "natural" conditions. Environmental regulations have been designed to *repair* and *reverse* human-induced changes in ecosystems or natural systems. Natural resources rules have tried to *preserve* places and natural objects that have not yet been sullied by anthropogenic action.[49]

What Chapter 6 has revealed is that humans are certainly not separate from their environmental surroundings, where they can, like a puppet master, hovering over Earth, manage and manipulate Nature for selfish anthropocentric purposes. Instead, humans are very much a part of, and integrated within, their surroundings. The Earth is a series of unified symmetrical social-ecological systems – the Earth-based SES. And this SES is not prone to stationarity; rather, it is an unpredictable, nonlinear complex adaptive system, a CAS. The SES-CAS that is the biosphere of Earth is most fundamentally characterized by *change*. Environmental policy addressing aspects of the SES-CAS that seem to threaten humans (e.g., climate change) needs to be centered not on bringing the Earth back to

---

[46]   *Id.* at 119–120.
[47]   See notes 26–27, *supra.*
[48]   See notes 36–38, *supra.*
[49]   *Craig, supra* note 5 at 18–20, 31–35.

some static pre-human natural baseline. Instead, policy needs to value the concept of dynamic change. Workable, effective environmental laws must embrace the two central and symmetrically paired qualities of the Earth-based SES-CAS: resilience and adaptive capacity. Such laws should seek to *increase* both the resilience and adaptive capacity of the SES.

Environmental laws that incorporate a far more flexible view of Nature and the natural world will realize that the natural systems and environmental goals that are the subject of these laws are themselves constantly changing. Therefore, the laws too will need to be flexible, requiring an adaptive, structured, iterative management decision-making methodology. This methodology may be termed "adaptive management," which has been described as "management that recognizes uncertainty in its consequences, and seeks to improve understanding so as to improve decision making [by] learning about management outcomes and incorporating what is learned into ongoing management."[50] Adaptive management may also be seen as *pragmatic* management. There should not be just one fixed decision made by policymakers, but many recurrent iterative decisions. Uncertainty about management impacts will inevitably be high when addressing the Earth-based SES, which is also a constantly changing CAS. Pragmatism and flexibility should guide policy.

As policy, adaptive management should become a co-strategy with mitigation efforts, rather than replacing mitigation. For example, the Intergovernmental Panel on Climate Change explicitly states that "mitigation and adaptation are complementary approaches for reducing risks of climate change impacts over different time-scales."[51] However, adaptive management seems particularly well-suited to addressing social-ecological systems, since adaption efforts may increase the adaptive capacity of both humans and the ecological systems on which they depend.[52] A non-fixed adaptive management policy can also permit decision-makers to revise their plans or legal regimes when it becomes apparent that policy goals for the SES are in fact unattainable.[53]

[50] B. K. Williams & E. D. Brown, Adaptive Management: The United States Department of the Interior Applications Guide (2012).

[51] IPCC Panel on Climate Change, supra note 44 at 17.

[52] James D. Ford, Supporting Adaptation: A Priortiy for Action on Climate Change for Canadian Inuit, 8 Sustainable Dev. L. & Policy 25, 29 (2008).

[53] Todd Sanford, Peter Frumhoff, Amy Luers, & Jay Gulledge, The Climate Policy Narrative for a Dangerously Warming World, 4 Nature Climate Change 164 (2014) (policymakers need to adopt "adaption options" because the prospects of realistically achieving the policy target of limiting global warming to 2°C are becoming "vanishingly small"). See also Robert Glicksman and Alejandro Camacho, Legal Adaptive Capacity: How Program Goals and Processes Shape Federal Land Adaptation to Climate Change, 87 Univ. of Coloradao L. Rev. 711 (2016).

7

Failed Model #3: How Humans Behave

In order for environmental policy to be successful, it must not only accurately take into account how the natural environment really works; it must also realistically reflect how humans behave when confronted with laws and rules affecting their behavior toward that environment. Unfortunately, traditional environmental policy has (1) perpetuated a false worldview of human's relationship to Nature[1]; (2) presumed a model of Nature that fails to conform to scientific reality[2]; and (3) embraced a conception of human behavior that now appears to be either misleading or just wrong.[3] Policymakers need to be particularly careful that their assumptions about human decision-making are sound. If environmental policy presumes that anthropomorphic decisions are driven by biases and influences that in fact are not affecting behavior, then those policies will fail.

For centuries, it has been an article of faith among policymakers that humans made decisions in a predictable, ordered, rational fashion – similar to how we used to think that Nature operated in a predictable, logical, linear way. Humans were seen as *optimizing* their individual welfare, in markets seeking equilibrium – similar to how we used to think that Earth's systems made adjustments so as to optimize life and bring about a condition of stationarity. But just as we did not realize until recently just how chaotic, and unpredictable, Nature is (it is best described as a "complex adaptive system"), we too did not see until very recently that humans are likewise often irrational. We sometimes make decisions contrary to orthodoxy, in a counterintuitive manner. We are not just focused on optimizing and maximizing individual welfare. And we may be ineffectively influenced by policy that orders us *not* to do something; we may respond far better to policy that urges us *to do* something.

[1] See Chapter 4.
[2] See Chapters 5 and 6.
[3] See Yannis Papadogiannis, The Rise and Fall of Homo Economicus: The Myth of the Rational Human and the Chaotic Reality (2014).

For environmental policy to work, it should be based on an accurate conception of human behavior. It should not be solely based on the prevailing model that has been most powerful when it comes to influencing public policy – economic theory. Standard traditional neoclassical economic theory rests on certain premises, but these premises appear to be seriously flawed.[4] Other theories, such as behavioral economics, seem better capable of both explaining human choices and affecting environmental policy.[5]

A.   The Myth of Homo Economicus

Environmental policy has long been influenced by economists and economic theory. Of all the social sciences, economics has been the undisputedly most powerful discipline when it comes to shaping public policy.[6] Economics' prominence is due in part to a decision by academic economists to establish their field not just as a discipline but as a hard science. "Economic science" emerged, whose central premise was that human behaviors could be understood by a series of laws and mathematical methodologies deployed as rigorously as Newtonian physics.

The origins of economic science as an explanation for human behavior began with neoclassical theory in the early twentieth century. This new theory sought to formulate general laws governing human behavior, such as the idea that most micro and macro human actions can at their essence be explained on the basis of individual choices and individual behavior. Famous economists such as Alfred Marshall, A. Pigou, V. Pareto, and Lionel Robbins all sought to ensure that economic theory was grounded in scientific foundations. These economists gave power to economic theory by providing to policymakers (and some social science academics) a core theory from which predictions about and explanations of human behavior could follow. This core theory was thought to be as scientifically and mathematically sound as physics. This seeming legitimacy justified the notion that economists, particular neoclassical economists, were uniquely capable of giving policy advice to lawmakers.[7]

---

[4] Richard H. Thaler, The Making of Behavioral Economics 6 (2015).
[5] Daniel Kahneman & Amos Tversky, Choices, Values, and Frames (Cambridge Univ. Press 2000); Philip N. Meyer, Psychological Shortcuts, ABA Journal 26 (Jan. 2016).
[6] *Papadogiannis, supra* note 3 at x; *Thaler, supra* note 4 at 5.
[7] *Thaler, id.,* at 4–5.

The central theory underlying economic "science" has been that "all social interactions are ... interactions among individuals."[8] The individuals that populate the world of economists are not normal, run-of-the-mill, ordinary homo sapiens, but a specific kind of individual, who behaves in a particular way, and who has certain immutable traits. *Homo economicus* is (1) rational, (2) selfish, and (3) makes choices and decisions by optimizing. Much public policy, and a significant amount of environmental policy, has presumed a model of human behavior that is characterized by these three qualities. Market-based solutions to environmental problems, such as cap-and-trade systems deployed for pollution, or for when there is overexploitation of an open-access resource, rely on these three assumptions about how humans behave. The problem with this behavioral model, of course, is that humans in reality often do not act consistent with it.

Rational Choices – one of the items of faith among economists is to assume that human behavior is rational. Economists found that it was useful to assume a certain perfection in the rational decision-making of individuals, when social problems were to be solved by institutional or policy reform. Rational homo economicus thought "marginally," in that they compared marginal benefits to marginal costs when deciding whether to act or not. They also never acted unless the benefit from an action was greater than its cost. Rational choice theorists saw rational competitive decision-making by producers and consumers in markets. They then later extended rational choice analysis to behavior outside of traditional market structures otherwise comprised of goods, services, and prices.[9]

Selfish Choices – Another tenet of neoclassical economists, especially "welfare economists," is that individuals act to benefit themselves, not the greater and larger interests of the group. Indeed, it has been said that "the first principle of Economics is that every agent is actuated only by self-interest."[10] If selfish human behavior drives decisions, then it would follow that cooperation, altruism, and selflessness would be rare. When humans

[8] Kenneth Arrow, J. Methodological Individualism and Social Knowledge, *The American Economic Review*, 1–9 (1994).

[9] Bengt Knistrom & Per-olov Johansson, Economic Valuation Methods for Non-Market Goods, Oxford Bibliographies (Nov. 30, 2015); Andrew Schotter, Strong and Wrong: The Use of Rational Choice Theory in Experimental Economics, 18 Journal of Theoretical Politics 498 (2006); Roger Myerson, Nash Equilibrium and the History of Economic Theory, 37 Journal of Economic Literature 1067, 1068 (Sept. 1999); Gary Becker, The Economic Approach to Human Behavior (1976).

[10] F. Y. Edgeworth, *Mathematical Psychics: An Essay on the Application of Mathematics to Moral Sciences* 17 (1881).

did collaborate or strike a deal, it would be only out of self-interest. The general assumption was that when people were in competition with others, they inevitably acted to benefit their own individual welfare.[11]

Optimizing Choices – Homo economicus are not only rational and selfish; they choose by optimizing. Pursuant to the neoclassical economics model for human behavior, people only choose what they can afford when purchasing goods and services. Their choices are emotionally unbiased, with price and need driving virtually all decisions.[12] These choices seek to "optimize" individual welfare, in that they consistently reflect outcomes with higher payoffs compared to those with lower payoffs.[13] The standard model thereby assumes rational maximizing behavior of individuals when the individual is making decisions for that individual (sometimes known as "maximizing individual utility"). And when other competing individuals are involved, each person is thought to act, within that person's domain of control, to maximize welfare as that person evaluates it given the predicted behavior of others.[14]

Neoclassical economists did more than just populate the world with rational, selfish, optimizing people. They also assumed that, if left alone by government, this clan of homo economicus would achieve two goals: ①"perfect competition" in a free market, and ②"equilibrium." These two goals, central to the orthodoxy of neoclassical economics, would eventually become highly influential to those setting public policy, including environmental policy.

1.   Perfect Competition in a Free Market

The idea of a perfectly competitive free market dazzled economists and policymakers, because even an approximation of the qualities of perfect competition were thought to produce the best economic results. And if conditions yielding perfect competition became an ideal, then the study of imperfect markets suffering from imperfect competition could suggest policy changes that might steer homo economicus toward the elusive goal of perfect competition. In a hypothetically perfectly competitive

---

[11] Amartya K. Sen, Rational Fools: A Critique of the Behavioral Foundations of Economic Theory, 6 Philosophy and Public Affairs 317 (Summer 1972).

[12] Jonathan Knee, In "Misbehaving," An Economics Professor Isn't Afraid to Attack His Own, New York Times (May 5, 2015); *Thaler, supra* note 4 at 5.

[13] Douglas Baird, Robert Gertner, & Randal Picker, Game Theory and the Law 11 (1994)

[14] Roger B. Myerson, John Nash's Contribution to Economics, 14 Games and Economic Behavior 287 (1996).

market: (1) the price of a good is influenced by a large number of buyers and sellers; (2) these market actors are rational and knowledgeable, aware of market conditions and available alternatives; (3) there is freedom of market entry and exit for buyers and sellers; and (4) everyone behaves consistent with the homo economicus model – rationally, in order to optimize self-interest.[15] An imaginary market experiencing perfect competition has been important to environmental policymakers because it has helped flag how, in the real market, there are imperfections that cause market breakdowns, which might be then addressed by government policy.

For example, in a perfect market, everything has a price, and all market actors are charged an appropriate (market-clearing) price for their actions. If a firm is not charged an adequate price for using up clean air, and contributing dirty polluted air, then the firm's pollution becomes an unpriced component of the firm's product. That product is underpriced because some of its real costs – the pollution costs – are borne by others outside of the market transaction. The cost of pollution becomes a negative externality, in that it is a cost external to the market cost, which is then underpriced. Without government intervention, there is no economic incentive to temper the firm's selfish interest in supplying pollution to the atmosphere as part of the product's manufacture. The price of the product does not reflect its real cost to be made, and there is no accurate price to guide the firm's decision-making. Because of information and transaction costs, the parties to a transaction generating negative externalities cannot bargain among themselves to remove the externality.[16]

Standard neoclassical economic science would argue that when goods are persistently underpriced because of the presence of negative externalities, such as pollution, policymakers should tax or charge market actors so that the true price of the product is reflected in the market transaction. And while that response seems logical and mathematically correct, in reality it may not account for how humans in fact behave. Take the case of a state in the United States that imposes a special gasoline tax on car owners when they fill up their car, because they are consuming a scarce resource and polluting the atmosphere when they drive. If this environmental policy works as intended, drivers who now experience the true higher price of driving a car that uses gasoline should change their behavior – they

---

[15] Papadogiannis, supra note 3 at 50.

[16] Avinash Dixit & Barry Nalebuff, Thinking Strategically: The Competitive Edge in Business, Politics, and Every Day Life 224–225 (1991); Ronald Coase, The Problem of Social Cost, 3 Journal of Law & Economics 1 (1960).

should begin to purchase fuel-efficient hybrid cars that do not use as much gasoline.

Unfortunately, as the State of Oregon realized with its anti-pollution gasoline tax, when drivers react to the tax by buying more fuel-efficient cars, the drivers are taxed less, and there are fewer revenues available from the tax that had been used by Oregon to pay for highway maintenance. To make up for less tax revenue from gasoline, Oregon is experimenting with a program that taxes drivers *by the mile*, not by the gallon of gasoline. But by decoupling the experimental mileage tax from fuel efficiency, the Oregon program ironically now *reduces* the incentive to purchase fuel-efficient cars.[17] Oregon's environmental policy did not account for (1) how humans might behave when faced with that policy (the tax on gasoline), and then (2) how humans would respond to the follow-up policy (the mileage charge) that was necessitated when policymakers realized the unintended consequences of their original policy.

2.   Natural Equilibrium

Neoclassical economists believed that under conditions of perfect competition, the individual actions of market actors would lead to a "natural" equilibrium. At that point, there would be an optimum distribution of resources. When a nation's economy was at this point of equilibrium, which was the best possible point it could ever reach, it would then have achieved a condition called Pareto optimality. Economists said that Pareto optimality or Pareto efficiency existed when no other improvement or redistribution could be made in the allocation of resources to one individual without causing some loss to others.[18] It was thought that the free, unfettered operation of the market mechanism would lead an economy to this optimum point. And the goal of public policy should be to try to create conditions where Pareto optimality could, in theory, be achieved.[19] In some ways, Pareto optimality was, for resource economists, the functional

---

[17] Stephen Carter, Oregon Mileage Tax a Drag, The Denver Post 5D (July 12, 2015).

[18] Yang Yang, What Is Pareto Efficiency?, Intro to Economics, www.econguru.com.

[19] In game theory, an equilibrium can also occur, especially in situations involving "non-cooperative games," when players are choosing a strategy that will benefit that player individually. This equilibrium exists when each player makes the "optimal choice" given what the other players might choose, even though these choices do not necessarily result in the best outcomes for everyone, or even for any one player. Such a Nash Equilibrium (named after John Nash, who discovered it) is present if neither player can unilaterally switch to another strategy without reducing its payoff. Scott Borg, Finding Sanity with Game Theory, Strategy & Business 2, www.strategy-business.com.

equivalent of "stationarity," which to biologists was thought to be how Nature would self-regulate to a natural equilibrium if humans did not interfere.[20]

It soon became apparent that Pareto optimality and natural equilibrium could only occur (and be proved mathematically) by making a series of wildly unrealistic assumptions. One would have to presume that markets were perfectly competitive where prices could freely move up and down, fluctuating in a way so that supply always equals demand. Markets also need to be "complete," in that every future transaction in the market, which depends on the future status of the economy, may be "discounted" today.[21] Theories influencing environmental public policy thereby became based on sophisticated mathematical models that were often divorced from how people behave, and instead became grounded in the fictional choices of homo economicus.[22]

B. Humans as Masters and Degraders of Nature

In addition to economists, historians have also played a role in explaining human behavior. Political and ecological historians have increasingly defined humans in a way that calls for policy that "commands" humans to halt their destructive ways. Such policy also seeks to "control" our decisions about our environmental surroundings by threatening sanctions if we stray from an array of mitigation rules. Much of environmental policy has therefore been characterized by command-and-control laws.

Environmental historians argue that we cannot, and should not, rule out the role of anthropogenic ecological destruction as a major factor in world history. Their thesis is that a number of the world's great civilizations declined or even collapsed in large part due to the overutilization and eventual destruction of natural capital and environmental goods.[23] When organized humans gradually destroy a region's soils, watersheds, forests, wildlife, and ecology, these civilized cultures must transform themselves or risk extinction.[24] Most of the time, this transformation does not occur,

---

[20] See Chapter 5.
[21] *Thaler, supra* note 4 at 5–6; *Papadogiannis, supra* note 3 at 52
[22] Wassily Leontief, Theoretical Assumptions and Nonobserved Facts, 61 American Economic Review 1, 3 (March 1971).
[23] Jared Diamond, Collapse: How Societies Choose to Fail or Succeed 159–160, 169–170 (2005).
[24] Sing C. Chew, The Recurring Dark Ages: Ecological Stress, Climate Change and System Transformation (2007).

and populations are either conquered by more adaptive cultures or simply wither away.[25]

Historical perspectives on humans' behavior towards their environmental surroundings have not only described *how* we have treated environmental goods. These studies have also sought to explain *why* we have seen the environment as our adversary, where humans needed to conquer and manage Nature. Environmental historians have seen two root causes for our dominant species' odd, and ultimately self-destructive, desire to overwhelm and control the biosphere. First, religion, particularly Christianity, seems to have influenced anthropocentric "arrogance" toward ecological surroundings. Second, it has been posited that human nature itself demands that we "dominate" the natural world around us.[26] Environmental policymakers have often fashioned rules that respond to these two assumptions about human behavior.

1.   Humans as God's Favorite Creatures

Some environmental historians have argued that we should not discount the influence of the Judeo-Christian worldview on Europeans' harsh treatment of Nature.[27] This religious view assumed divine creation where humanity, selected out from among other living parts of the biosphere, was given dominion over all creatures of the Earth, for selfish anthropomorphic use. Christianity rejected animism and disregarded notions of the intrinsic value of Nature. Western Europeans therefore could "mistreat" their environmental surroundings because non-anthropomorphic life seemed to have neither soul nor value, except as a resource to be exploited by humans.[28]

As a consequence of this perspective, Christian peoples between 500 AD and 1500 AD had used up many of the natural resources of western Europe. This destructive behavior nonetheless seemed justified by the fact that humanity was God's favorite creature inhabiting Earth, and the Earth itself had been designed by God for humanity.[29] It was God's will and command that humans dominate the biosphere and all of its components. Between 1500 and 2000, a combination of a Christian sense of human

---

[25] *Id.* at 112–137.
[26] See generally Gilbert F. La Freniere, The Decline of Nature: Environmental History and the Western Worldview (2008).
[27] Lynn White, Jr., The Historical Roots of Our Ecological Crisis, 155 Science 1203 (Mar. 1967).
[28] *Id.* at 1207.
[29] *La Freniere, supra* note 26 at 345.

dominion over Nature and a utilitarian need to manipulate the Earth's bounty for economic development led to a peculiarly Western destructiveness toward Nature.[30]

Other environmental historians have explained Western civilization's attitude of dominance and arrogance toward the Earth as being influenced by the Augustinian Christian worldview. "Christians were ... acting upon that [Earth] as if it were a passive configuration of matter devoid of its own interior life ... and existing only to be 'civilized' for gain."[31] Augustinian Christian attitudes of dominion, whether from a Catholic or Protestant perspective, provided a rationalization for brutal and ruthless actions toward both indigenous people and natural objects.[32]

2. Humans as the Masters of Nature

Many environmental historians have commented that humans have traditionally not just wanted to utilize their natural environment; they have resolved to be its *masters*. For example, one prominent scholar, Oswald Spengler, wrote in *The Decline of the West*: "Till [the discovery of the steam-engine], Nature had rendered services, but now she was tied to the yoke as a slave."[33] This human desire not only to use but to dominate Nature has been explained by human nature itself.

As the most successful species on this planet, homo sapiens have consistently exhibited one remarkable quality – the ability to adapt to the great variety of ecosystems found of the Earth. One notable example is how humans adapted to post-Pleistocene climate change and an increasing human population to create the Neolithic Revolution, where we first manipulated our surroundings through agriculture and grazing practices. The argument is that the particular genetic makeup of homo sapiens still permits us to adapt to virtually any ecological circumstance on Earth, and that we therefore "own" an entitlement to dominate, and to manage, for anthropogenic ends, our natural world.[34]

---

[30] Carolyn Merchant, Reinventing Eden: The Fate of Nature in Western Culture 77–84, 88–89 (2003).

[31] Frederick Turner, Beyond Geography: The Western Spirit Against the Wilderness 176 (1983).

[32] Max Oelschlaeger, The Idea of Wilderness (1991). Conversely, some scholars have argued that theologically derived concepts of salvation, redemption, and spiritual progress might explain, in the United States, why Americans developed a passion for protecting "Nature" and encouraging environmental cleanups, especially in the 20th Century. Evan Berry, Devoted to Nature: The Religious Roots of American Environmentalism (2015).

[33] Oswald Spengler, The Decline of the West 502 (1926).

[34] William Leiss, The Domination of Nature (1972).

In the United States, this faith in the human capacity to change natural landscapes to suit human short-term needs was manifested in nineteenth-century agricultural imperialism. Open western lands, populated by waves of settler farmers, were thought able (by Thomas Jefferson) to produce food and sustenance capable of supporting a population explosion. Perceived human dominance of Nature reached an unprecedented level when contemporaries of Jefferson began to argue that anthropomorphic agricultural change could actually change the climate itself, not just the land. Francois Volney, a friend of Jefferson, traveled to the United States in the early 1800s and observed that human "cultivation" of the land had caused "longer summers, later autumns, shorter winters, and lighter and less lasting snows."[35] New England naturalist Samuel Williams argued in 1809 that settlement and agricultural development could bring about a wholesale transformation of the American climate.[36]

Policymakers have not been unaware of these historic traits of arrogance and dominance that seem to drive human behavior. Their response has been, when it comes to environmental policy, to seek to overcome and suppress these powerful emotions of superiority by imposing on humans an equally powerful set of uniquely negative laws that order us ("command" us) not to do certain acts: Don't Pollute! Don't Overfish! Don't Contribute to Greenhouse Gas Emissions! Don't Drive Fuel-Inefficient Cars!

Environmental policy has traditionally imposed on humans negative duties. The thinking has been that laws should tell us what *not* to do. Environmental laws have been premised on the notion that rules should both stop us from doing more damage to the Earth and prevent us from engaging in behavior that seems to adversely impact our environmental surroundings.

C.   The Rise of Behavioral Economics

Neoclassical economists explained human behavior with reference to the fictional homo economicus model – whose rational, selfish optimizing actions in a perfectly competitive market would inexorably lead to natural equilibrium and Pareto optimality. Environmental policy has been influenced by this view of humans, leading to market-based solutions to environmental problems, such as (1) the creation of property interests for

[35] Constantin-Francois Volney, View of the Climate and Soil of the United States of America 215–216 (London 1804).
[36] Samuel Williams, Natural and Civil History of Vermont 70–71 (2d ed. 1809). See also Gillen D'Arcy Wood, Tambora: The Eruption that Changed the World 215–216 (2015).

commons, (2) cap-and-trade systems for open-access goods; and (3) taxes and charges to price the real environmental cost of economic growth and to disincentivize human choices generating negative externalities. Environmental historians have also contributed to a particular portrait of humans – the rapacious, arrogant destroyers of ecosystems and environmental goods, who seek to ensure anthropocentric dominance over Nature. Environmental policy has reflected this view of humans by instituting command-and-control rules that have told humans what not to do.

By the latter part of the twentieth century, scholars and researchers began to cast doubt about these two traditional explanations for human behavior. Observed behaviors seemed inconsistent with the orthodoxy of predictors set forth by economics and history. Groundbreaking insights into human behavior began to emerge from psychology and other social sciences.[37] A new discipline arose that seems equally able to explain human choices involving our environmental surroundings – *behavioral economics*. For environmental policies to succeed, they should also take into account the insights gained from this emerging discipline.

1.   How Do Human Really Behave?

Psychologists and social scientists have conducted research and undertaken observations to provide policymakers with a better understanding of how we make choices. What follows is a synthesis of some of their surprising and counterintuitive discoveries.

Human Use Heuristics When They Think – Behavioral economists, such as Daniel Kahneman, Cass Sunstein, and others, argue that people's behavior displays not homo economicus rationality, but rather "bounded rationality."[38] We tend to choose well in environments for which certain "rules of thumb," or "mental shortcuts," or *heuristics* are well suited.[39] Rarely do we think rigorously about something before we make choices. Effortful, overt, systematic thinking, which rationally balances costs and benefits, and which considers the marginal gains of choices, almost never guides our judgments. Instead, we oversimplify and employ biases and

---

[37] Amos Tversky & Daniel Kahneman, Judgment Under Uncertainty: Heuristics and Biases, 185 Science 1124 (1974); Richard H. Thaler, The Winner's Curse: Paradoxes and Anomalies of Economic Life (1992); Richard H. Thaler, Psychology and Savings Policies, 84 American Economic Review 185 (1994).

[38] Cass R. Sunstein, Why Nudge? 11 (2014); Daniel Kahneman, Thinking, Fast and Slow (2011).

[39] Hueristics: The Foundations of Adaptive Behavior (Gerd Gigerenzer et al., eds. 2011).

undertake quick, automatic thought.[40] As a result, human errors are common, and choices are made that in the long run may be harmful to the choice-maker.[41]

Humans Are Not Necessarily Rational – One of the totemic principles of neoclassical economics is a theorem (called the Coase Theorem),[42] which posits that an initial distribution of property rights will always be Pareto efficient (i.e., result in Pareto optimality or equilibrium) if certain assumptions are true. One of these assumptions is that people will rationally value goods and rights, which means the value will be stable and insensitive to logically irrelevant circumstances.[43] In reality, however, experiments in cognitive psychology and behavioral economics reveal that people will often value an item they have *just acquired* at a significantly higher dollar amount than the price they would have paid for that same item *before* they acquired it. In other words, the mere fact of ownership somehow adds value. This phenomenon is called the endowment effect, and it suggests that, contrary to standard neoclassical economics, people sometimes price goods and rights irrationally.[44]

Humans Cooperate With Other Humans – The prevailing wisdom among resource economists is that humans tend not to cooperate with each other, especially when there is competition for public goods or common pool resources or resource commons.[45] However, researchers such as Elinor Ostrom have shown that cooperative collective management can arise in these cases, without the need for formal legal rules.[46] Communities of people with a mutual interest in the sustainability of the resources in a commons (rangeland, irrigation systems, fisheries, forests) can work together to ensure that those resources are not depleted or exhausted. Cooperation is not antithetical to human behavior; it may be built into us.[47]

---

[40] *Kahneman, supra* note 38.

[41] *Thaler, supra* note 4.

[42] *Coase, supra* note 16.

[43] Herbert Simon, Rationality in Psychology and Economics, 59 J. Business 5209, 5211 (1986).

[44] Daniel Kahneman, Jack Knetsch, & Richard Thaler, Experimental Tests of the Endowment Effect and the Coase Theorem, 98 J. Pol. Econ. 1325, 1342–1346 (1990); Owen Jones & Sarah Brosnan, Law, Biology, and Property: A New Theory of the Endowment Effect, 49 Wm. & Mary L. Rev. 1935 (2008).

[45] Garrett Hardin, The Tragedy of the Commons, 162 Science 1243 (1968). See generally Amity Doolittle, Tragedy of The Commons, Oxford Bibliographies (Sept. 29, 2014).

[46] Elinor Ostrom, Governing the Commons: The Evolution of Institutions for Collective Action (Cambridge Univ. Press 1990).

[47] J. M. Burkart, et al., The Evolutionary Origin of Human Hyper-Cooperation, 5 Nature Communications #4747 (July 21, 2014); Carl Sagan, Cosmos 347 (1980).

Humans Behave Altruistically – Although selfishness, self-interest, and optimizing self-welfare define the mythical homo economicus, evolutionary anthropologists have concluded that early humans could not have survived without altruism and the social reciprocity of a larger group.[48] Moreover, fundamental tendencies toward altruism are not found just in our evolutionary history. The aftermath of natural disasters is typically characterized by selflessness, heroism, and the sharing of resources, not selfish panics. Altruism is also seen by many as the best way for individuals to live ethically.[49]

2.   Policy Implications

The standard neoclassical economic model for human behavior does not tell the entire story about why humans make the choices they do. Nor do environmental historians complete the tale of anthropogenic behavior. One needs also to add an overlay of what psychologists, sociologists, and other social scientists have discovered about the realities of human behavior. When behavioral economics is considered, government intervention is no longer justified by simply pointing to "market failures," such as the absence of property rights in an open-access commons, or by noting the harmful effects on third parties that follow from the creation of unpriced negative externalities. Environmental policy should obviously respond to these market failures. But policy also needs to reflect the behavioral realities of human beings.

One environmental policy that is consistent with behavioral economics is one that uses the mildest and most choice-preserving forms of government intervention. Scholars call these forms of intervention "nudges."[50] These are policy initiatives that maintain freedom of choice while steering individual decisions in a desired direction by having individuals judge what choices to make. Environmental nudges could include disclosure of information (e.g., mileage-per-gallon estimates for all new cars), warnings (e.g., energy consumption on a consumer's utility bill comparing a consumer's energy use with other neighbors), and default rules that establish

---

[48] Matthieu Ricard, Altruism (2015); Maia Szalavitz, Is Human Nature Fundamentally Selfish or Altruistic?, Time (Oct. 8, 2012).

[49] Samuel Bowles, Why Good Incentives Are No Substitute for Good Citizens (2016); Peter Singer, The Most Good You Can Do: How Effective Altruism is Changing Ideas about Living Ethically (2015).

[50] See, e.g., Cass R. Sunstein, Why Nudge? (2014); Richard Thaler & Cass Sunstein, Nudge: Improving Decisions about Health, Wealth, and Happiness (2009).

what happens if people do nothing (e.g., failure to opt out of a solar installation program means a utility will add solar panels to your residence and charge you monthly on your utility bill for the cost).[51]

The central idea behind "nudges" as a policy choice is due to social science research suggesting that "soft" government paternalism (e.g., policies that persuade) might be more effective than "hard" paternalism (e.g., policies that compel). Behavioral economists have found that soft paternalism is more libertarian in that it tends to preserve freedom of choice, which means that people exercising that choice are promoting their own ends, as they understand them.[52] Environmental policies that mandate *what not to do* may find more resistance than policies that persuade people *what to do*. Similarly, policies that impose affective or psychic costs, such as graphic health warnings, might provide better results than threats of steep fines or jail time.

Behavioral economics might also influence environmental policy alerting policymakers of the "identifiability bias" in human perceptions. The identifiability effect, as developed by psychologists, is the tendency to have stronger emotions regarding identifiable individuals or groups than for more abstract, less specific, unidentifiable ones.[53] Environmental law and policy is particularly susceptible to one-directional systemic bias because usually only those economically harmed by environmental laws are identifiable (e.g., consumers will have to pay more for "green products"; segments of the carbon energy workforce, such as coal miners, will have to be laid off). The beneficiaries of these laws (i.e., everyone who breathes air, drinks water, eats agricultural products, or lives on land) tend to be too numerous, not sufficiently specific, and less identifiable. As a result, the identifiability effect works *against* the adoption of environmental policy.[54]

For environmental policy to be accepted, policymakers need to come to grips with the reality of the identifiability bias. It might be useful to target some stakeholder groups with interests similar to the environmental goal, in an attempt to clarify exactly who will benefit from the environmental law, so that more than just the law's economic "victims" are known. It might also be helpful to place environmental benefits on the same level

---

[51] *Sunstein, id.* at 17.
[52] Riccardo Rebonato, Taking Liberties: A Critical Examination of Libertarian Paternalism (2012).
[53] Deborah A. Small & George Lowenstein, The Devil You Know: The Effects of Identifiability on Punishment, 18 J. Behav. Dec. Making 311 (2005).
[54] Shi-Ling Hsu, The Identifiability Bias in Environmental Law, 35 Fla. State Univ. L. Rev. 433 (2008).

playing fields as economic costs. Traditionally, the cost of compliance with environmental rules is a measurable and present value. But the benefits are more diffuse (e.g., avoiding inchoate harm), and are realized in the far future. If the benefits of avoiding future human health and environmental damage can be known in the present, then the justification for environmental action can better compete with inevitable fears over that action's economic costs.

Another example of how behavioral economics should affect environmental policy involves the question of how policy should seek to get people to take an interest in, and do something about, climate change. For years, the standard prevailing wisdom was to prod people into thinking about how they were responsible for causing climate change problems, and to make them feel so guilty that they would take action to address the problem. But behavioral research suggests that this assumption about how best to trigger action in people about climate change is misguided. It appears that environmental policy should frame the problem not as an issue involving personal responsibility, but as a collective problem threatening all of us. Once we believe that we are part of a larger collective environmental difficulty, we are more likely to require policy to be effective.[55]

D.   An Essential Property of Human Behavior: Symmetry

In Chapter 6, it was pointed out that one of the essential qualities of Nature is "symmetry."[56] For example, the Earth itself exhibits symmetry, since it consists of social-human systems that parallel ecological systems. The combined social ecological system (the SES) defines the twenty-first-century Earth. The "social" and "ecological" systems symmetrically interrelate. Policy, especially environmental policy, will fail if it views the "social" and "ecological" systems separately, instead of as an interrelated, symmetrical, SES whole.

Human behavior displays a similar tendency toward symmetry. Policymakers are often faced with a choice of diametrically opposed options when they are trying to bring about a change in human behavior for some larger goal. For example, the goal of preventing human action

---

[55] Nick Obradovich & Scott Guenther, Collective Responsibility Amplifies Mitigation Behaviors, 136 Climatic Change 1 (May 4, 2016).
[56] See Chapter 6, Section ID.

from exceeding "planetary boundaries" seems worthy if humans wish to live on a planet where conditions support human life.[57] But for environmental policy to succeed in restoring these planetary boundaries, policy choices need to reflect the symmetrical nature of human decision-making. These are usually two options available to policymakers seeking to change behavior, which are mirror images of each other. While both policy options will have some effect on humans, the one that will have the best chance of actually bringing about the sought-after human change will be the one that best resonates with the reality of how humans behave.

Carrots versus Sticks – When seeking to bring about behavioral change, environmental policymakers are often faced with the symmetrical choice of either "punishing" humans to deter them from harming, depleting, or polluting a natural resource, or "incentivizing" and "rewarding" humans who make decisions that preserve or conserve resources. The question is: Which policy will be more likely to bring about the needed behavioral change? The city of Santa Fe, New Mexico, has experimented with both the carrot and the stick approach in its attempt to impose a water use conservation policy that reduces consumption. As part of the "stick," the city decided to make the heaviest users of water pay more – much more – for the water they consumed. Santa Fe employed "tiered" pricing, where above a certain point water users pay four times more per gallon than consumers using less than that point. Such pricing techniques are consistent with traditional market-based systems that rely on consumers acting like homo economicus to avoid the incremental cost of water use.

But Santa Fe does more to reduce usage. It also relies on sticks and carrots that appeal to behavioral economists. To deter excessive use, the Santa Fe Water Department makes public the names and addresses of the city's top ten water users. Consistent with behavioral economics, such public "shaming" has had a powerful effect on water guzzlers – most of these water users quickly reduce consumption.[58] In some California cities, public shaming of water guzzlers has led to near-vigilante searches for excessive water users.[59] Santa Fe also relies on carrots – residents who

---

[57] Stockholm Resilience Center, The Nine Planetary Boundaries, www.stockholmresilience .org/21/research-programmes (2014); Will Steffen, et al., Planetary Boundaries: Guiding Human Development on a Changing Planet, 347 Science #6223 (Feb. 13, 2015).

[58] Nelson D. Schwartz, Water Pricing in Two Thirsty Cities: In One, Guzzlers Pay More and Use Less, New York Times (May 6, 2015); *Sunstein, supra* note 50 at 57–61.

[59] Elizabeth Day, Anger Drives Hunt for "Criminal" Water Guzzler During California Drought, The Guardian (Nov. 7, 2015).

buy low-water washing machines automatically get a $200 credit on their water bills. Again, as with the shaming technique, behavioral economists have predicted that low-cost default rules (e.g., an automatic credit upon making a purchase consistent with conservation) can be as effective as command-and-control laws as means of achieving a policy end.[60]

Altruism versus Self-Indulgence – When humans make choices, these decisions are not made in a vacuum, but rather tend to follow from other previous choices. A prior choice tends to influence a current choice. Behavioral economists have discovered a symmetrical connection that links the prior choice to the current choice, which has been called "the licensing effect."[61] This effect predicts that if individuals make a prior choice that boosts a positive self-concept, that prior, more altruistic choice may subsequently "license" a follow-up choice that is the symmetrical opposite of the first one – a choice that is self-indulgent. In other words, a previous intent to act in a virtuous way may inadvertently encourage a subsequent action that is selfish and harmful. The first "virtuous" choice subconsciously licenses the next "destructive" choice.[62]

The licensing effect should be a warning to environmental policymakers. If policy successfully nudges individuals to act green by virtuously driving only fuel-efficient cars, or by conserving energy at home, or by installing solar panels, those same individuals may believe these prior altruist choices license a subsequent self-indulgent choice that impairs environmental quality (e.g., buying a diesel-powered pickup truck to pull a mobile home). Human "nature" may sabotage policy if success in bringing about short-term environmentally sensitive behavior ironically yields future long-term policy failure due to the licensing effect.

Loss Aversion versus Gain Seeking – Another symmetrical quality of humans affecting behavior involves this classic policy choice: Is it

---

[60] *Sunstein, supra* note 50 at 36, 59; Eric Johnson & Daniel Goldstein, Decisions by Default, in The Behavioral Foundations of Public Policy 417 (Eldar Sharif ed. 2013).

[61] Uzma Khan & Ravi Dhar, Licensing Effect in Consumer Choice, XLIII Journal of Marketing Research 259 (May 2006).

[62] For example, if someone eats healthy food like vegetables and salmon and quinoa, that consumer may as a result feel like there is now license to eat cheese or pastries or candy. Some economists call this "licensing effect" a "crowding out bias." See Gernot Wagner & Martin Weitzman, Climate Shock: The Economic Consequences of a Hotter Planet 133 (2015). In other words, when an environmental threat like climate change motivates people to take action, such as recycling, that one action might "crowd out" other, more ambitious actions, such as installing solar panels. The one action assuages people's worries and prevents them from taking more aggressive actions to address climate change.

preferable to try to bring about change in people by providing them with benefits if they comply, or by taking away from them something of value if they do not comply? The answer seems to be similar to the "endowment effect," discussed previously.[63] We tend to seek to avoid losses more than we seek gains.[64] If loss aversion is more powerful in people than its symmetrical counterpart, gain seeking, then effective policy might be weighted more toward threatening losses if there is noncompliance, rather than rewarding if there is compliance. In other words, if environmental policy wishes to reduce consumer usage of electricity, it would be more effective to take away a consumer's energy-gobbling air conditioner than to award a conservation-minded consumer a tax credit for the purchase of a more energy-efficient swamp cooler.

Reducing Demand versus Limiting Supply – If environmental policy intends to reduce global warming by lowering fossil fuel combustion, then such climate change policy is faced with a symmetrical choice involving human behavior: Should the goal of reduced fossil fuel burning be achieved by reducing demand for fossil fuels or by limiting fuel supply? Of course, this choice is not an either/or question, but one that asks which one might be more effective in light of behavioral economics. For decades, policymakers (and international agreements) have sought to reduce demand through energy efficiency measures, low-carbon technology, and carbon pricing and taxing. But since these demand reduction strategies do not seem to be working,[65] researchers are exploring the symmetrical mirror image of demand reduction – limiting supply.[66]

Supply-side policies have not been as vigorously pursued as demand reduction measures have been. However, supply-side options, such as the removal of producer subsidies, compensation of resource owners for leaving fuels unburned, or even outright prohibition, could be a useful alternative, or supplement, to traditional demand reduction policies.[67]

---

[63] See note 44 *supra*.

[64] Penelope Wang, How a Bowl of Cashews Changed the Way You Save for Retirement, Time (May 11, 2015).

[65] Agence France-Presse, World in "Uncharted Territory" as Greenhouse Gases Hit New High: UN, www.rawstory.com/2015 (concentrations of carbon dioxide and greenhouse gases in the atmosphere hit a new high in 2014, reaching levels not seen on Earth for more than a million years).

[66] M. Lazarus, P. Erickson, and K. Tempest, Supply-Side Policy: The Road Less Taken, SEI Working Paper No. 2015-13 (Oct. 29, 2015).

[67] For example, climate change activists have argued the U.S. president and Department of the Interior should simply ban all future leasing of federal fossil fuels – the "keep it in the ground" approach.

Supply-side policies might make it easier for low-carbon or no-carbon alternatives to compete economically with fossil fuels. Natural gas, wind, and solar producers could become far more dominant if environmental policy seeks to restrict the supply of fossil fuel use, instead of primarily encouraging measures that reduce the demand for these carbon-based resources.

Why Environmental Policies Fail II

A Critique of Existing and Proposed Strategies

In Part III, we summarized how environmental policies often fail because they have too often been built on models that are flawed, or simply wrong, as a matter of good science and empirical reality. In Part IV, we review the most commonly used or proposed policies and consider whether the policies themselves may have internal defects that might be preventing them from achieving external success.

This critique of environmental policies is certainly not the first time that a commentator has sought to explain why decades of environmental law seem not to have had much of an effect on Earth systems that are rapidly making this planet inhospitable to homo sapiens. A review of environmental literature reveals that there have been a number of explanations offered for the odd, and persistent, inability of policies and laws to have much of an impact on the litany of Earth-based woes listed in Chapter 3. Here is a sampling (by no means comprehensive) of some of the reasons why other thoughtful commentators believe environmental strategies continue to fail to do the job.

Misguided strategies of environmental funders – Those who provide grants to environmental organizations have favored top-down "elite" strategies that have neglected to support a robust grassroots infrastructure. Underwriting grassroots groups is essential for any large-scale environmental success.[1]

Political refusal to ratify two key international treaties on eliminating toxic chemicals – The United States has failed to adopt two treaties – the Stockholm Convention and the Rotterdam Convention – on eliminating chemicals the international community has agreed are extremely dangerous

---

[1] Sarah Hansen, Why the Environmental Movement Is Not Winning, National Committee for Responsive Philanthropy (Feb. 2012).

to human health and the natural environment.[2] The United States also is reluctant to update and fix loopholes and gaps in one key federal toxic chemical statutes, Federal Insecticide, Fungicide, and Rodenticide Act.[3] Nor does U.S. environmental policy regarding chemicals, and dangerous pollutants adequately reflect the "precautionary principle." As a result, the United States has a more lax approach to toxics and poisonous pollutants than the approach to chemical policies prevalent in Europe, which holds that action should be taken even in the absence of full scientific certainty when a chemical threatens irreversible damage.[4]

The law of unintended consequences – Although countries support laws designed to protect the natural environment, too often these laws are adopted without regard for whether the measure actually achieves the desired outcome. And, instead of benefiting environmental quality, the laws produce unplanned secondary consequences that create a separate set of environmental problems.[5] For example, when the state of California realized it was facing an unprecedented catastrophic drought, the state's governor ordered cities and water utilities to cut consumption of water. When residential lawns and grass around homes were not watered, so too were city trees denied water. As a result, the state is losing millions of trees that beautify cities, improve air quality, offer shade, and provide urban habitat for squirrels and birds. Even worse, as customers cut back on the length of their showers and the number of times they flushed their toilets, they lowered the outflow of water needed to push waste through the sewage pipes. The solids that are flushed cannot move because there is not enough water to carry the material.[6]

Excess consumerism and unlimited economic growth – Capitalism and an unquestioning society-wide commitment to economic growth at any cost produce an economic and political reality that is highly destructive environmentally. Traditional markets tend to systemically create negative

---

[2] Kristin S. Schafer, One More Failed U.S. Environmental Policy: Washington's Policy on Toxic Chemicals is Also, Well Toxic, http://fpif.org/authors (Sept. 1, 2006).
[3] John S. Applegate, Jan G. Laitos, Jeffrey M. Gaba & Noah M. Sachs, The Regulation of Toxic Substances and Hazardous Wastes 229–311 (2d ed. 2011)
[4] Id. at 33–36
[5] Alexander Neubacher, Green Extremes: Germany's Failing Environmental Projects, Spiegel Online International (Mar. 15, 2012).
[6] Darryl Fears, California's Drive to Save Water is Killing Trees, Hurting Utilities and Raising Taxes, The Washington Post (Feb. 27, 2016).

externalities and environmental costs unless corrected by difficult-to-enact government rules.[7]

Failure to take into account where the law will govern – When natural conditions prove disastrous to humans, such as when there is a drought, sometimes the consequences to human populations can be avoided *if* the planners and policymakers account for the environmental conditions of the place itself where the law will apply.[8] In the case of the chronic water drought affecting California, some commentators have argued that the disaster is "man-made" and caused by "misguided environmental policies."[9] These commentators allege that "environmentalists" have caused the drought by ignoring the locational reality of California river drainage. According to this argument, environmental groups have stopped construction of water storage and delivery systems, which means that much of California's rainfall is not captured, but instead is released into rivers to flow downstream to boost fish populations, or into delta reservoirs to dilute salinity.[10]

Too many government regulations – Environmental quality has not been enhanced because of the bureaucratic, top-down approach that has fostered too much policy. Although there is debate among policymakers about the utility of different legal tools in addressing anthropogenic changes to global systems essential to human survival, there is a powerful argument that no matter which legal strategies are adopted (e.g., alterations of property rights, taxes and subsidies, or direct government regulation), there will be dramatic increases in government intervention in individual lives. This inevitable increase in government intervention in human society "will test a range of legal doctrines that are intended to protect individual rights against government overreaching."[11] Such "overreaching" in environmental policy will fail until there is strict enforcement

[7]   James Gustave Speth, Environmental Failure: A Case for a New Green Politics, Environment 360 (Yale, Oct. 28, 2008).
[8]   John Copeland Nagle, Law's Environment: How the Law Shapes the Places We Live (2010).
[9]   Malia Zimmerman, "Man-Made Disaster": Critics Say California Drought Caused by Misguided Environmental Policies, www.foxnews.com/us/2015/04/16.
[10] Other commentators make the case that California's drought is due to rising temperatures, ground water depletions, and a shrinking Colorado River. Environmental 360 (Yale, June 15, 2015).
[11] Eric Biber, Law in the Anthropocene Epoch 3 (unpublished manuscript, 2016).

of private property rights, combined with environmental entrepreneur-ship that "humanizes" environmental laws.[12]

While there may be a certain amount of truth in each of these expla-nations of policy failures, it seems that it would also be useful to divide up the universe of distinct environmental policies that have been tried or proposed, and to critically examine their utility as well as their flaws. One can identify ten main categories of policy that are designed to alter, affect, or influence human behavior that impacts natural resources, environmen-tal goods, and Earth-based natural systems. Each of these is discussed in Chapter 8. Each has promise, yet each also has self-limiting characteristics.

[12] Re-Thinking Green: Alternatives to Environmental Bureaucracy, The Independent Institute (R. Higgs & Carl Close eds. 2005).

8

A Narrative of Failed Environmental Strategies

A. Introduction

Environmental policy often supports, encourages, or compels human behavior. The hope is that the policy will somehow affect or change behaviors so that humans will be less likely to cause large-scale Earth problems that threaten anthropomorphic existence. The policy must do more than simply express concern about, or increase public awareness of, Earth problems such as climate change, pollution, biodiversity loss, and natural resource depletion. To be effective the policy needs to realign people's usual preoccupation with economic growth and individual advancement, so that we are equally motivated to minimize anthropogenic harm to our environmental surroundings.[1]

Over the past several decades, ten main categories of environmental policy strategies have either been implemented or proposed. Based on the grim results summarized in Chapter 3, one can logically presume that these strategies have failed. They have not deterred human behaviors that have caused critical planetary boundaries to be exceeded.[2] And to the extent certain proposed strategies have not been adopted, failure to implement them is likely because they are unrealistic politically, or are too complicated or cumbersome for policymakers to embrace.

The ten categories of environmental policy strategies are:

1. **Direct Government Action** – a public entity undertaking the responsive action directly.
2. **Command and Control (Regulatory)** – rules that prevent or limit or sanction certain behaviors, and that tell humans what not to do.

---

[1] A. Kollumuss & J. Agyeman, Mind the Gap: Why do People Act Environmentally and What are the Barriers to Pro-Environmental Behavior?, 8 Environmental Education Research. 239 (2002).
[2] Johan Rockstrom, et al., A Safe Operating Space for Humanity, Stockholm Resilience Centre (Jan. 22, 2015), www.stockholmrsilience.org.

3. **Economic Policies** – market-based instruments that influence human behavior by relying on prices, taxes, and cost-based systems, where such market tools presume individual welfare maximization as a primary motive behind resource choices.

4. **Information** – rules requiring disclosure of environmental effects of human or governmental choices, or information helpful to consumers wishing to make decisions conducive to sustaining Earth-based conditions consistent with human survivability.

5. **Adjustments to Property and Tort Law** – expansion of property and tort rights into previously unowned or communally owned global systems.

6. **Legal Rights for Nature** – creation of legally enforceable rights in natural objects, natural resources, or environmental goods, either through a public "trust" theory or by conferring on the natural object/resource/good a right to resist human intervention.

7. **Preservationist Rules** – protection of natural resources or critical ecological spaces by forbidding human access to, or human development of, these preserved objects or places.

8. **Human-Nature Linkages** – either adoption of policies that mimic the processes and essential attributes of Nature, or conversely, decoupling of human well-being from human choices that impair natural systems.

9. **Behavioral** – influencing human behavior so that individuals will be more likely to make choices that are less destructive to their environmental surroundings, and so that individuals take affirmative action that is environmentally remedial.

10. **Delegate to Private Parties** – either empowering humans with a right to a safe and sustainable environment, or relying on private parties to undertake response efforts on their own.

Each of these policy strategies is discussed in Chapter 8. Some are traditional, such as "direct government action," "command-and-control," "economic," "informational," "preservationist," "rights-based," and hortatory "defer to private initiative" policies. Some are relatively recent, such as "behavioral" tools, which are slowly being integrated into positive law after being broadly accepted.[3] Some are theoretical only, such as "human-nature linkages." Some policies, such as those calling for "adjustments to property and tort law," or "legal rights for Nature," seek to stretch existing

---

[3] Linda Steg & Charles Vlek, Encouraging Pro-Environmental Behavior, 29 Journal of Environmental Psychology 309 (2009).

legal doctrine to adapt to large-scale environmental issues. None seem to be able to fully address the ravages of the Anthropocene Era, in which human actions have altered the Earth and Nature to the point where the forecasted future for human survival appears problematic.[4] Each policy strategy contains within it inherent limits that make the policy less successful, or even an abject failure.

B.   Direct Government Action

Government entities can most easily use their public powers, or ownership of public lands, or their power of the purse, to bring about direct change in natural global systems.[5] For example, a government forestry department might plant trees on its lands to absorb greenhouse gases and generate oxygen. At a local level, a municipally owned electricity utility that is coal-fired could decide to shut down its coal-burning power plant and replace it with a wind farm. Or a government agency might use its procurement powers to purchase solar panels for government buildings.[6] Government can financially incentivize private parties to undertake actions that mitigate anthropogenic changes in the biosphere or restore natural conditions that have been impaired by human choices. The government could subsidize private actions by paying homeowners to install solar panels or to plant trees to absorb carbon dioxide.[7]

Such direct public action is costly. First, any government purchase or procurement of items that ameliorate climate change (e.g., constructing

[4] Will Steffen, et al., The Anthropocene: Conceptual and Historical Perspectives, 369 Philosophical Transactions of the Royal Society 842 (2011); Will Steffen, Paul Crutzen, & John McNeil, The Anthropocene: Are Humans Now Overwhelming the Great Forces of Nature? 36 Ambio: A Journal of the Human Environment 614 (Dec. 2007).

[5] Climate Change 2014, Mitigation of Climate Change, Intergovernmental Panel on Climate Change, Working Group 3 at 94, 97 (IPCC).

[6] Id. at 1156.

[7] Eric Biber, Law in the Anthropocene Epoch 36 (unpublished manuscript, 2016). A macro example of a multi-nation subsidy to address climate change is the Green Climate Fund. This fund was created in 2009, and its goal is to have the world's rich nations, responsible for most of the greenhouse gases that cause climate change, provide money to poor nations to support clean energy, low-emission agriculture, and sustainable forestry. There is a serious question as to whether or not the Fund can ever achieve these goals, or even how the Fund, with its unwieldy governance structure, can ever do business. For example, it is highly contentious whether the Fund should make grants, low-interest loans, market-rate loans, or equity investments. There is also a question as to whether any money from the Fund should go to governments, businesses, or nonprofits. Marc Gunther, Rich Countries Have Pledged Billions in Climate Aid. Why Has Progress Been So Slow? http://ensia.com/features (April 28, 2016).

wind farms to generate electricity instead of burning coal, or retrofitting government buildings with solar panels, or planting trees) will cost the taxpayers who generate revenue for the government. And there is incurred both an up-front acquisition/construction/installation cost and an ongoing maintenance and operation cost. Second, public subsidization of private-party action involves extensive state involvement in private activities. Government subsidies require that some bureaucrat give benefits to some but deny benefits to others; subsidies also need government audits to ensure that recipients are complying with the conditions of the grant.[8] Since subsidies should only be paid for private activities that would otherwise not occur except for the subsidy, there should in theory be some difficult-to-demonstrate baseline establishing what private parties would do in the absence of the subsidy.[9]

On the other hand, government policy could be directed at government-owned lands to ensure that climate change is accelerated and even worsened! The United States owns about one-third of the lands in this nation. For these lands, federal policy could encourage the development and extraction of carbon-based energy fuels, such as coal, oil, and gas. For example, a moratorium on leasing federal coal could be lifted, so as to encourage coal mining, as well as the construction of coal-burning fossil fuel electrical power plants on federal lands. Since the lands are owned by the federal government, and since the relevant federal energy resource statutes are implemented at the discretion of "the Secretary of Interior" or the "Secretary of Agriculture," two officials appointed by the President, federal carbon-based fuel policy on federal lands could be determined entirely by politics.

C.   Command and Control (Regulatory) Policies

The most traditional form of environmental policy is regulatory policy. Regulations from government policymakers usually just directly order a particular behavior, which often takes the form of "commanding" individuals or firms on what not to do. Pollution control laws are typically regulatory, in that they ban or limit or "control" polluting activities, or command that the polluter comply with the conditions of a permit. These

---

[8] *Id.* at 38.
[9] *IPCC, supra* note 5 at 1251; Irina Slav, Are Subsidies Killing US Solar Companies?, oilprice. com (May 12, 2016) (The unintended consequence of subsidies for purchasers of solar power equipment is that companies relying on the subsidy are tempted to grow too big, and too fast, and ultimately may be unable to cope when demand for their product diminishes).

requirements are enforced in a variety of ways, ranging from criminal prosecution[10] to fines[11] to administrative penalties[12] to court-imposed injunctions.[13] If the polluter ignores these sanctions, the regulatory body can try to shut it down.[14]

Command-and-control anti-pollution regulations tend to be either technology-based or performance-based. The former specifies the methods and equipment that firms must use to meet the target. Performance standards, on the other hand, set an overall target for each firm, or plant, or individual, and give them some discretion in how to meet the standard. These performance standards are either "end of the pipe" solutions or ambient standards that must be met everywhere in the environment.

American pollution control law relies on regulatory command-and-control statutes to reduce and remediate water pollution, air pollution, and land pollution of hazardous wastes. The water and air laws essentially say to polluters: Do not discharge unless you comply with regulatory standards. The Clean Water Act requires dischargers to install best available control technology that is economically achievable.[15] Another part of the Clean Water Act provides authority for the denial of permits for the discharge of dredged and fill material into navigable waters, when such discharges would have adverse impacts on aquatic ecosystems, such as wetlands.[16] The Clean Air Act makes it unlawful for any operator of a stationary source of air pollution to operate that source in violation of a preestablished "standard for emissions."[17]

In order to prevent contamination of land by hazardous waste, American pollution law first directly regulates the handling, discharge, or disposal of solid, liquid, or chemical material that poses a substantial threat to human health or the environment.[18] In order to clean up abandoned hazardous waste sites, American law does not deploy a regulatory statute. Instead, it authorizes the federal government, states, Indian tribes, and private parties to clean up sites, and to use a statutory liability scheme to hold others

---

[10] See, e.g., 33 U.S.C. § 1319 (c).
[11] See, e.g., 33 U.S.C. § 1319 (d).
[12] See, e.g., 42 U.S.C. § 7413 (d).
[13] See, e.g., 33 U.S.C. § 1365.
[14] Amoco Production Co. v. Campbell, 480 U.S. 531, 545 (1987).
[15] 33 U.S.C. § 1311 (b).
[16] 33 U.S.C. § 1344 (a) (b); 40 C.F.R. § 230.10 (a).
[17] 42 U.S.C. § 7411 (e). Between 1980 and 2014, the Environmental Protection Agency in America estimates that the Clean Air Act was responsible for reducing total emissions of the six principal air pollutants by 63 percent. http://www3.epa.gov/airtrends (2014).
[18] The Resource Conservation and Recovery Act, 42 U.S.C. §§ 6901 et seq.

responsible for the costs incurred in the necessary cleanup effort.[19] Both approaches rely on government environmental law and policy to protect citizens from harmful hazardous water and toxic substances, although there is widespread disagreement on how to measure and manage the risk from these dangerous substances.[20]

Traditional command-and-control rules, such as those used in American pollution laws, are sometimes a preferred policy. For example, they may be appropriate where the activity regulated is so immediately dangerous that abatement demands outweigh any concerns over the economic efficiency of a blunt command. For example, environmental policy could, in theory, "command" that carbon-based energy sources on which we have relied be replaced with solar and wind power. Such a draconian command could be justified if there is a consensus about impending planetary doom if we continue to use coal, oil, and gas for electricity and transportation.

Regulations may also be acceptable when there are significant societal benefits experienced from an initial reduction in the amount of a pollutant, or from the initial halting of a destructive activity, especially where the marginal benefits of continued reductions, or further prohibitions, are highly inelastic. On the other hand, any rules-based policy often suffers from the possibility of weak enforcement, low acceptance rates, high administrative and information costs for the regulator, and high compliance costs for regulated firms. A rules-based environmental policy also depends on the rules being technologically, economically, and scientifically sound, which too often is not the case.

Another problem with command-and-control performance-based standards is that there is no reward for beating a target. Rather, there is the risk that the policymaker will raise the standard if there is new and better technology in place. It is true that the first round of command-and-control regulations was likely successful in securing reductions in pollution emissions from previously unregulated industries. However, over time standards have become more restrictive and businesses, firms, and individuals have to bear the burden of meeting these more strict standards. Sometimes, but not always, the cost and suitability of alternative technologies can be considered when pollution standards are being set. Another weakness of command-and-control regulations is that they have tended to focus on

[19] The Comprehensive Environmental Response Compensation and Liability Act, 42 U.S.C. § 9601 et. seq.
[20] John S. Applegate, Jan G. Laitos, Jeffrey M. Gaba, & Noah M. Sachs, The Regulation of Toxic Substances and Hazardous Waters (2d ed. 2011) at v.

large point sources, because these were obvious first targets. But what is not being regulated are diffuse pollution sources, which are contributing just as much environmental damage as the large sources are.[21]

D.   Economic Policies

Because of the drawbacks of regulatory tools, policymakers, academics, and many economists have favored market-based instruments that appear more efficient than a rules-based approach. Market-based economic policies would include financial incentives and disincentives to influence behavior, such as subsidies, grants, penalties, and taxes. They would also encompass tools that deploy market-and-property-right mechanisms such as cap-and-trade programs with tradeable pollution permits. A cap-and-trade system seems particularly well suited as a policy to address the global reality of climate change and worldwide greenhouse gas pollution.[22]

These economic policies grew from the popularity of microeconomics as a methodology for understanding the decision-making of individuals. For most of the twentieth century, and beyond, microeconomics was underpinned by neoclassical economic theory. As noted previously in Chapter 7, this theory was grounded in several broad assumptions about humans, affectionately known as homo economicus.

Rationality – Individuals have rational preferences and the ability to make rational decisions. Rational behavior means that each individual understands the implications of their choices; each individual bases that individual's choices on a personal "utility function," which is optimized given perceived opportunities.[23]

Optimizing – Individuals will always maximize their utility for both monetary and nonmonetary gains. Individuals are self-interested, seeking to maximize their own welfare. They act to obtain the highest possible well-being for themselves, given available information about opportunities and constraints.[24]

---

[21] William Andreen, No Virtue Like Necessity: Dealing With Nonpoint Source Pollution and Environmental Flows in the Face of Climate Change, 34 Va. Envtl. L. J. 255 (2016); Daniel H. Cole & Peter Z. Grossman, When Is Command-and-Control Efficient? Institutions, Technology, and the Comparative Efficiency of Alternative Regulating Regimes for Environmental Protection, 1999 Wisconsin L. Rev. 887 (1999).

[22] OECD, Evaluating Economic Instruments for Environmental Policy (1997); Duncan Austin, Economic Instruments for Pollution Control and Prevention – A Brief Overview, World Resources Institute (Sept. 1999).

[23] Gary Becker, The Economic Approach to Human Behavior (Chicago 1976).

[24] John Elster, Nuts and Bolts for the Social Sciences (Cambridge Univ. Press 1989).

Amoral – Social values are ignored unless adhering to them provides individual utility. Motivation is extrinsic, not intrinsic, in that rewards and punishment are the primary inducements of behavior. Decisions and judgments are made to lead to an expected or planned end yielding the highest self-satisfaction, irrespective of larger societal implications.[25]

Deliberate – Individual behavior is the result of conscious deliberative thought. All decisions are made by weighing costs and benefits of alternative courses of action. Most problems, even global ones, are seen as risk management problems.[26]

In a world populated with homo economicus, private property exists primarily to protect the subjective expectations that particular owners of property have in particular things. The purpose of property law is to protect owned things from the interference by others, and to promote autonomy, security, and the ability to maximize the long-term value of the property for the owner. Economic value dominates all the values associated with the property.[27]

Traditional neoclassical economic theory also appears well tailored to addressing global environmental issues like climate change. With nearly every nation on Earth now "pledged" to the 2015 Paris Agreement to gradually reducing emissions of heat-trapping greenhouse gases that are warming the planet, the next question is *how* these countries should take concrete steps needed to deliver on their vows. Many countries have agreed that nation-specific legislation is essential to set the ground rules for the marketplace, proposing market-based economic tools, such as a carbon tax or a cap-and-trade system, as the preferred policy to implement their pledges.[28] Academics have also uniformly embraced market-based approaches for global climate change.[29]

---

[25] T. Lawson, The Nature of Heterodox Economics, 30 Cambridge J. of Economics 483 (2006).

[26] Genot Wagner & Martin Weitzman, Climate Shock: The Economic Consequences of a Hotter Planet (2015).

[27] Thomas W. Merrill, Melms v. Pabst Brewing Co. and the Doctrine of Waste in American Property Law, 94 Marquette Law Review 1055, 1059 (2011).

[28] Sewell Chan, Leaders Move to Convert Paris Climate Pledges Into Action, www.nytimes.com/2015/12/14.

[29] William Nordhaus, The Climate Casino: Risk, Uncertainty, and Economics for a Warming World (Yale University Press 2014); Shi-Ling Hsu, The Case for a Carbon Tax: Getting Past Our Hang-Ups to Effective Climate Policy (Island Press 2011); David Schoenbrod, Richard Stewart, and Katrina Wyman, Breaking the Logjam: Environmental Protection That Will Work (Yale University Press 2010). But see Brendan Haley, Ontario's Climate Plan and the Promise of Mobilizing Markets and Society, The Broadbent Blog, broadbentinstitute.ca/brendanhaley/Ontario (June 28, 2016) ("The sooner we dispel ourselves from the myth that the market alone will solve the climate change problem, the sooner we can start to ensure more technology and sector specific policy approaches are implemented …. ").

Unfortunately, despite the popularity and broad acceptance of market-based instruments as efficient environmental policy, evidence has emerged that suggests that reliance on economic policy may be problematic, especially policy grounded in standard neoclassical theory. First, as noted in Chapter 7, the neoclassical economic model itself may be flawed because it is built on assumptions about human behavior that are inaccurate. Second, although the problem of climate change seems suitable to being addressed by market-based tools,[30] use of these policy tools raise difficult questions of distributive and corrective justice.[31]

The *first* of these two problems with neoclassical economic theory arose when behavioral economists challenged each of the traits characterizing homo economicus.[32] Using integrated insights from psychology and economics and empirical data about human behavior, a new and more realistic model of humans arose that was contrary to the premises grounding homo economicus.

Irrational – Human behavior is often irrational, and the pressure to maximize profits in markets carries with it a strong incentive to appeal to the worst sides of human nature. Human choices are often driven by nonrational influences such as risk aversion, loss aversion, anchoring, or status quo bias.[33]

Altruistic – Humans are not necessarily selfish in their decisions. They will act altruistically sometimes, especially when a larger team or collective benefit might result. Intrinsic motivation can in some cases "crowd out" extrinsic rewards and punishments.[34]

Social – Humans make choices based in part on social context. They are not simply amoral utility-driven automatons, but rather individuals who have emotions, family ties, and connections to the community. Social norms help influence behavior.[35]

---

[30] Willaim D. Nordhaus & Joseph Boyer, Warming the World: Economic Models of Global Warming (MIT Press 2003).

[31] Cass R. Sunstein, Conspiracy Theories and Other Dangerous Ideas 115–138 (2014).

[32] Daniel Cohen, Homo Economicus: The (Lost) Prophet of Modern Times (Polity Press 2014); Richard Thaler, From Homo Economics to Homo Sapiens, 14 Journal of Economic Perspectives 133 (2000).

[33] George Akerlof and Robert Shiller, Phishing for Phools: The Economics of Manipulation and Deception (Yale University Press 2015); Daniel Kahneman & Amos Tversky, Prospect Theory: An Analysis of Decision Under Risk, XLVII Econometrica 263 (1979).

[34] Amos Tversky & Daniel Kahneman, The Framing of Decisions and the Psychology of Choice, 211 Science 453 (1981).

[35] C. Bicchieri, Norms, Preferences, and Conditional Behavior, 9 Politics, Philosophy, and Economics 297 (2010).

Judgment Heuristics – Humans often do not calmly deliberate costs and benefits, or risks and benefits. Instead, they use mental shortcuts to solve problems rapidly, even though these shortcuts might seem irrational.[36]

This more modern view of human behavior also suggests that property does not exist primarily to protect the subjective expectations of selfish individual owners, but rather to maximize the value that *society* ascribes to particular things. In other words, property may be less an individual right and more a social institution. If individuals are not just self-interested welfare-optimizing independent actors, but social beings equally influenced by the welfare of others, then the purpose of property law may be to permit exchanges and transfers of wealth that are more congruent with the larger interests of human society.[37] Similarly, environmental policy should align its goals not just with human interests, but with the interests of Earth's broadest possible environmental entity – the social ecological system (SES) that makes up the human-Nature continuum on this planet.

The *second* difficulty with market-based instruments involves difficult questions of distributive and corrective justice, particularly when economic tools seem the best policies to choose for truly global environmental issues, such as climate change. *Distributive* justice issues become important then, because the United States has the highest gross domestic product of any country in the world. Does this wealth mean that America has a special duty to reduce the effects of climate change? Are the obligations of a wealthy country such as the United States different from those of a country such as China, which is an even bigger emitter of greenhouse gases but which is less wealthy than the United States? Principles of *corrective* justice focus on wrongful behavior occurring in the past. Because of its past contributions of greenhouse gases, does the United States owe remedial action or material compensation to those nations that have been thereby harmed?[38]

To address global climate change, nearly 200 nations in 2015 adopted a global pact, calling on the world to collectively cut and then eliminate greenhouse gas pollution.[39] The so-called Paris Agreement aims to keep global temperatures from rising another degree Celsius between 2015 and 2100. The countries to the pact pledge to limit the amount of greenhouse

---

[36] C. F. Camerer, Behavioral Economics: Past, Present, Future, in Advances in Behavioral Economics 3–5 (2004).

[37] See, e.g. Kelo v. City of New London, 545 U.S. 469 (2005).

[38] See *Sunstein, supra* note 31 at 116.

[39] Karl Ritter, Seth Borenstein, & Sylvie Corbet, Deal Sets Stage: Nearly 200 Nations Open Doors to First Global Accord to Fight Climate Changes, The Denver Post 2A (Dec. 13, 2015).

gas emitted by human activity. Of course, a "pledge" is not the same as a requirement, or an enforceable duty. If a nation chooses to "opt out" of the Paris Agreement, as the post-Obama United States President has threatened to do, then there is nothing to prevent a key nation from simply ignoring in the future any 200 nation, non-binding agreement that occurred long ago, in 2015.

Although the Paris Agreement countries pledge to "reach global peaking of greenhouse gas emissions as soon as possible," the agreement does not tell countries *how* to get there. Most economists, academics and several political leaders believe that to reduce greenhouse gas emissions, one of two market-based approaches should be taken: (1) an emissions tax on carbon emissions designed to capture the externalities (i.e., the social cost) associated with climate change; (2) a cap-and-trade system to create a worldwide cap on aggregate emissions. Such a system would require a consensus on the appropriate cap, as well as an initial allocation of emissions rights.

Distributive Justice Issues – If a worldwide carbon tax were adopted, then the largest carbon emitters, such as the United States, would bear the largest burden. But difficult questions then arise. Should the tax paid by the United States take the form of an in-kind benefit to poor nations, or would it be better for America to simply make a cash transfer to poor nations so that these countries may use the money however they see fit? And who in the United States would pay the carbon tax? If the poor in the United States would be hit hardest (by higher prices for goods that require carbon-based energy), then the tax is regressive.[40]

If a cap-and-trade program is adopted, if the initial allocation of entitlements were allocated on a per capita basis (i.e., each nation has a right to emit a specified amount per person), then the United States would have far less emission rights than more populous countries, such as India and China. U.S. emitters would then have to purchase emission rights from these other countries, resulting in an enormous worldwide redistribution of wealth.[41]

Corrective Justice Issues – If one assumes that the United States has historically used most, or a disproportionately large share, of the carbon emissions now threatening human life on the planet (because greenhouse gases emitted more than a hundred years ago are still in the atmosphere), then

---

[40] *Sunstein, supra* note 31 at 126–127.
[41] *Id.* at 137–138.

one can make the argument that the United States is particularly to blame for the problem of climate change. Therefore, as a matter of corrective justice, the United States should devote significant resources to remedy the problem. Indeed, some countries want the United States to pay reparations for extreme weather.[42] However, the U.S. share of greenhouse gases in the current atmosphere is a result of behavior of U.S. emitters from the past, where most of the emitters are now dead. Holding Americans today responsible for the actions of their ancestors seems neither fair nor reasonable on corrective justice grounds.[43]

E. Information

An important non-regulatory tool is environmental policy that attempts to influence behavior by providing information to policymakers and individual consumers so that they can make good choices. Informational approaches, unlike market-based approaches, do not attach a price to environmentally harmful activity directly. But they nonetheless create incentives. The mandated disclosure of accurate information about agency practices that affect our environmental surroundings, or about consumer products that might add to greenhouse gas emissions, influence both private market actors and government decisions.

There are three classes of environmental policies that seek to improve choices by forcing the disclosure of information pertaining to environmental quality. The first class, and most well known, is the policy that requires government entities involved in resource management, project development, or agency administration of environmental laws to analyze and disclose the environmental impacts of their actions *before the fact*. The statute best embodying this policy is the National Environmental Policy Act of 1969 (NEPA), America's first comprehensive environmental law.[44] NEPA requires federal agencies to prepare environmental impact statements for federal actions that will "significantly affect ... the quality of the human environment."[45]

---

[42] Thomas Kostigen, Poor Nations Want U.S. to Pay Reparations for Extreme Weather, www.msn.com/en-us/news/world (Sept. 12, 2015).

[43] *Sunstein, supra* note 31 at 132. Nonetheless, the 2015 Paris Agreement does explicitly provide that developed countries, including the United States, "shall provide financial resources to assist developing countries with respect to both mitigation and adaptation ..." *Karl Ritter, supra* note 39.

[44] 42 U.S.C. §§ 4321, 4331.

[45] 42 U.S.C. § 4332 (2) (c).

The rationale behind NEPA is to require government agencies to describe the environmental impact of proposed actions before those actions are implemented, in the hopes that the agencies will then take steps to avoid adverse impacts to environmental goods, and to consider alternatives to the proposed action. However, such impact disclosure policies have a number of inherent limitations. First, laws such as NEPA do not require that federal agencies make the best environmental decisions, or even any corrective and preventative decisions. The only requirement is a procedural one, which is for the government entity to articulate the likely impacts of the proposal action. Once the impacts have been disclosed, the government's legal obligation has been fulfilled.[46]

Second, when litigants have attempted to challenge impact statements for failing to consider the effect of proposed government action on global problems, like climate change, such lawsuits have generally failed. As a matter of constitutional standing, it has been difficult for environmental plaintiffs to prove any connection between their individual injuries and the government's alleged failure to consider the "effects" of climate change when approving pollution limits.[47] And even if standing can be established, it has been nearly impossible to convince courts that governmental agencies must be required to include in their impact statements an analysis of how climate change will affect the outcome of the proposed action.[48]

Third, the very idea of assessing and disclosing the "impact" on the natural environment of a proposed government action presumes that the government entity contemplating the proposal can ever fully know what the effects of human actions are on natural conditions. As noted in Chapter 4, Earth systems are far more complicated and complex than we have realized. We may never be able to accurately predict or disclose what consequences follow from human actions that intersect with natural processes. Moreover, the notion of an "environmental impact statement" presumes a certain separation between the human "action" and the resulting environmental "effect." But, as was pointed out in Chapter 6, there really is no separation between humans their environmental surroundings: "Nature" is a symmetrical synthesis of integrated anthropocentric

---

[46] Robertson v. Methow Valley Citizen's Council, 490 U.S. 332 (1989); Stryker's Bay Neighborhood Council v. Karlen 444 U.S. 223 (1980).

[47] See, e.g., Conservation Law Foundation, Inc. v. U.S. E.P.A., 964 F. Supp. 2d 175 (D. Mass. 2013); Summers v. Earth Island Inst., 555 U.S. 488, 491 (2009).

[48] *Conservation Law Foundation*, *id.* at 191–192. But see Center for Biological Diversity v. California Dept. of Fish & Wildlife, 361 P. 3d 342, 541-354 (Cal. 2015).

human-social systems and eco-centric environmental systems, making up a unified social ecological system – an SES.

Another class of "information" policy includes laws that require private companies to report and disclose their release of toxic chemicals. Such laws, like the Emergency Planning and Community Right-to-Know Act, encourage private decision-making based on information provided by private entities that may be polluters or generators of toxic substances.[49] These kinds of disclosure laws are grounded in utilitarian rationales: information about releases of hazardous chemicals should in theory encourage those directly responsible for the chemicals to take precautionary measures, while simultaneously deterring chemical firms from making toxic releases because of fear of litigation or adverse decisions by investors and government regulators.

On the other hand, some commentators are skeptical about whether "community right-to-know" laws really have much effect:

> What the public is to do with the information to which it has a right is less clear. The knowledge of presence of hazardous substances in the community seldom brings with it the ability to do anything about them ... Citizens generally ... are in a much poorer position to reduce risk themselves. Moreover, it is questionable whether consumers or workers are in a position to make intelligent use of the information.[50]

A final class of environmental policy involving informational disclosures includes laws that place labels on consumer products, which in turn informs the potential purchaser about whether the product is either costly to operate or inefficient. For example, fuel economy labels on new cars inform car buyers about the relative expense of fuel during the lifetime of the vehicle, as well as the amount of carbon-based fuel that will be used to operate it.[51] Appliances with labels disclosing energy efficiency information to consumers alert purchasers about the energy efficiency of a product.[52]

Such labels may at once be too much and too little. They may reveal "too much" in that, as noted previously, individuals often do not make decisions in a deliberate, measured fashion. Instead, they often use heuristics and mental shortcuts that bypass the information on the labels.[53] Conversely, they may reveal "too little" in that, to be thorough, the labels should also reveal (which they do not) the costs of making products that

---

[49]   42 U.S.C. §§ 11001 et seq.
[50]   John S. Applegate, The Perils of Unreasonable Risk: Information, Regulatory Policy, and Toxic Substances Control, 91 Colum. L. Rev. 261, 295–298 (1991).
[51]   49 U.S.C. § 32902.
[52]   42 U.S.C. § 6294.
[53]   See note 36, *supra*.

use less energy, as well as the economic and environmental benefits from lower energy use over the lifetime of the product.

F.   Adjustments to Property and Tort Law

In order to avoid direct regulation of private parties, private law systems like property and tort law could be exponentially expanded to create private rights to environmental stability and quality. Individuals could have a property right to parts of the biosphere, like the oceans, giving them the right to sue in trespass those who transgress and do harm to natural systems that are part of the private property right.[54] Or the tort claim of nuisance could be dramatically expanded to permit lawsuits against those who adversely affect the global climate.[55] Such an unprecedented expansion of private law would create problematic conceptual and logistical issues if common law rights were extended to entire global systems, previously unowned or publicly owned, such as climate or biodiversity.

G.   Legal Rights for Nature

If environmental policy wishes to ensure that interests are protected in environmental goods and natural resources, this protection from human interference can occur either by granting to the "public" rights in an array of natural resources or by conferring such protective rights on the natural resources themselves. The common law "public trust doctrine" has been suggested as possibly providing an avenue for judicial intervention in the name of claimed *public* rights in natural resource interests. Another approach, derived from "deep ecology" and "Earth jurisprudence," would recognize and legitimate legal rights for Nature. Although both approaches seem to have promise, both have severe impediments that will frustrate their success as policy.

1.   *The Public Trust Doctrine*

In American law throughout much of the twentieth century, the public trust doctrine was an extremely limited idea that recognized a right, held in common by every member of the public, to navigate and fish on navigable-in-fact waters. The doctrine, grounded entirely in state law, thereby

---

[54] Eric Biber, A House With a View, Lee County v. Kiesel, 109 Yale L. J. 849 (2000). See also Eric T. Freyfogle, Natural Resources Law: Private Rights and Collective Governance (2007).
[55] *Biber, supra* note 7 at 42.

imposed on both public and private owners of riparian and submerged lands a duty not to obstruct the exercise of the right.[56] The doctrine held promise. It forced courts and legislatures to recognize the general public as an independent rights holder, and it suggested that there were long-term public interests, even public rights, in natural resources.[57]

The public trust idea seemed attractive to activists wishing to find doctrinal justification supporting state judicial intervention during the burgeoning environmental protection movement of the late twentieth century. Law review articles were written that pointed out two singular advantages of the public trust doctrine. First, the doctrine seemed to function as a limit on government when government acted contrary to public rights. Second, it provided a way to avoid takings clause limitations on regulations adopted to protect public rights; since the public trust rights were antecedent to any private rights affected, they superseded any property right interest that might otherwise be implicated by the assertion of the public trust.[58]

Despite the traditional public trust doctrine's modest beginnings, academics, particularly law professors, seized upon it as a creative and potentially powerful tool in the arsenal of environmental policy. A flood of law review articles argued that the doctrine should be stretched far beyond its initial protection of commercial navigation and fishing on navigable waters.[59] For example, some legal academics proposed that the doctrine be extended to include wildlife among the resources in which the public has rights pursuant to the public trust.[60] One especially far-sighted and imaginative law professor, Professor Mary Christina Wood, has sought to

---

[56] James L. Huffman, Speaking of Inconvenient Truth-A History of the Public Trust Doctrine, 18 Duke Envtl. L. & Pol'y 1 (2007).

[57] Robin Kundis Craig, What the Public Trust Doctrine Can Teach Us about the Police Power, Penn Central, and the Public Intersection. Natural Resources Protection, 45 Envtl. L. 519, 520 (2015).

[58] Joseph L. Sax, The Public Trust Doctrine Natural Resources Law: Effective Judicial Intervention, 68 Mich. L. Rev. 471 (1970); Joseph L. Sax, Liberating the Public Trust Doctrine from Its Historic Shackles, 14 U. Davis L. Rev. 185 (1980).

[59] See, e.g., Carol Rose, The Comedy of the Commons: Commerce, Custom, and Inherently Public Property, 53 U. Chi. L. Rev. 711 (1986); Richard Epstein, The Public Trust Doctrine, 7 Cato 411 (1987); Charles F. Wilkinson The Headwaters of the Public Trust: Some Thoughts on the Source and Scope of the Traditional Doctrine, 19 Envtl. L. 425 (1989); Michael C. Blumm, Public Property and the Democratization of Western Water Law: A Modern View of the Public Trust Doctrine, 19 Envtl. L. 573 (1989).

[60] Gary D. Meyers, Variation on a Theme: Expanding the Public Trust Doctrine to Include Protection of Wildlife, 19 Envtl. L. 723 (1989). See also Patrick Redmond, The Public Trust in Wildlife: Two Steps Forward, Two Steps Back, 49 Nat. Res. 249 (2009).

apply the trust to the atmosphere. In urging use of the public trust doctrine to protect the air resource surrounding this planet, she argues that states should deploy the doctrine to prevent appropriation of the atmosphere as a dumping ground for greenhouse gases.[61]

Some of these law professors even believe that the public trust doctrine should be an implied feature of federal constitutional law.[62] If so, then federal sovereign authority should also be subject to public trust limits. Such federal trust obligations should apply to protect the atmosphere against private appropriation as a disposal site for greenhouse gas pollution.[63]

Although some cases have taken the public trust doctrine beyond its original borders,[64] virtually all United States' efforts to expand the state common law public trust beyond water resources have been unsuccessful.[65] Moreover, the U.S. Supreme Court has strongly suggested that the public trust doctrine is a creature of state law alone, and therefore does not apply to the federal government.[66] And several courts have explicitly rejected the argument that the public trust doctrine extends to the atmosphere.[67] Other lower courts have narrowly interpreted the scope of the public trust doctrine, and a state's obligations under that doctrine.[68]

It should not come as a surprise that the public trust doctrine has not proven to be a viable widespread environmental policy for the twenty-first century. The original doctrine was quite narrow in scope, limited to the proposition that a state cannot alienate submerged lands affected by

---

[61] Mary Christina Wood, Nature's Trust: Environmental Law for a New Ecological Age (Cambridge Univ. Press 2014); Mary Christina Wood & Michael C. Blumm, The Public Trust Doctrine in Natural Resources Law (2013); Mary Christina Wood, Atmospheric Trust Litigation in Climate Change: A Reader 1018, 1021 (W. H. Rodgers et al. eds. 2011); Mary Christina Wood & Dan Galpern, Atmospheric Recovery Litigation: Making Fossil Fuel Industry Pay to Restore a Viable Climate System, 45 Envtl. L. 259 (2015).

[62] Michael Blumm & Lynn Schaffer, The Federal Public Trust Doctrine: Misinterpreting Justice Kennedy and Illinois Central Railroad, 45 Envtl. L. 257, 400–01 (2015).

[63] Nature's Trust, supra note 61 at 136.

[64] See, e.g., National Audubon Society v. Superior Court (Mono Lake), 658P. 2d 709 (Cal. 1983); Robinson Township v. Commonwealth, 83A. 3d 901 CPA. 2013); Owsichek v. State Guide Licensing & Control Bd., 763 P. 2d 488 (Alaska 1988); Just v. Marinette County, 201 N.W. 2d 761 (Wis. 1972).

[65] Erin Ryan, Public Trust & Distrust: Theoretical Implications of the Public Trust Doctrine for Natural Resource Management, 31 Envtl. L. 477, 490 (2001).

[66] PPL Montana LLC v. Montana, 132 S. Ct. 1215, 1235 (2012).

[67] Alec L. ex rel. Loorz v. McCarthy, 561 F. App'x 7 (D.C. Cir. 2014), cert. denied, No. 14–405, 2014 WL. 6860603 (2014); Sanders-Reed v. Martinez, 350 P. 3d 1221 (N.M. App. 2015).

[68] United States v. Walker River Irr. Dist., 2015 WL 3439122 (D. Nev. 2015) (public trust doctrine cannot be used to abrogate vested appropriative rights to the use of non-navigable waters); Chernaik v. Brown, No. 16-11-09273 (Or. Cir. Ct. Lane City, May 11, 2015) (public trust doctrine does not apply to waters of the state, beaches, or shorelands).

the public trust.[69] The public trust itself was only a common law right to commercial navigation and fishing on navigable waters, including access to submerged lands where necessary to the exercise of the common law right.[70] Any expansion of the traditional common law public trust could result in the confiscation or "taking" of private property rights.[71]

2. Nature's Rights

Some commentators, and even some countries, have either urged or adopted environmental policy that does not just value Nature and environmental systems for the benefits provided to humans. This environmental policy rejects the obsessively anthropocentric worldview of a dominant species that reserves only to this species all the rights and privileges to use and enjoy Earth. An eco-centric approach to environmental policy does not define natural law and natural rights in anthropocentric terms. It does not define the relevant "community" as just the "human" community. Rather, this policy contemplates laws that acknowledge Nature's rights. These laws fall into two categories: (1) those that concern themselves with issues affecting Nature and the natural world for its own sake, for its intrinsic worth, irrespective of humans[72]; and (2) those that provide legal rights for *all* members of the Earth Community, from rivers and trees to birds and humans.[73]

Protecting the Intrinsic Worth of Eco-centric Values – Many commentators have recognized the anthropocentrism inherent in traditional responses to environmental calamities such as global warming and species extinction, especially when legal protections are framed in human but not necessarily environmental terms.[74] These commentators challenge human-centered value systems, and instead embrace the intrinsic worth of plants, animals, ecosystems, and natural resources irrespective of

---

[69] Illinois Central RR v. Illinois, 146 U.S. 387 (1892).

[70] *Id.* at 452–53.

[71] Barton H. Thompson, Jr., The Public Trust Doctrine: A Conservative Reconstruction and Defense, 15 Southeastern Envtl. L. 47 (2006); Barton H. Thompson, Jr., Judicial Takings, 76 Va. L. Rev. 1444, 1507–08 (1990).

[72] See, e.g., Jan G. Laitos, The Right of Nonuse (Oxford Univ. Press 2012).

[73] See, e.g., Cormac Cullinan, Wild Law: A Manifesto for Earth Justice (97) (2d ed. 2011) ("the rights of the members of the [Earth] Community an indivisible – there cannot be rights for some without there being rights for all").

[74] Gunther Handl, Human Rights and Protection of the Environment, in Economic, Social and Cultural Rights 303–305 (Asbjorn Eide, Catarina Krause, & Allan Rosa eds., 2001).

instrumental or economic worth.[75] Acknowledgment of eco-centric values suggests that legal norms should not be defended in purely anthropocentric terms, but must also accept and legitimate the eco-centric worth and benefit of natural resources when they are left alone by humans.[76]

The assertion of Nature's intrinsic value has already made its way into the lawmaking of international environmental instruments. In 1992, the United Nations approved the Convention on Biological Diversity, whose preamble explicitly recognized "the intrinsic value of biological diversity."[77] In 2008, Ecuador's citizens voted their approval of a new constitution that expressly provides "Nature ... the right to exist, persist, maintain, and regenerate its vital cycles."[78] In April 2010, a conference of more than 35,000 people in Bolivia proclaimed a Universal Declaration of the Rights of Mother Earth.[79] In 2012, New Zealand granted "personhood" rights to the Whanganui River, with both the indigenous Maori people and the national government appointing a guardian to protect it.[80] These pronouncements reflect a realization, supported by environmental ethicists, that humankind should not be the sole yardstick against which the utility of resources should be measured. Nature, natural processes, and the environment surrounding humans should have a legally protected integrity independent of human interest.[81]

Earth Rights – A far more encompassing environmental policy does more than just bestow legal legitimacy on Nature; it instead sees Nature and humans as one Earth Community and grants legal rights to this integrated entity – in effect, rights are given to the SES that makes life possible on this Earth.[82] This policy, termed Earth Jurisprudence or Wild Law, believes that every component of the larger Earth Community should have certain legal rights (e.g., the right "to be," the right "to habit," and the right "to fulfill its

---

[75] Christopher J. Preston, Saving Creation: Nature and Faith in the Life of Holmes Rolston III (2009); David Takacs, The Idea of Biodiversity 249–254 (1996).

[76] *Laitos, supra* note 72 at 67.

[77] United Nations Environmental Programme Convention on Biological Diversity 5 (Jun 1992), 1760 U.N.T.S. 143–146.

[78] http://blogs.nature/thegreatbeyond/2008/ecuador

[79] www.guardian.co.uk./environment/2011/bolivia

[80] Daniel Stone, Rivers as People Too, 223 National Geographic 24 (May 2013).

[81] Environmental ethicists term non-anthropocentric environmentalism as "deep ecology." Arne Naess, The Shallow and the Deep, Long-Range Ecology Movement: A Summary, 16 Inquiry 95 (1973); Bill Devall, The Deep Ecology Movement, in Key Concepts in Critical Theory Ecology 125 (C. Merchant ed. 1994).

[82] See Chapter 6, *supra*.

role ... in the Earth Community").[83] While humans would still have rights, these human rights would not be superior to the rights of other parts of the Earth Community to exist in their natural state, unaffected by anthropogenic action.[84] Indeed, human rights are by necessity limited by the rights of other members of the Earth Community.[85]

Of course, whether the right is conferred solely on nonhuman natural objects or every component of the Earth Community, there is an inevitable problem of enforcement. It is difficult to imagine how Nature's interests can be protected from human use demands without humans raising their own human concerns.[86] Indeed, any law focused on protecting non-anthropocentric interests would likely have to be both asserted and enforced by very anthromorphic humans. Accordingly, many commentators have persuasively argued that natural objects should *not* be accorded their own rights.[87] Others have maintained that humans asserting anthropocentric interests can provide the same protection of Nature as purely eco-centric and biocentric laws.[88]

Moreover, even if enforcement issues were resolved, four central questions would have to be answered before a "Nature's Rights" approach could become viable policy: (1) If Nature has "rights," would humans have a duty toward Nature?[89] (2) Which components of Nature should have rights?[90] (3) What should be the purpose and content of the right?[91] (4) Who would have legal standing to raise the right?[92] Each of these issues raise serious, perhaps unsolvable problems for any environmental policy advancing the idea of creating legal rights for natural objects or environmental goods.[93] And

---

[83] *Cullinan, supra* note 73 at 103.

[84] *Id.* at. 104–105

[85] Emilio F. Moran, People and Nature: An Introduction to Human Ecological Relations 129–130 (2006).

[86] J. E. de Steiguer, The Age of Environmentalism 143 (1997).

[87] J. G. Merrills, Environmental Protection and Human Rights: Conceptual Aspects, in Human Rights Approaches to Environmental Protection 25, 31, 34 (Alan E. Boyle & Michael R. Andersons eds. 1996).

[88] James L. Huffman, Do Species and Nature Have Rights?, 13 Public Land L. Rev. 51, 75 (1992); P. S. Elder, Legal Rights for Nature: The Wrong Answer to the Right(s) Question, 22 Osgoode Hall. L.J. 285, 291 (1984).

[89] Robert Elliot, Environmental Ethics, in A Companion to Ethics 112 (Peter Singer ed. 1993).

[90] *Huffman, supra* note 88 at 55–56; Aldo Leopold, A Sand County Almanac (1949).

[91] Mary Anne Warren, The Rights of the Non-Human World, in Environmental Philosophy 115 (Robert Elliot & Arron Gare eds. 1983).

[92] Christopher D. Stone, Should Trees Have Standing? Law, Morality, and the Environment (3d ed. 2010).

[93] See *Laitos, supra* note 72 at 124–127. Chapter 10 attempts to answer several of these questions, while simultaneously offering its own proposed "rights/duties" solution to the problem of how to create protectable interests for the Earth-based SES.

even if answers were forthcoming, it seems improbable that any eco-centric right could ever realistically veto a human right to use natural resources.

H. Preservationist Rules

If anthropocentric decisions threaten wildlife, wildlife habitat, or biodiversity, then one traditional environmental policy has been to "preserve" those spaces and places that contain natural flora and fauna, so that they remain free from human interference. Examples of such preservationist laws include UNESCO's World Heritage List of sites in the world that (1) are areas of "exceptional natural beauty," (2) are "examples of major stages of earth's history, including ... significant geomorphic or physiographic features," (3) represent "on-going ecological and biological processes in evolution," or (4) contain "significant cultural habitats for in-situ conservation of biological diversity."[94] In the United States, federally owned lands set aside for preservationist purposes include wilderness areas, national parks and monuments, and wildlife refuges.[95]

However, because of global climate change, the very act of setting aside preserves for plants and animals might ironically make it *less likely* that these species will thrive there. Global warming has caused shifts in the ranges of animals and plants, disrupting migrations and spawning, and stressing species confined to parks and reserves. When climate changes such as global warming makes their preservationist habitats unsuitable, surrounding human development often prevents them from migrating to more hospitable places.[96] To aid animals and plants otherwise trapped in preservationist islands no longer appropriate as habitat, managers could engage in "assisted migration" to places less affected by climate change. But then "all of a sudden, nothing is wild anymore."[97]

Another form of preservationist policy intended to reduce greenhouse gas emissions and the effects of climate change is the "Keep it in the Ground" proposal. The proponents of "Keep it in the Ground" are primarily law professors who argue that federal energy policy should ban all future leasing of federal fossil fuels.[98] Their logic is that a federal decision

---

[94] United Nations Educational, Scientific and Cultural Organization, World Heritage Convention, The Criteria for Selection (2005).

[95] Jan Laitos & Sandra Zellmer, Hornbook on Natural Resources Law 225–266 (2015).

[96] Anthony Barnosky, Heatstroke: Nature in an Age of Global Warming (2009).

[97] Robert Sanders, In Face of Global Warming, Can Wilderness Remain Natural?, www .berkeley.edu/news/media/releases/2009/04/13.

[98] Mark Squillace & Alexander Hood, NEPA, Climate Change, and Public Lands Decision Making, 42 Envtl. L. 469 (2012).

to open a public land area to oil, gas, coal, or tar sands development will have a direct impact on climate change because of the fossil fuels that are burned to develop the site, and the methane gases often released during development and production. If all federal leasing of fossil fuels is banned and the carbon-based fuels are "preserved" in the ground, then climate change may be slowed.[99]

Although a "Keep it in the Ground" policy may have initial appeal, its likelihood of success depends initially on whether there is legal authority for federal decision-makers (e.g., the U.S. President and Secretary of the Interior) to stop all federal coal leasing, as well as onshore and offshore oil and gas leasing. If one reviews statutes that authorize development of federal oil, gas, and coal deposits,[100] as well as pertinent case law,[101] this law strongly indicates that the intent of Congress has not been to "keep it in the ground," but to encourage and incentivize development of fossil fuels. Federal energy policy has been consistently premised on promoting extraction of fossil fuels, not preserving them in the ground.[102]

I.   Human-Nature Linkages

Thoughtful commentators reviewing environmental law and policy in a time of global climate change have concluded that traditional legal responses to climate change impacts demonstrate neither efficiency nor effectiveness.[103] In order to replace the failed environmental policies summarized thus far in this chapter, these scholars have proposed two quite different approaches. Law professors J. B. Ruhl and Robin Kundis Craig advocate that future environmental laws mimic and reflect the workings of the natural systems that are the objects of the laws. Conversely, a number of economists, biologists, and ecologists have countered with a policy

---

[99] Bobby Magill, Global Warming Casts Shadow Over Oil Leasing on Public Lands, Scientific American (Sept. 15, 2015).

[100] Mineral Leasing Act of 1920, 30 U.S.C. §181 et seq.; The Mining and Minerals Policy Act of 1970, 30 U.S.C. §226 (b)(1); Federal Land Management Policy Act of 1976, 43 U.S.C §1701 (a).

[101] Udall v. Tallman, 380 U.S. 1, 4 (1965); California v. Udall, 296 F. 2d 384, 388 (D.C. Cir. 1961); Mountain States Legal Foundation v. Andrus, 499 F. Supp. 282, 392 (D. Wyo 1980); Norton v. Southern Utah Wilderness Alliance, 542 U.S. 55, 58 (2004).

[102] Heidi Ruckriegle & Rebecca Watson, "Keep It In The Ground" – Part II, www.wsmtlaw .com/blog.html (Dec. 2, 2015).

[103] Robin Kundis Craig, "Stationarity is Dead" – Long Live Transformation: Five Principles for Climate Change Adaption Law, 34 Harv. Envtl. L. Rev. 9, 14 (2010)("American environmental law and policy are not keeping up with climate change impacts and the need for adaptation.").

proposal that seeks to "decouple" human well-being from anthropogenic uses of natural resources.

1.   Environmental Policy Reform That Reflects Natural Systems

One leading and influential commentator, Prof. J. B. Ruhl, has in several related articles argued that much of the current environmental regulatory structure is itself, like the environment being regulated, a complex adaptive system.[104] Therefore, government organizations and environmental laws need to become like Nature and environmental systems, more adaptive and resilient in the face of constant environmental change.[105] Because dynamic natural systems tend to respond to external sources of disturbances consistent with "complexity theory," Ruhl then makes the case for complexity theory being used by policymakers to produce the best strategies for regulatory reform.[106]

Similarly, another leading commentator, Prof. Robin Kundis Craig, has persuasively made the case that because American environmental law and policy has not kept up with climate change impacts, a new environmental law structure needs to emerge. This new policy paradigm must be able to respond to "the increasingly uncomfortable world of changing complex systems and complex adaptive management – a world of unpredictability, poorly understood and changing feedback mechanisms, nonlinear change, and ecological thresholds."[107] Like Ruhl, Craig argues that any new approach to environmental policy will need to mimic the changing natural world being regulated: "[T]he new climate change ... law needs to incorporate a far more flexible view of the natural world, because both the identity of the regulatory objects – the things such as rivers that such statutes

---

[104] J. B. Ruhl & Harold J. Ruhl, Jr., The Arrow of the Law in Modern Administrative States: Using Complexity Theory to Reveal the Diminishing Returns and Increasing Risks the Burgeoning Law Poses to Society, 30 U.C. Davis L. Rev. 405, 416 (1997). Complex adaptive systems are described in Chapter 5.

[105] J. B. Ruhl, Thinking of Environmental Law as a Complex Adaptive System: How to Clean Up the Environment by Making a Mess of Environmental Law, 34 Houston L. Rev. 933 (1997).

[106] J. B. Ruhl, Complexity Theory as a Paradigm for the Dynamical Law-and-Society System: A Wake-up Call for Legal Reductionism and the Modern Administrative State, 45 Duke L.J. 849 (1996); J. B. Ruhl, The Fitness of Law: Using Complexity Theory to Describe the Evolution of Law and Society and Its Practical Meaning for Democracy, 49 Vand. L. Rev. 1407 (1996).

[107] Craig, supra note 103 at 15.

are trying to protect – and the regulatory objectives will themselves be continually transforming, especially at the ecosystem level.[108]

Unfortunately, neither Ruhl's nor Craig's suggestions have yet been embraced by government decision-makers. Nor are they likely to be adopted in the future. Ruhl's specific proposal to apply complexity theory to environmental law and regulation has been called "theoretically and practically untenable, producing a worldview at odds with understandings of humanity, normative judgments, and democracy."[109]

Professor Craig is certainly correct in pointing out how existing environmental laws, espousing preservation and restoration of mythical environmental baselines, are both unrealistic and based on false models of how Nature really works.[110] However, her new policy paradigm, based on increasing adaptive capacity, carries with it the difficulties that will face policymakers who might find themselves paralyzed by so much uncertainty.[111] Since Nature itself acts in an unpredictable fashion, laws seeking to reflect Nature, even laws nimble enough to adapt to constant change, risk the formulation of a policy that becomes, in effect, no policy. Any policy decision that mirrors complex adaptive systems is bound to change frequently and constantly. Those subject to environmental policy must be able to rely on a predictable set of rules that govern present and future behavior. Rules cannot change frequently and constantly without producing societal and marketplace chaos.

2.   Decoupling Human Societies from Nature

A number of respected environmental scientists, policy analysts, and economists, calling themselves "ecopragmatists" and "ecomodernists," have drafted a document setting forth the counterintuitive proposition that human societies must *not* harmonize with Nature to avoid economic and ecological collapse. This document – "An Ecomodernist Manifesto" – instead affirms as a preferred environmental policy "that humanity must shrink its impacts on the environment to make more room for Nature."[112]

---

[108] *Id.* at 17. Craig calls for new "climate change adaption law ... based on principled flexibility," consistent with adaptive management theory. *Id.* at 63–68.

[109] Jeffrey Rudd, J. B. Ruhl's "Law-and-Society System": Burying Norms and Democracy Under Complexity Theory's Foundation, 29 Wm. & Mary Envtl. L & Policy Rev. 551 (2005).

[110] See Chapter 5 and Section H in this chapter.

[111] Rasmut Heltberg, Paul Siegel, & Steen Lau Jorgensen, Addressing Human Vulnerability to Climate Change: Toward a "No Regrets" Approach, 19 Global Envtl. Change 89, 94 (2009).

[112] An Ecomodernist Manifesto (Apr. 2015), www.ecomodernism.org.

This goal may be achieved not be reflecting or mimicking Nature, but by *decoupling* human well-being from environmental impacts.[113]

According to the "Manifesto," decoupling occurs when human environmental impacts rise at a slower rate than does overall economic growth. In other words, for each additional unit of economic output, there will be less environmental impact (e.g., pollution, deforestation). Such decoupling can occur when modern technologies use natural ecosystem services more efficiently. For example, efficiencies in agriculture mean that the amount of land required for growing crops and animal feed for the average person has declined by one-half in the past 5,000 years.[114] The amount of water needed for the average diet has declined by nearly 25 percent over the past half-century.[115] Modern energy can mitigate climate change by relying on zero-carbon technology, such as solar, wind, hydro, and nuclear fission and even nuclear fusion.[116]

When human impacts on the environment decline, caused in large part by future technology and innovation, then "humans have the opportunity to re-wild and re-green the Earth ... Decoupling [permits] societies [to] achieve peak human impact without intruding much further on relatively untouched areas. Nature unused is nature spared."[117] The Manifesto concludes that "any large-scale attempt at recoupling human societies to Nature ... would result in an unmitigated ecological and human disaster."[118]

This concept of "decoupling" humans from Nature belies three important realities. First, the Manifesto is premised on technology and scientific efficiencies accelerating to a point when there might be some separation between humans and their impacts on Nature. There is no guarantee, or even a reasonable probability, that technological change can occur that quickly. Second, as noted in Chapter 6, there is no separation between humans and their environmental surroundings. Instead, there is a unified and integrated social ecological system, an SES, that is the best description and accurate understanding of the Earth. Third, as noted earlier in this chapter, as well as by most environmental commentators,[119] any effective environmental policy needs to not ignore natural systems; to be effective, such policy needs to conform to the rules and laws of Nature.

---

[113]   *Id.* at 11.
[114]   *Id.* at 13.
[115]   *Id.*
[116]   *Id.* at 23.
[117]   *Id.* at 15, 19.
[118]   *Id.* at 16.
[119]   See *Craig, supra* note 103 and *Ruhl, supra,* notes 104 & 105.

J. Behavioral

In order to influence consumer behavior by leading (not compelling) individuals to make choices that are better for their environmental surroundings, environmental policy might consider behavioral tools that are perceived as less paternalistic. For example, the European Union (EU) has shown increasing policy interest in bringing about "green behavior" by relying on softer forms of intervention that encourage businesses and individuals to operate with less detriment to their natural environment.[120] These EU initiatives do not rely on administrative or regulatory commands, but rather seek public acceptance of environmentally conscious social norms.[121] Such environmental policy is intended to act in a "bottom-up" fashion, influencing behavior, where the actual choices affecting environmental conditions are made by individual businesses and consumers.[122]

Policy grounded in behavioral tools followed from behavioral economists who challenged neoclassical economic theory that assumed that individuals have rational preferences to maximize outcomes.[123] Psychologists such as Daniel Kahneman dismantled this notion of an arch-rational decision-maker and replaced it with a more realistic model of human behavior, according to which human irrationality is common, individuals do not always maximize utility, and cognitive biases influence judgment.[124] From these insights into the human condition came policy tools based on public acceptance of larger environmental goals and bottom-up, minimally paternalistic decision-making.[125]

Environmental policy based on human behavior relies on the disclosure of information so consumers may make better decisions (discussed in Section E earlier), such as fuel economy labels on cars. Default rules also are effective, such as automatically enrolling homeowners in energy audits,

---

[120] European Commission, Science for Environment Policy; Future Brief: Green Behavior (Oct. 2012).

[121] C. Bicchieri, Norms, Preferences, and Conditional Behavior, 9 Philosophy & Economics 297 (2010).

[122] P. Hallsworth Dolan, et al., Mindspace: Influencing Behavior Through Public Policy (2010); J. M. Hines, H. R. Hungerford, & A. N. Tomera, Analysis and Synthesis of Research on Responsible Environmental Behavior: A Meta-Analysis, 18 Journal of Environmental Education 1 (1986).

[123] H. Simon, A Behavioural Model of Rational Choice, 69 Quarterly Journal of Econ. 99 (1955).

[124] Daniel Kahneman, Thinking, Fast and Slow (2011). See also Chapter 7.

[125] See, e.g., R. H. Thaler & Cass Sunstein, Nudge: Improving Decisions about Health, Wealth, and Happiness (2008).

leaving them the choice of opting out. "Nudges" work too, when peer pressure goads or shames consumers into saving electricity by comparing (and publicizing) each homeowners' energy usage with their neighbors.[126] Even "green envy" encourages the fight against climate change; those who have neighbors with solar panels are significantly more likely to purchase solar panels themselves.[127] And environmental policy can be effective when it appeals to altruistic and collective values, contrary to the traditional neoclassical view of humans being self-centered welfare maximizers.[128]

Of course, while a realistic view of human behavior can be used by policymakers to encourage individual choices that are environmentally sensitive, certain entrenched human behaviors can also impede acceptance of choices that benefit our environmental surroundings. A list of these anti-environmental human behaviors suggests the extent of the uphill battle facing policymakers seeking to encourage more green behavior:

- *High Discount Rate* – Humans often fail to support environmental policies because they are hard-wired to downplay long-term risks. They are more concerned with present problems, and tend to downplay or ignore risks (like the effects of climate change) that will be far in the future.
- *Judgment Heuristics* – Humans make mental shortcuts that limit rationality. For example, "anchoring" is the tendency to rely too heavily on one trait. Anchoring can lead to branded or well-known products that are energy-consumptive, or carbon-based, being chosen over newer, environmentally friendly products. Or, "loss aversion" is the tendency for people to be more reluctant to give up something than to be content with a commensurate gain. Loss aversion can produce a reluctance to give up old products that may cause negative externalities, such as inefficient or polluting cars.
- *Lock-Ins* – When consumers do not initially choose environmentally better products (because of cost, or loss aversion), companies will not invest in product designs to reduce negative environmental impacts.
- *Rebound Effects* – Sometimes "green" products can cause consumers to behave so that they become less energy efficient. More efficient vehicles

[126] Jim Tankersleg, Will People Help Save Energy Just to Be Good Citizens? Actually Yes, The Washington Post (Oct. 27, 2014); Cass R. Sunstein, Why Nudge? The Politics of Liberal Paternalism (2014).

[127] Kenneth Gillingham & Marcello Graziano, Spatial Patterns of Photovoltaic System Adoption: The Influence of Neighbors, 15 Journal of Economic Geography 815 (Aug. 2014).

[128] Elinor Ostrom, Governing the Commons: The Evolution of Institutions for Collective Action (1990); Nicholas Christakis & James H. Fowler, Connected: How Your Friends' Friends' Friends Affect Everything You Feel, Think & Do (2009).

may lead drivers to increase driving distances when they commute to work; better insulation may lead to an increase in home energy use.[129]

- *The Limits of Communal Resource Management* – Although some communities can develop systems to successfully manage the extraction of natural resources, without the necessity of state management rules,[130] these communities typically have very limiting characteristics. They involve small-scale resources, such as fishing or discrete irrigation projects. The community can exclude outsiders from the resource. There are traditional feedback loops among members of the community.[131] Without these unique attributes, state action is necessary.[132]

K.   Delegate to Private Parties

A final environmental policy delegates to private individuals the right, or the discretion, to make choices that protect planetary boundaries from anthropogenic activities that alter Earth systems and the natural world. This delegation can occur in two, quite different, ways. First, policymakers may embrace a top-down, purely rights-based approach. Governments and legal institutions may grant to humans a legal, enforceable right to a clean and healthy environment (or a right that serves to preserve planetary boundaries necessary for human survival into the future). Conversely, as a matter of policy, legal institutions may choose to not confer on humans any special-rights based entitlement to a clean/healthy natural environment. Instead, the declared policy is a "hands-off," bottom-up approach. Consistent with this non-paternalistic philosophy, individuals, on their own, will then hopefully decide to do the right thing and make their own good choices for the environment.

1.   A Human Right to Environment

When human environmental surroundings seem threatened by human activities, it has been customary among academics and commentators to suggest that there should be created, not by moral norms, but by positive

---

[129] Kenneth Gillingham, David Rapson, & Gernot Wagner, The Rebound Effect and Energy Efficiency Policy, Review of Environmental Economics and Policy (Dec. 14, 2015).

[130] Elinor Ostrom, Governing the Commons: The Evolution of Institutions for Collective Action (1990).

[131] *Id.* at 26, 182, 189.

[132] Elinor Ostrom, Polycentric Systems for Coping with Collective Action and Global Environmental Change, 20 Global Environmental Change 550 (2010).

law, a legal "right" conferred on humans to a better, more sustainable-to-humans, natural environment. This legal right is given only to humans, not to Nature or natural objects.[133] And the right itself is to some kind of outcome regarding the "environment," ranging from a "clean" to a "safe" to a "viable" to a "sustainable," or to a "healthy" environment. Sometimes the right is simply for humans to have a "right to environment," or a "human right to environment."[134] And sometimes the right is "intergenerational," providing rights to future generations."[135]

Such a right to a natural environment conducive to conditions acceptable for human sustainability may be a recasting of general human rights guarantees, ensuring that the natural environment does not deteriorate to the point where the human right to "life," to "health," or other recognized human rights are seriously impaired.[136] It has been argued that such a human right to some level of environmental quality may even be inherent in the human condition, entitling us to such environmental protections simply by being human.[137] Despite claims that environmental human rights may be present in existing human rights, or inherently, most commentators believe that what needs to be adopted is an entirely new set of human rights, relating directly to environmental quality.[138]

A human right to environmental quality may be an emerging international right.[139] The right can be inferred from explicitly stated international

---

[133] Nature's Rights are discussed in notes 72–93 and accompanying text, *supra.*

[134] See, e.g., Human Rights and the Environment: Cases, Law, & Policy (S. Krauchenko & John Bonine eds. 2008); Sumudu Atapattu, The Right to Life or the Right to Die Polluted: The Emergence of a Human Right to a Healthy Environment Under International Law, 16 Tulane Envtl. L. J. 65 (2002); Dinah Shelton, Human Rights, Environmental Rights, and the Right to Environment, 28 Stanford J. Int'l L. 103 (1991).

[135] Beyond Environmental Law: Policy Proposals for a Better Environmental Future (Alyson C. Flournoy & David Driesen eds. 2010); Richard P. Hiskes, The Human Right To a Green Future: Environmental Rights and Intergenerational Justice (2009); Burns H. Weston, Climate Change and Intergenerational Justice: Foundational Reflections, 9 Vt. Envtl. L. 375 (2008). See also Burns W. Weston & David Bollier, Green Governance: Ecological Survival, Human Rights, and the Law of the Commons 51–57 (Cambridge 2013).

[136] Dinah Shelton, Environmental Rights, in People's Rights (Philip Alston ed. 2001).

[137] Linda H. Leib, Human Rights and the Environment: Philosophical, Theoretical and Legal Perspectives (2011).

[138] David R. Boyd, The Environmental Rights Revolution: A Global Study of Constitutions, Human Rights, and the Environment (2012); Symposium, The Confluence of Human Rights and the Environment, 11 Or. Rev. Int'l L. 225 (2009); Michael R. Anderson, Human Rights Approaches to Environmental Protection: An Overview in Human Rights Approaches to Environmental Protection (A. Boyle & M. Anderson eds. 1996); Melissa Thorme, Establishing Environment as a Human Right, 19 Denver J. Int'l L. & Policy 301 (1991).

[139] Prudence E. Taylor, From Environment to Ecological Human Rights: A New Dynamic in International Law, 10 Geo. Int. Envtl. L. Rev. 309 (2010); Linda A. Malone & Scott

human rights because the goal of environmental quality is to enhance the quality and dignity of human life.[140] Environmental human rights of one kind or another have been adopted in the national constitutions of more than one hundred countries, such as the constitutions of Colombia ("every individual has the right enjoy a healthy environment")[141] and Chile ("the right to live in an environment free from contamination").[142] Even some states in the United States recognize environmental human rights.[143]

Despite the popularity of environmental human rights, this rights-based approach has been criticized on several grounds. First, if this right is held just by humans, then it does not address threats to nonhuman species, or to natural resources and Earth systems. In other words, an environmental human right is anthropocentric. It focuses on a natural environment that is "safe" or "healthy" only for humans, but not necessarily for the environment surrounding humans.[144] Second, a flat, unconditional, unqualified human right is not capable of sorting out relative priorities among competing societal goals.[145] Third, a universal environmental human right could cause incursions into national sovereignty if a human right from one country was impaired by the actions of another country.[146] These concerns are why environmental rights for humans found in constitutions and other forms of positive law are usually seen as statements of broad aspirations rather than enforceable laws.[147]

Paternack, Exercising Environmental Rights and Remedies in the United Nations System, 27 Wm. & Mary Envtl. L. & Policy Rev. 365 (2002).

[140] W. Paul Gormley, The Legal Obligation of the International Community to Guarantee a Pure and Decent Environment: The Expansion of Human Rights Norms, 3 Geo. Int'l Envtl. L. Rev. 85, 97 (1990); Luis E. Rodriguez-Rivera, Is the Human Right to Environment Recognized Under International Law? It Depends on the Source, 12 Colo. Int'l L. & Policy 1, 20–37 (2001). For example, in 2010, the United Nations General Assembly recognized the human right to water.

[141] 4 Constitutions of the Countries of the World 20 [art. 79 of the Colombia Constitution] (R. Wolfrum & R. Grote eds. 2005).

[142] 4 Constitutions of the Countries of the World 42 [art 19 (8) of the Constitution of the Republic of Chile] (A. Blaustein & G. Flanz eds. 1991).

[143] Sunburst v. Texaco, Inc. 165 p. 3d 1079 (Mont. 2007); Montana Envtl. Info. Ctr v. Dept. of Envtl. Quality, 988 P.2d 1236, 1244 (Mont. 1999).

[144] Anderson, supra note 138.

[145] Gunther Handle, Human Rights and the Protection of the Environment (A. Eide, C. Krause, & A. Rosas eds. 2d ed. 2001).

[146] Jan G. Laitos, The Right of Nonuse 115 (Oxford 2012).

[147] For an example of a persuasive and thoroughly researched non-aspirational environmental human right, see Burns H. Weston & David Bollier, Green Governance: Ecological Survival, Human Rights, and the Law of the Commons, chapters 2–4 (Cambridge 2013).

2.   Defer to Private Initiative

This policy is really a non-policy – a government decision to rely on private party initiatives to address changes and impairments to global systems that adversely impact ecosystems and human societies. Individuals could purchase fuel-efficient hybrid cars, or install solar panels on their residence, or plant trees on their property, simply because these individuals have concluded, on their own, that such private actions incrementally help restore environmental conditions conducive to human survival. The extent of de-minimus government influence in these decisions could range from providing information about the environmental consequences of private choices (e.g., energy efficiency reporting requirements for new cars) to announcing government-sponsored "voluntary programs" for firms to be more green (e.g., encourage industry sectors to install low-cost emission reduction measures).[148]

Unfortunately, there are many reasons why such voluntary private action seems unlikely. First, anthropogenic harms to collective resources, such as global systems like climate, or global resources like the oceans, entail all the traditional problems associated with collective action; individuals who take their own steps to address a collective problem run the risk of free-riding by other individual actors. Second, although social norms could in theory change to the point where a carbon-based energy system is socially unacceptable, residents in developed and developing countries will be unlikely to forgo the net present benefits that flow from a modern industrial society that relies on carbon (e.g., cheap electricity and even cheaper cars).[149] Third, government-sponsored voluntary programs rarely succeed when they are seeking to bring about green behavior; to be effective, such voluntary programs need to be integrated within mandatory regulatory standards.[150]

---

[148] *IPCC, supra* note 5 at 1173.
[149] *Biber, supra* note 7 at 45.
[150] *IPCC, supra* note 5 at 1171–72.

V

Environmental Policy Must Obey the Fundamental Laws of Nature

The object of environmental policy is to alter humans' behavior toward their non-anthropocentric environmental surroundings. The policy would be considered effective when human behavior no longer adversely interferes with human environmental surroundings necessary for anthropogenic survival, and when this natural context is again conducive to human sustainability. And to achieve this level of effectiveness, which current policy does not, environmental policy must conform to, and be consistent with, certain universal truths of Nature. One of the central realizations about traditional environmental policies is that they were fashioned to satisfy anthropocentric needs, and anthropomorphic assumptions about how Nature works. But to succeed, environmental policy must reflect and be consistent with the "Laws of Nature." To prevent failure, environmental policy and laws flowing from such policy must "obey" the laws of the natural environment.

Chapter 9 describes these truths, or "laws," that must be obeyed by human positive law if that environmental law and policy is to stand any chance of achieving its goal. And that goal, once again, is to return Earth to a condition where humans as a species can live and survive.[1] This goal can be achieved when human laws follow the same path as the laws of Nature, and the laws of Nature inevitably obey the rules of symmetry. Chapter 9 summarizes these rules, which are always followed by Nature, and which should also be followed by environmental policy.

Chapter 10 suggests an environmental policy that conforms to the rules of symmetry and is consistent with accurate, realistic models of "how Nature works"[2] and "how humans behave."[3] The policy outlined in

---

[1] It is important to recall, as noted in earlier chapters, that the "Earth," or "Nature," are not being harmed by anthropogenic activities affecting the planet, such as greenhouse gas pollution or deforestation. The Earth, and Nature, will eventually adapt to these human actions that have changed the biosphere. It is the humans who exist within this biosphere who may not be able to survive the environmental effects of their actions.

[2] See Chapters 5 and 6.

[3] See Chapter 7.

Chapter 10 has a chance of succeeding, compared to other policies that have been tried or proposed. Such previous policies either have failed or failed to be adopted.[4] Chapter 10 describes an environmental policy that obeys the same universal truths that Nature obeys, which is tailored to *coupled* human-natural social-ecological systems, and that does not presume anthropogenic separation from, or superiority to, Nature.[5]

[4] See Chapter 8.
[5] See Chapter 4.

9

Nature and Symmetry

For purposes of this book, "Nature" is equivalent to "Earth." Both terms describe an integrated human-natural system on this planet consisting of humans and all the other nonhuman members of the larger Earth Community.[1] A critical nonhuman member of the Earth Community is the complex adaptive system (CAS), characterized as ecological processes that thrive on biocomplexity, adaption, change, resilience, feedback mechanisms, nonlinearities, and emergent properties.[2] Humans exist within CASs, and affect ecosystems and natural capital that are drivers of a CAS. This coupled human-natural system is sometimes known as a social ecological system, or SES. The SES consists of interactions of human and natural processes. The Earth is, for humans and the biosphere, an SES.[3] And, since for our purposes Earth is the equivalent of Nature, the question is: What environmental policy would most effectively impact Nature (i.e., the Earth we inhabit) so that it remains a safe operating space for humanity?[4]

For environmental policy, or environmental laws, to be effective (with respect to the CASs, ecosystem services, natural systems, and environmental goods that comprise Nature), such a policy must respect the laws of Nature. In other words, environmental policymakers should start with the universal truths of Nature and the fundamental secrets of the natural systems. Environmental policy should be consistent with these laws followed

[1] S. T. A. Pickett, M. L. Cadenasso, & J. M. Grove, Biocomplexity in Coupled Natural-Human Systems: A Multidimensional Framework, 8 Ecosystems 225 (2005).
[2] S. Levin, Self-Organization and the Emergence of Complexity in Ecological Systems, 55 Bioscience 1075 (2005).
[3] S. J. Walsh & D. McGinnis, Biocomplexity in Coupled Human-Natural Systems: The Study of Population and Environment Interactions, 39 GeoForum 773 (2008); Emilio F. Moran, People and Nature (2006).
[4] Will Steffen, et al., Planetary Boundaries: Guiding Human Development on a Changing Planet, 347 Science #6223 (Feb. 13, 2015); John Rockstrom, et al., Planetary Boundaries: Exploring the Safe Operating Space for Humanity, 14 Ecology and Society 32 (2009).

by Nature. So, then, what are the "laws" of Nature? What "rules" are followed by natural systems?

A.   The Laws of Nature Deduced from the Requirement of Symmetry

One of the most important discoveries about Nature was the realization that if one is attempting to learn the immutable laws of the natural world, what one needs to do is *start with symmetry*. Symmetry originates the laws of Nature. Nature has an underlying design, which is symmetry. In mathematics, physics, and biology, it is inevitably best to work from symmetry toward truth.

In other words, an observer seeking to unlock universal truths about Nature should not start with an enormous amount of data about Nature, infer equations and theories, and then find that these equations and theories are obeying symmetry principles. Instead, it is best to realize that symmetry requirements come first, and typically dictate the laws Nature has to obey. The laws of Nature may be deduced from the requirement of symmetry.[5]

The modern meaning of symmetry, in the precise mathematical sense, is "immunity to change." Or as Nobel laureate Frank Wilczek writes, symmetry is "change without change."[6] For example, the equation X=Y is symmetrical because if one changes X into Y, and Y into X, so that the equation is now Y=X, there has been a definite change in form. But there has not been a change in content. When we transform X=Y into Y=X, there has been a "change without change." The equation is symmetrical.

When most people think of symmetry, they often take it to mean the identity of the two sides of something symmetrical, like a butterfly. This kind of symmetry is called mirror reflection symmetry, or bilateral symmetry, which is only one example of a large variety of possible symmetries. The more scientific meaning of symmetry is a principle of "invariance," which tells us that something does not change its appearance when we make certain changes in our point of view – for instance, by rotating it

---

[5] Frank Wilczek, A Beautiful Question: Finding Nature's Deep Design 139 (2015); Mario Livio, The Equation That Couldn't Be Solved: How Mathematical Genius Discovered he Language of Symmetry 43, 205, 231 (2005). In the Richard Rodgers – Oscar Hammerstein musical, "The Sound of Music," there is a famous song called "Do-Re-Mi." One lyric in the song says, "When you know the notes to sing, you can sing most any thing." Symmetry provides the "notes" that permit us to deduce, and then "sing," the music of Nature.

[6] *Wilczek, id.* at 137, 238.

or moving it.[7] Or as mathematician Herman Weyl once put it, "A thing is symmetrical if there is something you can do to it so that after you have finished doing it, it looks the same as before."[8]

A valuable key to Nature's secrets is therefore the realization that the laws of Nature evidently obey certain principles of symmetry, such as change without change. If we start with the requirements of symmetry, we can infer the existence of a symmetry if we make observations, and then predict, based on symmetry, what further observations should be made. For example, in 1928, Paul Dirac discovered an equation that combined quantum theory and special relativity to describe the behavior of an electron inside an atom, which always has a negative charge. Although Dirac's equation won him the Nobel Prize in 1933, it posed another problem: it could have two solutions, one for an electron with negative energy, but also with an electron having positive energy. However, in classical physics, the energy of a subatomic particle like an electron was always negatively charged.

Dirac interpreted this paradox consistent with the requirements of symmetry. He presumed that for every subatomic particle there must be a corresponding "antiparticle," exactly matching the particle, but with an opposite charge. For the electron with a negative charge, for instance, there should be, in light of symmetry ("change without change"), an "anti-electron" identical in every way but with a positive charge.[9] In his Nobel Lecture, Dirac speculated on the existence of the anti-electron when he predicted a completely parallel yet symmetrical world made out of antimatter.[10]

In 1932, a professor at the California Institute of Technology, Carl Anderson, was studying showers of cosmic particles in a cloud chamber and saw a track left by something positively charged and with the same mass as an electron. Anderson decided the tracks were actually Dirac "anti-electrons," each produced alongside an electron from the impact of cosmic rays in the cloud chamber. He called the anti-electron a "positron" for its positive charge. The discovery gave Anderson the Nobel Prize in 1936 and confirmed the existence of anti-electrons, predicted by symmetry, and by Dirac in 1933. Subsequent discoveries succeeded in further

[7] *Id.* at 74, 238; Steven Weinberg, Symmetry: A "Key to Nature's Secrets," The New York Review of Books (Oct. 27, 2011).

[8] Hermann Weyl, Symmetry 3 (1983).

[9] Rosy Mondardini, The History of Antimatter, http://livefromcern.web.cern.ch (June 4, 2008).

[10] Paul A. M. Dirac, Theory of Electrons and Positrons (Nobel Lecture, Dec. 12, 1933).

proving the essential symmetry of the natural universe, between matter and antimatter.[11]

thesis :   Another example of how symmetry predicts how Nature behaves comes from biology. Bilateral symmetry (mirror image symmetry) is so prevalent in animals that one may presume that evolutionary processes and natural selection prefer animals that exhibit this kind of symmetry. Of all the different configurations that animals could have taken, mirror image symmetry was somehow selected for its many advantages (symmetrical wings, or legs, permit motion, and bilateral symmetry is also economical; two organs are better than one if the species is to survive).[12] Moreover, key biological reactions on Earth rely on molecules with the property called "chirality" – compounds that can form two different varieties that are mirror images of each other, sort of like left and right hands. Although the molecules are made of the same components, one cannot flip one around to make it exactly match the other. Because of that reality, most of the important chiral molecules on Earth, like amino acids, have the same "handedness" as each other.

Because symmetry, especially bilateral symmetry, is so common in animals and biology, the scientists who discovered the structure of the DNA molecule, James Watson and Frances Crick, knew that previously proposed structures would be incorrect that presumed the molecule would consist of *three* intertwined chains.[13] Instead, Crick and Watson correctly deduced that the DNA molecule consisted of two symmetrical strands of a double helix: "This structure has two helical chains each coiled round the same axis."[14] Crick and Watson also realized the advantages of this symmetrical structure: "It has not escaped our notice that the specific pairing we have postulated immediately suggests a possible copying mechanism *efficiency* for the genetic material."[15] In other words, it is the symmetry of the DNA molecule that permits life on Earth to grow and to reproduce. The laws

---

[11] Physicists have found antiprotons and antineutrons, and an antideuteron a nucleus of antimatter made out of an antiproton plus an antineutron. *Mondardini, supra* note 9.

[12] *Livio, supra* note 5 at 6–7.

[13] Linus Pauling had proposed a three-chain model for DNA. See J. D. Watson and F. H. Crick, Molecular Structure of Nucleic Acids, 171 Nature 737 (Apr. 25, 1953).

[14] *Id.* at 737.

[15] *Id.* The other researcher responsible for discovering the DNA structure, Rosalind Franklin, also concluded that in the DNA molecule there would be a double helix, not a triple helix or a singular helix. Rosalind Franklin & R. G. Gosling, Molecular Configuration in Sodium Thymonucleate, 171 Nature 740 (Apr. 25, 1953) ("It therefore seems probable that there are only two co-axial molecules and that these are unequally spaced along the fibre axis.").

of Nature obey certain principles of symmetry, and environmental policy affecting Nature should do so as well.

B.   Three Principles of Symmetry and the Environmental Policies That Should Follow from Them

Since Nature appears to be governed by certain universal laws, such as symmetry, it is possible for us to decipher what may be a "grand design" for the natural world and for our environmental surroundings.[16] Policymakers wishing to adopt and implement effective, successful environmental policy should pay particular heed to the principles of symmetry: the natural environment these legal policies affect will certainly obey the laws of Nature, where one central law is the central presence of symmetry.[17] Three manifestations of symmetry in Nature should play an important role when environmental policy is being fashioned. Such policy should conform to the principles of (1) conservation, (2) equivalence, and (3) unification.

1.   The Law of Conservation

An important truth observed from the natural world is the *Law of Conservation*. This law reflects the fact that some quantities can neither be created nor destroyed, and they have the same values whether they are measured today or tomorrow. This principle is sometimes called the First Law of Thermodynamics, which holds that the quantity of matter and energy remains the same. It can change from solid to liquid to gas to plasma,[18] or from potential to kinetic energy,[19] but the total amount of matter/energy in the universe remains consistent.

The Law of Conservation is connected to symmetry through *Noether's Theorem*. In the early twentieth century, German mathematician Emmy

---

[16] Joe Rosen, Symmetry Discovered: Concepts and Applications in Nature and Science (2011); Macus du Sautoy, Symmetry: A Journey into the Patterns of Nature (2009); John Conway, Heidi Burglel, & Chaim Goodman-Strauss, The Symmetries of Things (2008).

[17] *Symmetry: A "Key to Nature's Secrets," supra* note 7 at 2.

[18] The law of conservation of a mass dates from Antoine Lavoisier's 1789 discovery that mass is neither created nor destroyed in chemical reactions. The mass of one element at the beginning of a reaction will equal the mass of that element at the end of the reaction. R. W. Sterner, G. E. Small, & J. M. Hood, The Conservation of Mass, 3 Nature Education Knowledge 20 (2011).

[19] The law of conservation of energy holds that the amount of energy remains constant, and energy is neither created nor destroyed, even when it is converted from one form (potential) to another (kinetic). Conservation of Energy, Glenn Research Center, National Aeronautics and Space Administration, www.grc.nasa.gov/www/k-12.

Noether united the two conceptual pillars of physics: symmetry in nature and the universal laws of conservation. What Noether's Theorem says is that wherever one finds symmetry in Nature, what will also be found is a corresponding conservation – for example, a conservation of momentum or a conservation of energy.[20] Noether's Theorem fused together the laws of symmetry and conservation, such that we now understand symmetry and conservation are nothing but different perspectives of the same fundamental property.[21]

What has become apparent, then, is that Nature (and the natural world, and humans' environmental surroundings) tends to obey two universal and interlinked rules: symmetry and conservation. The idea of "conservation" in Nature means more than the realization that neither matter nor energy is ever lost. "Conservation" also suggests the concept of "economy," which has been defined as "producing an abundance of effects from very limited means."[22] In other words, when Nature is faced with a problem – for example, what should be the shape of all snowflakes, or what should be the structure of the DNA molecule – Nature will inevitably opt for the simplest, most economical solution. And consistent with Noether's Theorem, that solution will employ symmetry. A snowflake is most stable when its shape is symmetrically six-sided; the sturdy DNA molecule is a symmetrical double helix.

What does all of this mean for environmental policy? If policy affecting Nature should reflect, and be consistent with, the fundamental laws of Nature, and if symmetry and conservation are two such laws, then it would follow that *policy should obey the rules set forth by conservation/symmetry*. One of those rules is that Nature will often favor the simplest, most economical approach, especially where that approach produces "an abundance of effects from *very limited means*."[23] In other words, environmental policy should seek to achieve the maximum effect with the least effort.

This principle is also known as Occam's razor, or the principle of parsimony. Occam's razor admonishes that when one has to choose from a set of otherwise similar models, or explanations, of a given phenomenon,

---

[20] Natalie Angier, The Mighty Mathematician You've Never Heard Of, The New York Times (March 27, 2012) ("Noether's theorem shows that a symmetry of time – like the fact that whether you throw a ball in the air tomorrow or make the same toss next week, will have no effect on the ball's trajectory – is directly related to the conservation of energy.").

[21] *Livio, supra* note 5 at 217.

[22] *Wilczek, supra* note 5 at 11, 15.

[23] *Id.* Emphasis added.

the "simplest" one is usually the correct one. The Occam's razor principle underlies all scientific modeling, and it in turn is consistent with how Nature usually prefers the simplest solution: "Although the symmetries are hidden from us, we can sense that they are latent in nature, governing everything about us ... Nature is much simpler than it looks."[24]

Occam's razor is particularly pertinent when law and policy is addressing matters involving human environmental surroundings – the natural systems, environmental goods, natural capital, and biosphere that are inexorably being altered by anthropogenic actions. These environmental surroundings are usually seen as subjects of policy that are of unlimited complexity.[25] Indeed, this natural environment is best described as a "complex" adaptive system.[26] Occam's razor holds that when the subject domain of a theory or policy is excessively complex, the theory or policy itself should *not* be complex. Rather, the policy should be the simplest one possible.[27] In other words, environmental policy will likely fail if it is too complex or complicated.[28] Conversely, environmental policy opting for the *simplest solution* to the Earth-based issues laid out in Chapter 3 should have the greatest likelihood of success.

2.   The Equivalence Principle

Another manifestation of symmetry in Nature was discovered (or announced) by Albert Einstein in 1907 when he pointed out that two

---

[24] *Id.* at 165, quoting physicist Steven Weinberg. Occam's razor has been confirmed and repeated, in different ways, by a variety of commentators. Kelly Johnson, lead engineer of the Lockheed "Skunk Works," which designed the most sophisticated airplanes of a generation, called it the KISS principle (Keep It Simple, Stupid). Architect Mies van der Rohe urged that "less is more." Contemporary economist Steven Levitt and journalist Stephen Dubner argue that "contemplated problems don't necessarily require complicated solutions; simple solutions are often better." Levitt & Dubner, Think Like a Freak, chapter 5 (2014).

[25] Navigating Social-Ecological Systems: Building Resilience for Complexity and Change (F. Berkes, J. Colding, & C. Folke eds. 2003); J. Liu, et al., Complexity of Coupled Human and Natural Systems, 317 Science 1513 (2007); J. H. Holland, Hidden Order: How Adaptation Builds Complexity (1995).

[26] See Chapter 5.

[27] F. Heyligher, Occam's Razor, Principia Cybernetica Web (July 7, 1997).

[28] See, e.g., J.B. Ruhl, Complexity Theory as a Paradigm, for the Dynamical Law-and-Society System: A Wake-Up Call for Legal Reductionism and the Modern Administrative State, 45 Duke L.J. 849 (1996). Take the example of the United States Clean Air Act, 42 U.S.C. § 7401-7671q, which is the federal air pollution control law. This one statute takes up 319 single-spaced pages of a book devoted to "Selected Environmental Law Statutes" (Thomson Reuters 2015). And that is just a single environmental *statute*, not its endless regulations.

seemingly different forces – gravity and acceleration – are in fact the same. This insight that acceleration and gravity are simply two demonstrations of the same force has been termed the *equivalence principle*.[29] Einstein's realization was that a weightless person inside a free-falling closed elevator cannot tell if the feeling of being weightless is because the force of gravity has been switched off, or because the elevator is accelerating downward. Both would yield the same feeling of weightlessness inside a closed elevator. And this is because the forces of gravity and acceleration are symmetrically equivalent.

Nature's penchant for pervasive symmetry, accompanied by the equivalence principle, led to Einstein's theory of general relativity. Einstein knew that the length of moving bodies, as measured by observers at rest, contracts along their direction of motion, and the contraction increases with an increase in speed and acceleration. In other words, acceleration of an object through space and time distorts or warps the object. Einstein then deduced that if acceleration warps or curves objects in space and time, then it would follow, according to the equivalence principle, that *gravity* produced by a large object like a star would also warp or bend spacetime. And that is how the sun exerts a gravitational pull on the Earth almost a hundred million miles away – the Earth is seeking the most direct route through the curved geometry of spacetime that has been warped by the sun's mass.

Einstein's general theory of relativity taught us that to understand Nature, and the laws governing natural processes, we must *put the symmetry first*.[30] Symmetry originates the rules that Nature obeys, such as the equivalence principle.[31] Acceleration and gravity are the same; they are equivalent. Similarly, so too are mass and energy the same. They are equivalent when one realizes, as Einstein did in 1905, that energy equals mass times the speed of light squared.[32] Einstein proposed that the equivalence of mass and energy was simply a consequence of the symmetries of space and time.[33]

The equivalence principle is not only an important truth that Nature obeys; it should also be a working presumption for policymakers determining the laws intended to affect human behavior toward environmental

---

[29] Markus Possel, The Elevator, the Rocket, & Gravity: The Equivalence Principle, 1 Einstein Online 1009 (2005).

[30] Graham Hull, Symmetries and Curvature Structure in General Relativity (2004).

[31] *Livio, supra* note 5 at 231.

[32] David Bondanis, E=mc²: A Biography of the World's Most Famous Equation (2000).

[33] John S. Rigden, Einstein 1905: The Standard of Greatness (2005).

surroundings. As noted in Chapters 2 and 4, for too many years that relationship was defined by laws that tended to assume an anthropocentric
moral superiority to the environmental surroundings of humans. Human
exceptionalism was the norm. Environmental policies often began with a
central premise: superior humans can manage, and ultimately master, the
Earth's natural processes and systems.[34]

The equivalence principle presumes the opposite. Consistent with the
principle's grounding in equality, humans are not considered superior to
Nature, but rather a part of a larger social ecological system. Environmental
policy should similarly begin with the idea that humans and their environmental surroundings are equivalent, and bound together, interlinked on a
level playing field. Indeed, the equivalence principle is the starting point
for modern ecological thought presuming that humans and Nature are a
coupled human-natural system best described as a social-ecological system, an SES.[35] Environmental policy should reflect the equivalence principle by formulating laws that address the Earth-based SES, not laws where
superior social humans seek to dominate ecological systems.

3. The Unification Principle

A third manifestation of symmetry occurs when there is a unification of
apparent opposites. When reconciliation is possible among apparently
opposite forces in Nature, or opposite agents in natural systems, they
become complimentary aspects of an underlying unity.[36] And while these
forces, or agents, may appear to be separate, and opposite, the unification
principle suggests that they are in fact just different when one observes

[34] See e.g., The Adaptive Challenge of Climate Change (K. O'Brien & E. Selboe eds. 2015);
Charles Perrings, Our Uncommon Heritage: Biodiversity Change, Ecosystem Services,
and Human Wellbeing (2014); Adapting to Climate Change (W. Adgers, I. Lorenzoni, & K.
O'Brien eds. 2011).

[35] F. Berkes, J. Colding, & C. Folke, Navigating Social-Ecological Systems: Building Resilience for
Complexity and Change (Cambridge Univ. Press 2003); B. Walker, C. S. Holling, S. Carpenter,
& A. Kinzig, Resilience, Adaptability and Transformability in Social-Ecological Systems, 9
Ecology & Society #5 (2004); P. Olsson, C. Folke, F. Berkes, Adaptive Comanagement for
Building Resilience in Social-Ecological Systems, 34 Envir. Management 75 (2004).

[36] *Wilczek, supra* note 5 at 391. The unification principle is quite similar to one of the fundamental principles of Taoism. One of these principles is that beneath the apparent separateness of "the ten thousand things" of everyday life is a deeper underlying unity. Taoism
believes that life on this planet, whether it be human life, plant life, animal life, or even
ecosystem functioning, is an organic whole, making up a web of interconnectedness. Ted
Kardash, Taoism – Ancient Wisdom for a Modern World: The Tao of Daily Living, www
.pacificcollege.edu/news/log/2015.

them, but possessing similar unified properties. The unification principle is similar to "systems theory," which focuses on the arrangement of, and relations between, the parts that connect them into a whole. The unified system itself is different than its independent components, which may consist of forces that appear to be opposites.[37]

The unification principle exhibits the symmetry of the laws of nature by unifying separate and opposing entities into one system, one theory, or one natural property. There are several examples of the unification principle that have emerged from mathematics, physics, and natural sciences:

- The systematic use of coordinates pioneered by Rene Descartes's unified algebra and geometry.
- Isaac Newton's universal law of gravitation and laws of motion symmetrically connected two kinds of motion that seemed quite different: an apple falling toward the center of the Earth and the moon orbiting the Earth – both are examples of objects falling due to gravity. The forces keeping objects on the Earth's surface and the force holding moons and planets in their orbits are the same.[38]
- Michael Faraday and James Maxwell realized that electricity and magnetism are simply symmetrical manifestations of a single physical essence – electromagnetism. And Maxwell's equation provided a unification of electromagnetism and light.[39]
- Einstein's special theory of relativity connected space and time, so that we see them as two elements of a unified time-space.[40]

Policymakers should heed the unification principle because so much of environmental policy assumes that one superior life form – homo sapiens – is insulated from, and separate from, that species' environmental surroundings. Legal norms presume a perceived duality between humans and Nature, where humans are both superior to and separate from the biosphere.[41] Humans traditionally view Nature and natural processes from a place that is outside of and apart from humans, where humans can manipulate and manage Nature to serve anthropocentric ends.[42] This perspective is

---

[37] F. Heylighen & C. Joslyn, What Is Systems Theory?, Principia Cybernetica Web (Nov. 1, 1992).
[38] Wilczek, supra note 5 at 106.
[39] Id. at 127
[40] Id. at 200–201; 392.
[41] See Chapter 4.
[42] Environmental Law and Contrasting Ideas of Nature: A Constructivist Approach (K. Hirokawa ed. 2016).

embedded in environmental policies and regulations. Environmental protection laws become, in effect, an anthropomorphic police force designed to assist a "victim" (the Earth), which has been harmed or wounded by human actions, but remains alien to, and apart from, humans.[43]

Consistent with the unification principle, humans and their environmental surroundings are in fact not separate. They are united in one Earth-based system, the social-ecological system (SES) that comprises humans and all natural processes that affect, and are affected by, human actions. The SES is a *coupled* human-natural system characterized by biocomplexity, nonlinear dynamics, and heterogeneity.[44] Environmental policy must address not just the "environment" but the coupled, integrated SES, where humans and their environmental surroundings are considered an underlying unity.

---

[43] Simon Hailwood, Alienation and Nature in Environmental Philosophy (2015).
[44] J. Liu, T. Dietz, & S. R. Carpenter, Complexity of Coupled Human and Natural Systems, 317 Science 1513 (2007).

10

Toward a New Legal Alignment of Humans and Nature

Previous chapters have shown that planetary boundaries necessary for the continuation of human life are being breached by anthropogenic activity.[1] Environmental policies have failed to curb human behaviors that transgress these life-sustaining boundaries.[2] Any alternative policy paradigm will need to be sensitive to, and address the reasons for, this historic policy failure.[3] There appear to be four central explanations for why environmental laws just do not work very well.

- Environmental policy is too often premised on a belief in human exceptionalism and superiority with respect to our environmental surroundings, as well as a sense of anthropocentric separation from Nature.[4]
- Environmental policy has been based on an inaccurate model of how Nature works.[5]
- Some environmental policies are based on a false model for how humans behave.[6]
- Environmental laws and policies have not been consistent with a universal truth obeyed by the natural environment – symmetry.[7]

What is needed, then, is environmental policy that avoids each of these four missteps that have dogged most rules and laws designed either to influence or control how humans affect Nature. Such a policy is outlined in this chapter. It would be a policy that creates (or legitimates) a

---

[1] See Chapters 1 & 3.
[2] See Chapter 8.
[3] See Chapter 2. See also Thomas Rudel, Defensive Environmentalists and the Dynamics of Global Reform (Cambridge 2014).
[4] See Chapter 4.
[5] See Chapters 5 & 6.
[6] See Chapter 7.
[7] See Chapter 9.

particular type of legal right. This would not be the typical right that so many espouse – an environmental right granted to individuals to clean air and water. The right proposed here would be granted not just to humans,[8] and not just to Nature (or natural resources or environmental goods or natural systems),[9] but to the integrated social ecological system (the SES) that encompasses *both* humans and all their environmental surroundings. The right would be to a set of environmental conditions that permit the Earth's natural systems to operate so that critical planetary boundaries are restored in order for humans to have a safe operating space.[10] And it would be a "positive" right, which is a right that provides something to the right-holder.

There is also a corollary to this right, and this corollary obeys the principle of symmetry that is central to the laws of Nature. Consistent with the laws of symmetry, the aforementioned positive right also requires that there be a corresponding affirmative *duty*. There must be an affirmative duty to support natural systems so that humans as a species will be able to survive on this planet. The current level of anthropogenic impact on Earth systems risks destabilizing the Holocene state in which modern human societies evolved.[11]

Unlike the positive right, which is held by the unified SES, the affirmative duty imposes an obligation only on humans. Humans bear the sole burden of the affirmative obligation because, in the Anthropocene Era, it is not Nature, but only one species – humans – which is affecting natural systems and the biosphere. This anthropogenic impact on global systems is so dramatic that human long-term viability cannot be assumed.[12]

---

[8] See, e.g., James May & Eria Daly, Global Environmental Constitutionalism (Cambridge 2015) (individuals should have rights to a clean environment).

[9] Suzanne Goldenberg, Pope Francis Asserts "Rights of the Environment" in Speech to U.N., The Guardian (Sept. 25, 2015); Jan Laitos, The Right of Nonuse (Oxford 2012).

[10] Katherine Richardson, et al., Planetary Boundaries: Exploring the Safe Operating Space for Humanity, 14 Ecology and Society #32 (2009); Johan Rockstrom, et al., A Safe Operating Space for Humanity, 461 Nature 472 (2009).

[11] Will Steffen, et al., Planetary Boundaries: Guiding Human Development on a Changing Planet, 347 Science 6223 (Feb. 15, 2015) ("There is increasing evidence that human activities are affecting Earth System functioning to a degree that threatens the resilience of the Earth System … ability to persist … in the face of human pressures and shocks.").

[12] Will Steffen, et al., The Anthropocene: From Global Change to Planetary Stewardship, 40 Ambio 739 (2011); Will Steffen, et al., The Anthropocene: Are Humans Overwhelming the Great Forces of Nature? 36 Ambio 614 (2007).

A. A Positive Right for the Earth's SES

Improved, workable, more efficient environmental policy begins with a legal "right" created for the Earth's macro SES.[13] Such a "rights assertion" requires that potential environmental policymakers understand several critical features of this particular right. First, it is important to know what the legal right is: What exactly does it provide the right-holder? Is it a positive or negative right? And what is its source? Second, who, or what, has the right, and why? Third, the right-holder is entitled to what actions, to what ends? Fourth, what is the effect of the right on others? And finally, since the right pertains to Nature and Earth's systems, is the right consistent with the rules of symmetry that govern the natural world?

1. A Rights-Based Environmental Policy

A legally recognized right may be either a positive or negative right.[14] A positive right is one that provides something to the right-holder; the right is positive in the sense that it becomes a claim on legal grounds to have or obtain something, or to act in a certain way. It may also be a claim for the positive action and assistance of others in fulfilling the basic purpose of the right-holder. That basic purpose becomes an entitlement for the right-holder to perform certain actions, as well as an entitlement that others perform certain actions consistent with the purpose of the right. Consistent with the "Hohfeldian Analytical System" for rights, a positive right may either be "privilege" endowing its holder with the ability to engage in an activity, or a "power" enabling the right-holder to alter the privilege if circumstances demand a change.[15]

The "right" here would be to the restoration and protection of the Earth system in a resilient and accommodating state, so as to create "a global safe operating space" for continued societal development. The relatively stable, nearly 12,000-year-long Holocene epoch provided the only conditions on Earth that we know can support contemporary human societies. There is overwhelming evidence that strictly human activities, not

[13] H. M. Leslie, et al., Operationalizing the Social-Ecological Systems Framework to Assess Sustainability, 112 Proc. Nat'l Acad. Science USA 5979 (May 12, 2015) (acknowledging the importance of integrative coupled system analyses when implementing spatial planning and other ecosystem-based policies).

[14] R. M. Hare, The Language of Morals (Oxford 1952).

[15] Wesley Hohfeld, Fundamental Legal Conceptions (Yale 1919). Nigel Simmonds, Introduction in W. N. Hohfeld, Fundamental Legal Conceptions as Applied in Judicial Reasoning (David Campbell & Philip Thomas eds. 2001).

the normal fluctuations of the Earth system, are so threatening the resilience of Nature and Earth's systems that the Holocene state is becoming destabilized to the point that human societies may no longer be supported. Planetary boundaries, defined as the environmental limits within which humanity can safely operate, are being breached by anthropogenic impacts.[16] Four such boundaries – climate change, biosphere integrity, biochemical flows, and land system change – have been so compromised by human actions that the Earth will soon not be able to provide humanity with a safe operating space.[17]

The purpose of the positive right, then, is to ensure that, as a matter of law and policy, the Earth's planetary boundaries are restored. The purpose of the right is to enable the Earth system again to support the continued sustainability, and survivability, of modern human societies. Note that the right is a positive right to obtain something – the Holocene-like conditions that make human life possible. It is a positive entitlement for Earth systems to perform so that modern human societies can continue to evolve. It is also an entitlement that humans engage in certain anthropogenic activities so that Earth systems can perform their Holocene-era role of creating a safe operating space for humanity.[18]

The right is *not* intended to primarily 'benefit,' "protect," or "save" natural resources or natural systems from anthropogenic acts. As has been noted repeatedly throughout this book, Nature and Earth systems will inevitably adapt to whatever humans do to their environmental surroundings. But humans may not be able to adapt to a post-Holocene, Anthropocene state.[19] So the positive right is directed only at human survival. The right is intended not to save the "natural" environment, but to save humans from humans.

Note also that this right is a "positive" right, and is to be contrasted to the other kind of right that is possible, a negative right. Negative rights are a claim by the right-holder that impose a negative *duty* on others. Usually that negative duty is a duty not to interfere with the right-holder's activities, or the right-holder's freedom to perform in a particular area.[20] The

---

[16] *Rockstrom, supra* note 10.

[17] *Steffen, supra* note 11.

[18] Will Steffen, Johan Rockstrom, & Robert Costanza, How Defining Planetary Boundaries Can Transform Our Approach to Growth, 2 Solutions: For a Sustainable and Desirable Future #3 (May 2011).

[19] *Steffen, supra* note 11. See also Colin N. Waters, et al., The Anthropocene is Functionally and Stratigraphically Distinct from the Holocene, 351 Science No. 6269 (2016).

[20] See generally Immanuel Kant, Grounding for the Metaphysics of Morals (James Ellington ed. 1985).

holder of a negative right has an entitlement that others not perform certain actions, and has a right to resist certain acts by others. The function of a negative right is to give its holder some control over someone else's duty, where that duty is a correlative negative duty to not act in some way.[21]

Virtually all existing environmental policies create negative rights that give rise to negative duties. For example, traditional command-and-control anti-pollution laws state: *Do Not Pollute without a Permit*. Laws that rely on economic tools, such as cap-and-trade rules on carbon taxes, are all negative – *Do Not Exceed the Cap*, or *Do Not Use Carbon-Based Fuels Unless You Pay the Tax*. Informational laws, such as America's National Environmental Policy Act, order government entities: *Do Not Proceed with the Proposed Action without Preparing an Environmental Impact Statement*. Preservation laws say, in effect: *Do Not Build Roads or Develop Resource Extractive Activities Here, or Don't Extract It, Keep It in the Ground*. Policies that rely on the Public Trust Doctrine argue that *Developers May Not Interfere with the Trust Interest*.[22]

By contrast, the proposed positive right suggested here is a right that *provides* something – a safe operating space for humanity. The positive right is also a claim for the positive assistance of others, especially humans, in fulfilling the constituents of the right – the restoration and maintenance of planetary boundaries that permit humans to evolve and survive.[23] Instead of having a negative right, entitling the right-holder to noninterference (e.g., don't interfere with global climate by adding too many greenhouse gases),[24] the holder of this positive right is entitled to either some "good" (e.g., a biosphere that is resilient and able to adapt to anthropogenic impacts)[25] or a "service" (e.g., sustainable natural capital and ecosystem services).[26] The right is not a right against certain self-destructive anthropogenic actions affecting the Earth system, but a right either to an eventual Earth system outcome or to positive human assistance in obtaining that outcome.[27]

---

[21] See general D. Ivison, Rights (2007); T. Campbell, Rights: A Critical Introduction (2006).
[22] Many of the negative rights and duties embodied in environmental policy are discussed in Chapter 8.
[23] Planetary Boundaries, Stockholm Resilience Centre (Jan. 2015).
[24] Ronald Dworkin, Taking Rights Seriously 46 (1999).
[25] *Steffen, supra* note 11.
[26] J. B. Ruhl, Steven Kraft, & Christopher Lant, The Law and Policy of Ecosystem Services (2007); R. Costanza, et al., The Value of the World's Ecosystem Services and Natural Capital, 387 Nature 253 (1997).
[27] J. Narveson, The Libertarian Idea (2001); Stephen Holms & Cass Sunstein, The Cost of Rights: Why Liberty Depends on Taxes 46 (1999).

There are two possible sources for this positive right. The first relies on a *status-based* justification that begins with the nature of the right-holder. If the right-holder is the Earth system consisting of all natural systems, resources, goods, and living organisms, in the Earth's biosphere, including humans, then the question is whether this entity has this positive right by the fact of its existence. The argument goes that since humans have rights because of their inherent nature as human beings,[28] and since humans are not separate from, but are a part of, their natural environment, then that which was, and still is, responsible for human existence – the environmental surroundings of humans – should have rights too.[29]

Another source of this positive right relies on an *instrumentalist* approach. This approach starts with the desired consequence and works backward to see which rights ascriptions will produce those consequences.[30] For environmental policy, the desired consequence of the right is that "safe operating space for humanity," which can only come about if critical planetary boundaries are respected.[31] So, whether the right is a status-based right or an instrumental right, the right is a positive entitlement to achieve something – stable planetary boundaries so that modern human societies can survive in Holocene-like conditions.[32]

2.   A Right Held by Social Ecological Systems

Environmental policies, as well as so-called resource-protective laws, have traditionally embraced a purely anthropocentric approach.[33] Consistent with this tradition, to the extent legal "rights" have been conferred by positive law, they have been granted only to humans. Legal regimes usually do not grant rights to Nature, natural systems or processes, or natural objects and resources. Legal systems prioritize human wants and needs over the integrity of our surrounding environmental and incidental ecological systems. Indeed, environmental policy traditionally values natural goods and services only insofar as these further anthropocentric interests. Such policy presumes that nature does not have intrinsic, non-human-centric worth: The assumption is that Nature's value is only derivative, permitting

---

[28] Robert Nozick, Anarchy, State, and Utopia (1974).
[29] Alan Boyle, Human Rights on Environmental Rights? A Reassessment, 18 Fordham Envtl. L. Rev. 471 (2007).
[30] Mark Tushnet, An Essay on Rights, 62 Texas L. Rev. 1363 (1984).
[31] *Planetary Boundaries, supra* note 23.
[32] *Steffen, supra* note 11.
[33] Fredric L. Bender, The Culture of Extinction: Toward a Philosophy of Deep Ecology (2003).

humans to have a relationship with their surroundings that may be characterized as parasitic.[34]

This human-centric tendency among environmental policies belies human dependency on the healthy functioning of the larger Earth-based natural systems within which the *homo sapien* species is embedded.[35] An anthropocentric approach in positive law has permitted great developmental and economic growth for human societies, but this growth has been accomplished at the expense of (1) many of Earth's life support systems, (2) the planet's reservoir of natural resources, and (3) a large percentage of global biodiversity.[36] Anthropogenic activity has also caused planetary shifts in ecosystem processes that are critical to the survival of the human species.[37] Human societal development and accompanying economic growth has actually led to a deterioration of human well-being, because this societal benefit has produced deleterious changes in the Earth-based systems that permit human life to evolve and thrive.[38]

From the perspective of environmental policy, we seem to have separated humans and their environmental surroundings. There has been a disconnect between the workings of human societies and the operation of natural systems that make it possible for the human species to emerge and prosper. Environmental policies tend to ignore the interests of the natural world and confer on humans the legal ability to exploit Nature. Instead, environmental policy should have focused less on human rights to the largess of Nature and more on recognizing as a matter of law that Nature has value for its own sake, and not just for its instrumental value to humans.[39]

As a result, any legal right to a safe operating space for humanity, and to the restoration of critical planetary boundaries, needs to be directed to an entity that *reconnects* human social systems to the functioning of the Earth's ecological systems.[40] That entity is a social ecological system, or an SES, which may range in size from a Wisconsin lake to the planet Earth.[41]

---

[34] Eccy De Jong, Spinoza and Deep Ecology: Challenging Traditional Approaches to Environmentalism 9–15 (2004).

[35] Comac Cullinan, Wildlaw 44 (2d ed. 2011).

[36] Carl Folke, et al., Reconnecting to the Biosphere, 40 Ambio 719 (2011).

[37] Emilio F. Moran, People and Nature: An Introduction to Human-Ecological Relations 11–13 (2006).

[38] Gary P. Kufinos & F. Stuart Chapin, III, Principles of Ecosystem Stewardship 59 (2009).

[39] Jan Laitos, The Right of Nonuse (Oxford 2012).

[40] Carl Folke, et al., Adaptive Governance of Social-Ecological Systems, 30 Ann. Rev. Envir. Rev. 441, 443–444 (2005).

[41] Michael D. McGinnis & Elinor Ostrom, Social-Ecological System Framework: Initial Changes and Continuing Challenges, 19 Ecology & Society #2 (2014).

The concept of an SES emphasizes the integrated concept of humans in Nature, where Nature is affecting humans and vice versa. The SES realizes that the delineation between social systems and ecological systems is artificial and arbitrary. Consistent with the "unification principle" outlined in Chapter 9, the SES "unifies" humans and their environmental context. All SESs should have the positive right outlined in this chapter, whether it be the Earth-based SES or more regional SESs.[42]

When the SES is protected by a positive right, human decisions and choices affecting their environmental surroundings will be limited. Anthropogenic choices will then be preferred that promote the resilience of complex SESs.[43] And because an SES is an integrated coupled system, ecosystem or environmental strategies will not foster any separation, or disconnect, between humans and Nature.[44] Instead of reflecting a condition of parasitism between humans and Nature, an SES holding the positive right fosters and legitimates a preferred state of "mutualism," where both humans and Nature benefit from each other.

3. A Positive Right Enabling the Holder with the Power to Alter the Right

Consistent with the Hohfeldian Analytical System of "rights," a primary right is a *privilege*, endowing its holder with the privilege to engage in an activity, and entitling its holder with the expectation that others will perform certain actions permitting the holder to engage in the activity subject to the right.[45] The proposal here is that the Earth-based SES should have a positive right, a privilege, ensuring that the SES provides humanity with a safe operating space on this planet. But Hohfeldian "privilege" also gives right-holders a "power" that enables them to alter the right.[46] The power to alter or change primary rights might be pragmatically necessary if the right-holder's normative situation is different than what it was when the initial right-privilege was first acknowledged.

---

[42] Jocher Hinkel, Pieter Bots, & Maja Schluter, Enhancing the Ostrom Social-ecological System Framework Through Formalization, 19 Ecology & Society #3 (2014).

[43] Navigating Social-Ecological Systems (F. Berkes, J. Colding, & C. Folke eds.) (Cambridge 2003); *Folke, supra* note 40.

[44] H. M. Leslie, et al., Operationalizing the Social-Ecological Systems Framework to Assess Sustainability, 112 Proc. Nat'l Acad. Science USA 5979 (May 12, 2015).

[45] See subsection A1 in this chapter.

[46] *Hohfeld, supra* note 15.

Since the right conferred on the Earth-based SES involves restoring and maintaining planetary boundaries and natural systems, it is important that the right has built into it a high degree of flexibility, because as was discussed in Chapter 5, Earth-based systems are nor predictable and static. Instead, Earth system processes are nonlinear, fluid, changing, and dynamic. They are best characterized as complex adaptive systems (CAS).[47] Nature is the quintessential CAS, as it is a series of complex micro-systems that are constantly adapting to their unpredictable environment.[48] Any legal right granted to the Earth-based SES should not be fixed and front-loaded, because the right itself is addressing a moving target – the many CAS that comprise Nature.

The right-holder, the Earth-based SES, cannot accurately predict the ecological effects of human actions on a CAS. Therefore, both the legal right and any environmental policies that flow from it must be provided a fair amount of pragmatic flexibility – the Hohfeldian "power to alter rules."[49] Policymakers respecting this positive right should be empowered to make adaptive changes or adjustments to resource management methods in order to promote resilience of ecosystems and natural processes.[50] Policymakers respecting or implementing the proposed legal right should adopt "adaptive management" as a policy tool. Adaptive management is a way of addressing natural resource decision-making in the face of uncertainty, where changes and alterations in policy are expected.[51]

4.   The Effect of the Right on Others

A right is not just an entitlement or privilege to perform certain actions (e.g., an entitlement to the Earth-system's ability to maintain planetary boundaries for humanity). A right is also an entitlement that others perform certain actions; it is in Hohfeldian terms, a "claim on others."[52] The

---

[47] Simon A. Levin, Ecosystems and the Biosphere as Complex Adaptive Systems, 5 Ecosystems 431 (1998).

[48] J. Stephen Lansing, Complex Adaptive Systems, 32 Annual Review of Anthropology 183 (2003); Simon A Levin, Complex Adaptive Systems: Exploring the Unknown, and the Unknowable, 40 Bull. American Math. Society 3 (2003).

[49] See, e.g., Robin Kundis Craig, "Stationarity Is Dead," Long Live Transformation: Five Principles for Climate Change Adaption Law, 34 Harv. Envtl. L. Rev. 9, 40 (2010).

[50] Lance Gunderson, Ecological Resilience – In Theory and Application, 31 Ann. Rev. Ecol. Syst. 433 (2000).

[51] Lucy Rist, et al., A New Paradigm for Adaptive Management, 18 Ecology & Society 63 (2013); C. J. Walters, Adaptive Management of Renewable Resources (1986); C. S. Holling, Adaptive Environmental Assessment and Management (1978).

[52] Hohfeld, supra note 15.

claim-right correlates to a duty borne by some duty-bearer. This duty is considered to be some obligation or responsibility to the right-holder. Where the right-holder is the Earth-based SES, the duty is borne by the "social" component of the SES, the humans. The SES should have, because it has a positive right, a justified claim on humans. Humans have a duty to the SES.

The duty that humans have to the Earth-based SES is explained in Section B of this chapter. Suffice it to say here that the claim on humans to the SES helps ensure the elimination of one flawed assumption of past environmental policy – the assumption that humans are an exceptional species superior to, and inherently more important than, environmental goods and services.[53] That the Earth-based SES has a claim on humans should help dispel the perception among environmental policymakers that short-term human needs always take precedence over the integrity and sustainability of natural systems.[54] A positive right held by the SES creates a claim on humans intended to replace notions of anthropocentric superiority. The claim on humans assumes that each of us have a personal responsibility toward our environmental surroundings.[55]

5.   The Right Obeys the Rules of Symmetry

Chapter 9 explained how Nature and environmental processes tend to follow several principles of symmetry. One key aspect of symmetry is that the parts are largely interchangeable with respect to the whole – they can be exchanged with one another while preserving the original figure. Because of this feature of symmetry, systems that are symmetrical have invariance, permitting scientists and ecologists to predict what the whole looks like (and how the whole operates) if one can identify central parts of the whole. Consistent with the principle of unification, if one knows these parts, we can predict with reasonable accuracy what the other parts will be in order for the parts be unified in a whole system. For example, space is simply "part" of the space-time continuum; matter is only part of a universe comprised of both matter and antimatter.[56]

---

[53] See Chapter 4.

[54] Holly Doremus, The Rhetoric and Reality of Nature Protection: Toward a New Discourse, 57 Wash. & Lee L. Rev. 11, 14–15 (2000).

[55] Hope M. Babcock, Assuming Personal Responsibility for Improving the Environment: Moving Toward a New Environmental Norm, 33 Harv. Envtl. L. Rev. 117, 123–124 (2009).

[56] T. Debs & M. Redhead, Objectivity, Invariance, and Convention: Symmetry in Physical Science (2007).

Besides unity (permitting predictions about the whole if one understands a part), symmetry also exposes two other principles that are characteristic in the physical and biological world: *equivalence* and *simplicity*. Both qualities of symmetry were discussed in Chapter 9. When one identifies a part of a symmetrical system, the other "missing" part is "equivalent" to the identified part, where the two parts form a unified whole. In physics, for example, time and space are symmetrically equivalent; so too are matter and energy, and electricity and magnetism.[57]

Another principle of symmetry involves simplicity. Symmetrical systems are inevitably non-complex, "simple" systems.[58] Even when the natural working of organisms seem complicated, there is often an underlying order and simplicity and conservation of effort that grounds what otherwise seems to be complex.[59] In Nature, for example, the rules of species interaction in an ecosystem may seem like a formidably complex problem. Yet macroscopic behavior of certain ecosystems displays a symmetry and simplicity that allow for analytical predictions for various distributions, such as relative species abundance and diversity.[60]

For environmental policy to be successful, and efficient, it should follow the same rules the environment follows. One of the most important of those rules, obeyed by natural systems and environmental processes, is symmetry.[61] A positive legal right bestowed on the Earth-based SES would, in order to be consistent with the symmetrical quality of invariance, (1) become only one part of a *unified* legal policy ensuring the continuation of Earth's planetary boundaries, (2) be the correlative *equivalent* to the right, and (3) be *simple* to understand and implement, and conserve legal resources. In other words, the other part, the non-right part, should be simply interchangeable with respect to the right. What is the symmetrical correlative of the positive legal right held by the SES that, when combined with that right, conserves legal implementation strategies and becomes a unified environmental policy?

In terms of standard Hohfeldian rights analysis, a *duty* would be that missing part of an environmental policy legitimating a right. Hohfeld arranged symmetrical "opposites" and "correlatives" in tables in order to

---

[57] P. J. Olver, Equivalence, Invariants, and Symmetry (Cambridge 1995).
[58] Victor J. Strenger, Timeless Reality: Symmetry, Simplicity, and Multiple Universes (2000).
[59] Klaus Mainzer, Symmetry and Complexity: The Spirit and Beauty of Nonlinear Science (2005).
[60] Sandro Azaele, et al., Dynamical Evolution of Ecosystems, 444 Nature 926 (Dec. 2006).
[61] See Chapter 9.

display the logical structure of his system.[62] If one had a right or privilege, then the creation of this right meant there was simultaneously created for the right-holder a justified claim on others. Such a claim would be, in effect, a duty to ensure the viability of the right. So, if there is a positive right held by the Earth-based SES to conditions that ensure planetary integrity and a safe operating space for humanity, then there must logically be a symmetrical duty, or obligation, to respect and perpetuate this right. A right to planetary boundaries and a duty to protect that right satisfy the requirements of equivalence and simplicity.

A law obviously cannot impose a duty on the "ecological systems" component of the SES (although ecological systems can benefit from the correlative right). But a law can impose a duty on the "social," human component. Since the right is positive, that positive right held by the SES symmetrically imposes on humans a positive duty to the SES, to which we now turn.

B. A Positive Duty to Nature Imposed on Humans

A "duty" may be defined as the obligation of someone, or some entity, to satisfy a claim made upon the one who owes the duty. Duty theories base the requirements of the duty on various deontological theories of obligation. One such theory was championed by seventeenth-century philosopher Samuel Pufendorf. He argued that humans have certain moral duties – to God, to oneself, and to others. This last duty was to promote the good of others, not just by not injuring others but also by seeking to affirmatively benefit them "so that I am glad that others who share my nature also live upon this earth."[63] In other words, Pufendorf believed as a matter of morality that humanity had an affirmative duty to benefit others, not just a negative duty to avoid harming others.

Another duty-based approach is grounded in *rights theory*. As noted in Section A, a "right is a justified claim against another," giving rise to a correlative, and symmetrical, duty. A right-holder impliedly may presume that another has a duty to that right-holder – there is a correlativity of rights and duties. Seventeenth-century philosopher John Locke argued that the laws of Nature give humans natural rights, as well as corresponding mandates (i.e., duties) that others not harm these rights.[64] If a positive

[62] *Hohfeld, supra* note 15.
[63] T. Irwin, Pufendorf, in The Development of Ethics. A Historical and Critical Study 332–352 (Oxford 2011).
[64] John Dunn, The Political Thought of John Locke (Cambridge 1969).

right is held by the Earth-based SES, then rights theory (and symmetry) predicts that an affirmative duty would be created as well.

Two deontological theories, one based on morality and the other based on rights, suggest that the existence, or creation, of a positive right in order to secure a safe operating space for humanity means there must be, or should be, a symmetrical affirmative duty to provide that safe space. Because the right is held by the Earth-based SES, the duty is imposed on the "social" component of the SES right-holder – the humanity. Humans have a duty to the SES to maintain planetary boundaries and natural systems so that life is sustained. And because the right held by the SES is positive, the duty also is positive. Respecting a positive right requires more than the duty to not act, which follows from a negative right. Positive rights impose on us the affirmative obligation to actively provide something to the right-holder.

This principle of the important role of affirmative duties was succinctly and aptly summarized by one of America's leading environmental law scholars, Professor A. Dan Tarlock:

> If environmental protection is to succeed as a legitimate, permanent policy, it must evolve from a *negative strategy* of simply trying to stop an action that disturbs a mythical natural baseline, to a pervasive affirmative one which provides incentives for creative ... protection solutions.[65]

Here is an example of Tarlock's point. A "minimum flow right" is a statutory right created to ensure that "perennial rivers and streams ... shall be retained with base flows necessary to provide for the preservation of wildlife, fish, scenic, aesthetic, and other environmental values."[66] The minimum flow right is a negative right held by the "perennial rivers and streams" giving rise to a negative duty – where there is established a minimum flow right, "lakes and ponds shall be retained substantially in their natural condition."[67] This kind of environmental policy is Tarlock's "negative strategy" because it prohibits withdrawals of water where there is a minimum flow right. Tarlock is arguing that there should also be an affirmative duty (an "affirmative ... strategy") that would incentivize the creation of additional environmental contexts where rivers, streams, and lakes continue to provide "preservation of wildlife, fish, ... and other environmental values."[68]

[65] A. Dan Tarlock, The Future of Environmental "Rule of Law" Litigation, 17 Pace Envtl. L. Rev. 237, 243 (2000) (emphasis added).
[66] RCW 90.54.020 (3)(a) (Washington State).
[67] Id.
[68] See Foster v. Washington State Dept. of Ecology, 362 P. 3d 959 (Wash. 2015).

An affirmative duty is an obligation to provide something, not a duty to prevent something. The affirmative duty that follows from this chapter's proposed positive right tells humans *what to do* instead of ordering them *what not to do*. A duty that tells humans what to do is consistent with science research revealing what motivates people to change. A meta-analysis of psychological studies showed that human behavior is more likely to change not when people are feeling scared or threatened, but when people believe they can do something, when their affirmative actions have power.[69] Consistent with Professor Tarlock's admonition, an affirmative duty that empowers humans to do something that benefits their natural surroundings has a better chance of success than a negative duty commanding them to not do something.[70]

Here are some examples of how humans might fulfill their affirmative duty *to do* something, and to *provide* something to the SES, so humanity has a safe operating space on this planet.

1.   A Duty to Create Public Goods and Positive Externalities

One obvious affirmative duty that could be imposed of humans is the active obligation to create public goods, or positive externalities that benefit and promote the sustainability of the Earth-based SES – that strengthen the Earth's planetary boundaries so humans can survive. An individual human could create both a public good and a positive externality by the simple act of planting a leafy deciduous tree where otherwise there would not be a tree. One of the planetary boundaries at risk is the atmosphere's ability to absorb greenhouse gases without causing (for human life) catastrophic climate change.[71] A leafy deciduous tree will both assimilate carbon dioxide, a ubiquitous greenhouse gas, and emit oxygen, thus incrementally helping stabilize climate change. Since the tree would not be there but for the individual planting the tree, the tree becomes both a public good and a positive externality.

---

[69] Gjalt-Jorn Peters, Robert Ruiter, & Gerjo Kok, Threatening Communication: A Critical Re-Analysis and a Revised Meta-Analytic Test of Fear Appeal Theory, Health Psychology Review S8–S31 (May 7, 2013). See also John Brandon, Is Your Culture One of Encouragement or Blame?, Chicago Tribune (Nov. 20, 2016).

[70] See, e.g., Erika Bolstad, How to Talk Global Warming in Plain English, www.scientificamerican .com/article (March 28, 2016) (instead of telling people what scientists knew about climate change, environmental policy should be more "interactive," which lays out the limited time people have to seize the initiative themselves to solve the climate change problem).

[71] Steffen, supra note 11 (anthropogenic perturbation levels of the Earth-system climate change process is about to exceed that system's boundary necessary for human society stability).

A public good is a benefit enjoyed by others that is both non-excludable and non-rivalrous. Non-excludability means that individuals cannot be effectively excluded from the use of the public good; a good is non-rivalrous where use by one individual does not reduce the availability of the good to others.[72] A public good generates "external benefits," or a "positive externality," in that the beneficiaries of the good are usually external to, or not responsible for, the creation of the good. Common examples of public goods include lighthouses, street lights, and environmental goods such as clean air. A newly planted deciduous tree is a public good because (1) humans cannot be excluded from the benefits produced by a living organism that marginally reduces planetary greenhouse gases, and (2) "consumption" of the environmental benefit produced from the leafy tree does not reduce the benefit enjoyed by another individual.

The planting of the leafy tree would also be a positive externality (sometimes known as a spillover, or neighborhood effect). Positive externalities increase the utility of third parties at no cost to them. A positive externality improves collective societal welfare, where the private provider of the externality (i.e., the person planting the tree) has no way of monetizing the benefit. If a homeowner builds a magnificent house next to a shabby outmoded house, the new house will likely increase the property value of the shabby house just by being there. That increase in property value is external to the magnificent house, and the owner of the magnificent house cannot capture the new gains in value for the shabby house. Similarly, if one plants a leafy tree, there is global benefit because of a marginal reduction of greenhouse gases, but the one responsible for the tree planting cannot directly capture that benefit.

Both the production of public goods and positive externalities result in societal benefits. In the case of the leafy tree, its planting by an individual will, in a barely noticeable way, have a positive effect on a planetary boundary (climate change) that is being assaulted by anthropogenic activity.[73] However, because the production of this global benefit is not remunerated by the tree planter, there may be no incentive for the tree ever to be planted. Consumers can take advantage of public goods and positive externalities without contributing to their creation. As a result, there is created what is termed the "free-rider" problem – if too many consumers of the public good or positive externality decide to ride free (i.e., not contribute to its

[72] Paul Samuelson, The Pure Theory of Public Expenditure, 36 Review of Economics and Statistics 387–389 (1954).
[73] See *Steffen, supra* note 71.

creation), then private costs exceed private benefits, and there then is no incentive for anyone to provide the societal benefit.[74]

As a matter of environmental policy, the question then becomes: What provisions are available for stimulating the private production of public goods and positive externalities that strengthen planetary boundaries? One answer to this question may be found in Chapter 7, where it was pointed out how the homo economicus model for humans may be wrong. The free-rider problem hinges on a conception of humans as being purely rational, individualistic, and selfish. Public goods urge homo economicus to be a free-rider. But Chapter 7 revealed that studies by behavioral economists suggest that people may be motivated by more than a rational, self-centered, cost/benefit analysis of choices. Altruism, social norms, and cooperation play an equally large role in how people behave.[75] If people on this planet become sufficiently educated about the threat posed to their existence by anthropogenic behavior affecting planetary boundaries, they might become the tree-planters, or creators of public goods, instead of free-riders.

Most economists and scholars discount the likelihood that individuals will create environmental goods or positive externalities simply because it is "the right thing to do" at a time when planetary boundaries are threatened. The argument is that external, societal benefits (i.e., a planet with less greenhouse gases in the atmosphere) will not affect a party's incentive to engage in the positive action (e.g., planting leafy trees). When the private costs of undertaking the benign action for humanity exceed the private benefits, parties will not engage in the beneficial action and instead will revert to being free-riders.[76] Instead, in the absence of a subsidy, or some other mechanism that permits a party to internalize a positive externality, most commentators are skeptical that humans will just do good deeds for the planet.[77]

---

[74] Gideon Parchomovsky & Peter Siegelman, Cities, Property, and Positive Externalities, 54 Wm. & Mary L. Rev. 211 (2012). See also Daniel B. Kelly, Strategic Spillovers, 111 Columbia L. Rev. 1641, 1716 (2011) (with positive externalities, a party may not have an incentive to engage in an activity because the activity's private costs exceed its private benefits, even though the activity is desirable as its social benefits exceed its social costs).

[75] Daniel Kahneman Thinking Fast and Slow (2011); Elinor Ostrom, Governing the Commons: The Evolution of Institutions for Collective Action (1990); S. A. West, A. S. Griffin, & A. Gardner, Evolutionary Explanations for Cooperation, 17 Current Biology R661 (2007).

[76] Brett M. Frischmann & Mark A. Lemley, Spillovers, 107 Columbia L. Rev. 257, 259 (2007).

[77] Thomas Sterner, Policy Instruments for Environmental and Natural Resources Management 167–180 (2003); Richard Cornes & Todd Sandler, The Theory of Externalities, Public Goods, and Club Goods 55 (1996); M. Theresa Hupp, Efficient Land Use and the

Subsidies are "carrots" when it comes to environmental policy – they are premised on the notion that if governments make individuals better off financially for cleaning up the environment – for example, by planting leafy trees – then those individuals will engage in environmentally benign activities that benefit others. The producer of the public good is compensated and the benefit is not "externalized." However, such financial carrots may crowd out voluntary efforts, burden the government's budget, and possibly be self-defeating if the subsidies are in cash, and the recipient (the public good producer) can take the cash and purchase something that undoes the environmental good of the public good (e.g., if the subsidy is used to buy an old diesel truck that aggravates greenhouse gas production).[78]

Instead of a carrot, environmental policy should acknowledge and create a "stick" in the form of a positive duty to assist the Earth-based SES so that planetary boundaries are restored and protected. A positive duty is the obligation actively to assist and support a right-holder's positive entitlement to something. Here, it is proposed that the SES has a positive right to environmental conditions that maintain and sustain the survival of humanity. From this right should follow and affirmative duty to provide those conditions necessary for humanity's safe operating space on Earth. Governments should impose on individuals the positive duty to provide public goods, to create positive externalities, to plant leafy trees. Instead of not acting, which would stem from a negative duty, the positive duty here is to act, to do what is necessary to shore up planetary boundaries, and to satisfy the positive right held by the Earth-based SES.[79]

2. A Duty to Reconnect Humans with the Reality of Nature

In addition to the imposition of duties to create environmental public goods and positive externalities, environmental policy should also take deontological steps that reconnect human activity to the real workings of Nature.[80] Three positive duties would help humans realize how, consistent

Internalization of Beneficial Spillovers: An Economic and Legal Analysis, 31 Stanford L. Rev. 457, 474–475 (1979).

[78] Brian Galle, The Tragedy of the Carrots: Economics and Politics in the Choice of Price Instruments, 64 Stanford L. Rev. 797 (2012).

[79] Galle, id. (sticks are better than carrots if one wishes to produce positive externalties).

[80] Carl Folke, et al., Adaptive Governance of Social-Ecological Systems, 30 Ann. Rev. Envir. Res. 441 (2005).

with Chapter 9's unification principle, they are part of their environmental surroundings, not apart from Nature.

a.   Real-Time Information about the Environmental Effects of Human Actions

One affirmative duty should be a requirement that individuals have accurate, and understandable, information about the environmental impacts of their actions, particularly their consumer choices. The impact of human consumer choices on our environmental surroundings is often felt far from the place where the original consumer choice was made. As a result of this disconnect between choice and effect, individuals remain unaware of the environmental repercussions of their consumer decisions.[81] To connect humans with their surroundings, they should be provided with realistic and real-time information about what planetary boundary was affected or what ecosystem was impacted by the production of the good about to be purchased. Such an information-based duty also has the advantage of being consistent with how humans behave.[82]

b.   Remove the Perception in Environmental Policy That Humans Are Separate from Nature

Many traditional environmental laws and statutes actually serve to insulate humans from the reality of the integrated SES. Most environmental statutes are grounded in a policy of "protecting" Nature from human interference. Laws that seek to protect Nature from humans assume that humans are somehow distinct from natural processes and systems, and therefore Nature is in need of some help and assistance from protective positive law.[83] This assumption ignores the reality of the Earth-based SES, where humans are integrated within the SES along with ecological systems. The SES is consistent with symmetry's unification principle, which holds that humans and Nature are a unified whole. Laws that represent Nature as that which is *other than human, and in need of human protection*, serve only to shield humans from scientific reality: We are part of the so-called "natural" world, so if our laws are aimed at protecting Nature, they in fact are aimed at protecting us.[84]

---

[81]   Emilio F. Moran, People and Nature 11–13 (2006).

[82]   R. Thaler & Cass Sunstein, Nudge: Improving Decisions about Health, Wealth, and Happiness (2008).

[83]   Daniel C. Esty & Marian R. Chertow, Thinking Ecologically: The Next Generation of Environmental Policy 1–3, 14–15 (1997).

[84]   *Moran, supra* note 81 at 8.

There should be an affirmative duty to adopt environmental laws that reflect the reality that humans are not just a part of the Earth-based SES; humans are also dependent on the functioning of the surrounding "ecological systems" component of the SES. This duty would be manifested in environmental policy acknowledging that anthropogenic alternation of planetary systems is a problem not primarily for Nature but for the humans who rely on natural, healthy ecological systems. Such a policy would encourage humans to change their behavior for their sake, and not just for the sake of Nature and its natural systems. The affirmative duty is required only of the human "social" component of the SES, not the "ecological systems" component, so that humans realize (1) they are not separate from ecological systems, and (2) their existence is dependent of the continued function of these systems.[85]

c. Address Natural Resources and Systems in Accordance with the Real Dynamics Governing Nature

For too long, resource managers have imposed environmental policies on natural systems that have been revealed to be in conflict with the real functioning of these systems.[86] Nature is not predictable, and inclined always to return to a stationarity equilibrium state. Rather, Earth systems processes are nonlinear, fluid, dynamic, and constantly adapting to change. As first noted in Chapter 5, Nature is best described as a complex adaptive system (CAS).

Human environmental policymakers should not "front-load" management tools, which are often, upon their implementation, outmoded or inapplicable. The object of the regulation, the CAS, may have changed by the time the regulation is deployed. Policymakers should instead have an affirmative duty to allow for policy alterations after the law is adopted, so that managers may make adaptive changes and adjustments as the CAS evolves.[87] This positive duty also has the advantage of conforming to how Nature works.[88]

---

[85] See *Doremus, supra* note 54.
[86] See *Craig, supra* note 49.
[87] Lucy Rist, et al., A New Paradigm for Adaptive Management, 18 Ecology & Society 63 (2013).
[88] See Chapter 5.

~

Epilogue

So, after many pages of explanation, and countless citations, why do environmental policies, environmental laws, and environmental rules fail? What this book has argued is that there appear to be recurrent mistakes made by environmental policymakers. When these mistakes are embedded in policy, which then becomes the basis for positive law, the results are disappointing, perhaps even frightening. A perusal of virtually any page in Chapter 3, which assesses whether environmental policies have been successful, reveals that the natural world is not becoming conducive to human survival; rather, the Earth is becoming unsafe for us. Indeed, several planetary boundaries have already been exceeded that are necessary for the Earth system's biophysical processes to provide a "safe operating space for humanity."[1] The message to policymakers is apparent – existing environmental policy has not prevented or deterred anthropogenic changes to Earth's biophysical boundaries that enable human civilization as we know it to exist. Some of the Earth's critical environmental parameters have now been altered that previously made the Holocene epoch so hospitable to human survival and growth.[2]

Our review of environmental policy revealed that the recurrent "mistakes" took place because our policies (1) relied on a false worldview of humans' fundamental relationship to Nature, (2) used models for Nature's processes and human behavior that were inaccurate, (3) adopted enforcement and implementation systems that had internal flaws that doomed their effectiveness, and (4) failed to be based on several universal truths

[1] Will Steffen, et al., Planetary Boundaries: Guiding Human Development on a Changing Planet, 347 Science Issue 6223 (Jan. 15, 2015).
[2] An international team of researchers concluded that human activities have now crossed four of nine planetary boundaries that may not be exceeded for humanity to be in a "safe operating space" on this planet. These four boundaries that have been crossed include climate change, loss of biosphere integrity, land-system change, and altered biochemical cycles like phosphorous and nitrogen runoff. *Id.* See also Fernando Jaramillo & Georgia Destouni, Comment on "Planetary Boundaries": Guiding Human Development on a Changing Planet, 348 Science Issue 6240 (June 12, 2015).

that are followed by the natural world. Here is a summary of these central mistakes found in environmental policy.

A. Anthropomorphic Superiority

We have long embraced a belief in human superiority to Nature. This belief is repeatedly legitimized and reflected through policy mandates and institutional decisions.[3] A belief in human superiority was particularly prevalent in American history during the nineteenth century. The American West was largely unpopulated, and human settlers assumed that Nature there was fearsome but capable of being "tamed" and brought under control by humans. Environmental policy should not constrain human exploitation of Nature; instead, laws should permit us to exercise dominion over, and to exploit, natural goods and systems.[4]

Another manifestation of human superiority is seen in a uniquely anthropocentric belief in our ability to actively "manage" natural resources and natural systems. Many of our natural resource management policies reflect assumptions of human exceptionalism. As God's chosen species, humans believed they could control and dominate Nature. We could assign to ourselves a duty to serve as "stewards" to certain natural resources and places within the Earth's biosphere where living organisms existed.[5] Human exceptionalism also permitted us to believe that the laws governing the rest of the natural world did not apply to humans. We were, for example, reluctant to abandon the long-held, but absurd, twin assumptions of an inexhaustible supply of natural resources and the unpollutability of the Earth's natural sinks.[6]

Of course, humans are *not* superior to Nature or natural forces, and humans are not so exceptional that they can successfully manage and control natural processes and Earth systems. A cursory review of Chapter 3

---

[3] Cormac Cullinan, Wild Law 63 (2d ed. 2011).

[4] J. Willard Hurst, Law and Conditions of Freedom in the Nineteenth-Century United States (1956); Jonathan Baert Wiener, Law and the New Ecology: Evolution, Categories, and Consequences, 22 Ecology L.Q. 325, 343 (1995). See also Jan G. Laitos & Lauren J. Wolongevicz, Why Environmental Laws Fail, 39 William & Mary Envtl. Law & Policy Review 1, 24–28 (2014).

[5] Jedediah Purdy, American Nature: The Shape of Conflict in Environmental Law, 36 Harvard Evtl. L. Rev. 169, 189–197 (2012); William Leiss, Modern Science, Enlightenment, and the Domination of Nature: No Exit?, www.vta.edu/humalagger (2014).

[6] Rachel Beddoe, et al., Overcoming Systemic Roadblocks to Sustainability: The Evolutionary Redesign of Woldviews, Institutions, and Technologies, 106 Proc. Natl. Acad. Sci. 28 (2009).

reveals that humans have been "dominant," but not in their ability to manage Nature, but in their success in altering Nature so that the Earth is shortly not going to provide us with a "safe operating space." Humans are not superior to Nature; they are entirely dependent on both Earth's natural resources and Earth's ecosystem services.[7]

B.   Human Separation from Nature

Another theme pervading environmental policy has been that humans are not a part of Nature, but instead are apart, and independent, from the natural world that surrounds us. Additionally, modern lifestyles further this myth of separation by masking the usual connections that typically cause humans to confront the natural systems surrounding them. Urban enclaves have disguised our connections to Nature, so that we notice neither our day-to-day dependence on Nature nor the effects our anthropogenic actions have on Nature.[8]

The reality is quite different from the myth. Humans and Nature exist interdependently.[9] Researchers now realize that humans and Nature co-evolve together, not as two forces, but as a *single system*. This unified system responds to the continuously changing dynamics between one species (*homo sapiens*) and the environmental surroundings in which that species exists. That single system is termed the social-ecological system, or SES.[10] When the dominant "social" component of the SES engages in too much of certain anthropogenic activities (like emitting greenhouse gases into the atmosphere), the "ecological system" component of the SES adapts in a way that may degrade its life-supporting ecological processes on which humans depend. There is no "separation" when human actions produce environmental consequences for natural systems, and when these systems in turn respond to the anthropogenic action by creating ecological systems that may no longer be consistent with human life.

---

[7] Carl Folke, et al., Reconnecting to the Biosphere 40 Ambio 719 (2011).

[8] Emilio F. Moran, People and Nature 7, 69 (2006); John Cairns, Jr., Eco-societal Restoration: Re-examining Human Society's Relationship with Natural Systems, chapter 2 in Goals and Conditions for a Sustainable World (ESEP Books 2002).

[9] P. Wesley Schultz, Inclusion with Nature: The Psychology of Human Nature Relations, in The Psychology of Sustainable Development 61 (P. Schmuck ed. 2002).

[10] Carl Folke, Thomas Hahn, Per Olsson, & John Norberg, Adaptive Governance of Social-Ecological Systems, 30 Annual Rev. Envir. Res. 441, 443 (2005).

C.   A False Model for the Dynamics of the Natural World

Humans, and their environmental policies, have too often relied on anthropogenic assumptions about the workings of natural systems. We have tried to impose on our environmental surroundings a human-skewed view of the way natural systems *should* work, instead of trying to learn as a matter of scientific fact how they *do* work. For example, many resource preservation laws, such as statutes protecting endangered species, or policies that set aside special places as parks or wilderness, presume a model of Nature that prefers a stable equilibrium state. In order to achieve this "natural" stable state, humans should be either prevented from interfering with natural systems or excluded from these special preserved places (or be allowed access only if they can walk in).

The scientific reality is that natural systems are not stable and they do not follow linear dynamics.[11] Such systems function as complex adaptive systems. They are dynamic, nonlinear, survivable in multiple stability configurations, and capable of absorbing disturbance while maintaining the same basic resilient structure.[12] The nonlinearity and unpredictable nature of ecological systems means that the effects of human intervention (or nonintervention) in Nature cannot be accurately foreseen. There could be unintended consequences if environmental policy tries to impose on our natural surroundings a model of the way natural systems should work (i.e., seeking equilibrium), instead of how they in fact do work (as complex adaptive systems).[13]

D.   A False Model for Human Behavior

Policymakers, academics, and economists have advocated a particular kind of environmental policy to help guide and alter the behavior of humans. Humans historically overuse, overpollute, and overextend natural resources and environmental goods. In order for law and policy to change this self-destructive behavior, the traditional thinking has been that the policy should be consistent with a specific model of human

---

[11] P. C. D Milly, et al., Stationarity Is Dead: Whither Water Management?, 319 Science 573 (Feb. 2008).

[12] Simon Levin, et al., Social-Ecological Systems or Complex Adaptive Systems: Modeling and Policy Implications, 18 Envir. and Dev. Econ. 111 (Apr. 2013).

[13] Matthis Wackernagel & William Rees, Our Ecological Footprint: Reducing Human Impact on Earth 4 (1998).

decision-making that purports to reflect how we make choices about our natural world. Policymakers have long embraced this model of behavior as the starting point for how we can best be steered toward more environmentally sustainable actions.

The model embraced by many social scientists and economists, and a sizable segment of the legal academic community, assumes that humans are a monolithic, undifferentiated mass of individuals who are (1) self-interested, (2) seeking to maximize their own utility, (3) rational, (4) amoral, and (5) able to make deliberate judgments toward their subjectively defined ends. The standard human decision-maker is known widely, and derisively, as homo economicus. This mythical human makes choices based on "utility" (and selfish human happiness), where utility is defined in terms of welfare maximization with the least possible cost.[14]

Homo economicus has roots stretching back several centuries. John Stuart Mill, Adam Smith, and David Ricardo relied on a model of individuals engaged in rational behavior influenced by choices that were made to maximize individual welfare. This model has dominated neoclassical economic theory and Western economic social theory. It is at the heart of standard environmental policy tools such as cap-and-trade systems, taxes and regulations designed to internalize negative externalities, and subsidies.[15]

Although the neoclassical economics model of homo economicus has anchored environmental policy for decades, modern behavioral economists and neuroeconomists and social scientists have challenged this model. Their empirical studies suggest that humans are not necessarily rational in their decision-making. Nor do humans always act on the basis of self-interest, after deliberately weighing the costs and benefits of alternative courses of action. Instead we also make choices based on other influences such as altruism, fairness, teamwork, and the collective choices of others.[16]

If the standard model for human behavior is not entirely accurate, and if there is another, competing model, which seems to portray better

---

[14] T. Lawson, The Nature of Heterodox Economics, 30 Cambridge J. of Econ. 483 (2006).
[15] Toshio Yamagishi, et al., In Search of Homo Economicus, Psychological Science, doi:10.1177 (Sept. 10, 2014); Steven D. Levitt & John A. List, Homo Economicus Evolves, 319 Science 909 (Feb. 2008).
[16] Amos Tversky & Daniel Kahneman, The Framing of Decisions and the Psychology of Choice, 211 Science 453 (1981); Daniel Kahneman & Amos Tversky, Prospect Theory: An Analysis of Decision Under Risk, XLVII Econometrica 263 (1979).

how and why humans make choices, then standard environmental policy based on the old model will be unsuccessful. If individuals make choices based on influences other than rational self-interest, and if "bounded" rationality is a more powerful motivator, then environmental policy should be less negative ("Don't pollute"), and more positive ("Here is a benefit you will experience if you drive an electric car"). And if humans are not necessarily obsessed just with self-interest, but are influenced by a desire to be cooperative and improve the natural world for all of us, then environmental policy needs to adapt to this new model of human behavior. Policy should rely less on rules that authoritatively tell us what not to do and instead rely more on prompts and incentives that help us understand what to do. And policy should be less fixated on imposing top-down rules on individuals and more inclined to further institutions of collective action.[17]

E.   The Limitations of Existing and Proposed
Environmental Policy

Chapter 8 summarizes most of the existing categories of environmental policy. It also considers environmental policy that has been proposed but has not yet been accepted or implemented. Many of the policy initiatives suffer from a flawed worldview about humans and their surrounding natural world. They may also be ineffective because they are based in part on inaccurate models of how Nature works and humans behave. But the purpose of Chapter 8 was to show that for each of both tried and proposed legal systems that make up the bulk of "environmental policy," there are several internal limits that make their success problematic. These inherent difficulties are not linked together with a common thread; each is unique to a particular policy. But since each environmental policy has its own limitations, by implication each policy carries within it the reasons why, ultimately, it will likely fail. Those limitations have all been identified and discussed in Chapter 8. All that needs to be repeated now is the more fundamental and universal reason for the failure of environmental policies. And this is a reason found in Nature's underlying design.

---

[17] Daniel Cohen, Homo Economicus: The (Lost) Prophet of Modern Times (2014); Cass R. Sunstein, Why Nudge? The Politics of Libertarian Paternalism (2014); Richard Thaler, From Homo Economicus to Homo Sapiens, 14 J. of Economic Perspectives 133 (2000); Elinor Ostrom, Governing the Commons: The Evolution of Institutions for Collective Action (1990).

F.   Failure to Conform to the Laws of Nature

If environmental policy is to succeed, it must, at a minimum, embody three qualities. First, it must accurately and realistically reflect and be responsive to the true character of the natural world (i.e., as a complex adaptive system that is part of a larger SES). Second, it must choose legal tools that will be effective in altering the otherwise environmentally destructive behavior of humans (i.e., tools that do not presume that individuals mimic homo economicus, but instead presume a more realistic and nuanced view of human choice-making). Much of this book has been devoted to explaining how traditional environmental policy has come up short with respect to these two requirements. And there is a third quality that will help cause environmental policy to succeed in creating conditions on this planet that are conducive to human sustainable survivability: policy designed to affect the natural "environment" needs to be consistent with the laws of Nature that guide and control our environmental surroundings.

It appears that Nature does have an underlying design, and the natural world, from a cosmic to a subatomic scale, does seem to follow certain rules. As laid out in Chapter 9, the laws of Nature follow symmetry. The requirement of symmetry underscores most observable phenomena in the universe and in our environmental surroundings. The laws of Nature may be deduced from the requirements of symmetry; symmetry requirements come first and should dictate the anthropomorphic laws that affect human behavior toward Nature. The pervasiveness of symmetry in Nature extends to three principles that follow from symmetry, which natural systems reflect, and which environmental laws should embody: the laws of equivalence, unification, and conservation.[18]

If environmental policy is to succeed, it must not ignore the critical role played by symmetry in the environmental systems that the policy is addressing. Much of existing environmental policy reflects notions of what humans should not do regarding their environmental surroundings. For this policy to succeed, it needs to alert, urge, or incentivize humans to do acts that are consistent with the laws of Nature, where these laws follow the requirements of symmetry. The environmental policy set forth in Chapter 10 is an attempt to fashion a human law or policy that conforms

---

[18]   Frank Wilczek, A Beautiful Question: Finding Nature's Deep Design (2015); Maio Livio, The Equation That Couldn't Be Solved: How Mathematical Genius Discovered the Language of Symmetry (2005); David J. Gross, The Role of Symmetry in Fundamental Physics, 93 Proc. Of the National Academy of Sciences 14256 (1996); H. Weyl, Symmetry (1952).

to Nature's law. A specialized positive "right" held by social-ecological systems, along with a correlative positive duty imposed on humans, seems a step in the direction of satisfying symmetry, and conforming human laws to Nature's laws. And when symmetry is put first, then the human laws can perhaps succeed in securing for us an Earth-based safe operating space that is now so threatened.

INDEX

American Clean Air Act, 56, 58
American Forestry Association, 49
AMOC. *See* Atlantic meridional
    overturning circulation
An Ecomodernist Manifesto, 162–164
Anderson, Carl, 175
Anthropocene Era, 7–8, 15, 34, 59, 76
anthropomorphic ethics, 20
anthropomorphic superiority, 204
application of law, 137
Atlantic meridional overturning
    circulation (AMOC), 73
atmosphere exploitation, 71–73

biodiversity, extinctions, 69–71
Bolivia, Universal Declaration of the
    Rights of Mother Earth, 157

California drought, 87–88, 137
carbon dioxide emissions, 71–73
CAS. *See* complex adaptive system
CEQ. *See* U.S. Council on
    Environmental Quality
Chile, environmental rights, 168
Clean Air Act, 143
climate change, greenhouse gases,
    global warming, 64–69, 146,
    148–149, 159–160
Coase Theorem, 127
Columbia, environmental rights, 168
command and control, regulatory
    policies, pollution control,
    142–145
commensalism, 47
communal resource management
    limits, 166

complex adaptive system (CAS),
    24, 38, 95–101. *See also* Earth
    system model
complexity theory, 161
Conservation Principle, 36
corrective justice issues, 149–150
Craig, Robin Kundis, 160, 161–162
Crick, Francis, 176

The Decline of the West (Spengler),
    124
decoupling human societies from
    Nature, 162–164
delegation to private parties,
    human right to environment,
    166–169
Descartes, Rene, 182
Dirac, Paul, 175
direct government action, 141–142
disclosure laws, 152–153
dynamics of natural world, false
    model, 206

Earth Jurisprudence, 13–14
Earth Rights, Earth Community,
    157–159
Earth system model, 5–9, 15
    anti-equilibrium, variety at edge of
        chaos, 99–100
    co-evolution, 98
    complexity, 96
    connectivity, 96–97
    Nature as complex adaptive system
        (CAS), 95–101
    resilience, adaptive connectivity,
        97–98